thankGodi...

Thank God I . ..® Triumphed Through Tragedy
Stories of Inspiration For Every Situation… Volume 3

Published by Inspired Authors, LLC
5348 Vegas Drive, Suite 1086
Las Vegas, NV 89108
http://www.thankgodi.com

ISBN–13: 978-0-9815453-2-5
Cover Design: Kim Brooks
Interior Design: Desktop Miracles, Inc.
Printed in the United States of America
Publisher's Cataloging-In-Publication Data
(Prepared by The Donohue Group, Inc.)
Special Thanks- David Gulick, Katherine Scherer, Kim Brooks
Thank God I…®— : stories of inspiration for every situation / created by John Castagnini.
v. ; cm.
ISBN: 978–0–9815453–9–4
ISBN: 978–0–9815453–1–8 (v. 2)
1. Gratitude—Religious aspects. 2. Life change events—Religious aspects. 3. Adjustment (Psychology) 4. Conduct of life. I. Castagnini, John.
BF575.G68 T43 2008
158.1

TABLE OF CONTENTS

Letter from the Founder

JOHN CASTAGNINI

Let's face it. You're probably NOT going to read this entire book.

If you're anything like me, you want to get STRAIGHT TO THE POINT, I get it. These days, none of us have time to waste.

I spent the last twenty years in the personal/spiritual development field. I'm forever thankful for the thousands of lessons and incredible teachers that I have been so fortunate to have shared time with on this journey.

Over the years I watched thousands and thousands of people attempt unsuccessfully to "get ahead." I deeply contemplated, why do so few people actually appear to get major results?

Yes there are so many ways to measure results, and of course we all get different results according to our individual values, but there was a specific key to fulfillment that only "the few" had found.

But why?

Along my road I discovered a single tremendous incongruence that was being perpetuated throughout the "spiritual development" field.

In an advertisement for Rhonda Byrnes' new book, *The Power,* a follow up to *The Secret*, it states, "You are not meant to suffer or struggle."

Do you suffer? Let's get REAL... Do you suffer? If you're being HONEST with yourself... You bet your ass you suffer!

WE ALL SUFFER. EVERY SINGLE ONE OF US.
Yes, some of us appear to have more challenging circumstances, but all of us suffer in different ways.

Why try to promise people that they can get rid of HALF of themselves (suffering)? Why set people up for the Impossible?

Don't get me wrong, I thank God for the personal/spiritual development field. It helped save my life, gave me a profession and provided for me an opportunity to share my heart.

That is why it's SO important for me to share with you a treasured truth that is the KEY to finally understanding "The Matrix."

WAKE UP!
YOU CANNOT BE HAPPY ALL THE TIME!
YOU CANNOT BE FREE FROM SUFFERING!
YOU CANNOT BE MORE POSITIVE THAN NEGATIVE!

Trying to get rid of half of yourself is like a cat chasing his tail. Eventually you will give up and be back reading this book. Hopefully some of the teachers spewing this "get rid of the negative" crap are reading this book. We will all chase "happiness," but it's impossible to be happy all the time. Wisdom is asking a new set of questions so that we may better understand the times when we aren't happy. Those times have just as much value in our lives as the happy times we seek.

Yes there is an underlying "PERFECTION" that exists, in every moment (even in you) But... That "Perfection" involves an equal amount of suffering and pleasure, happiness and sorrow, support and challenge.

What you can do is learn how to balance your opposite emotions, one by one. You can develop a more poised presence. You can gain wisdom in being more objective and balanced in your decision making. You can be more appreciative and fulfilled in honoring the actuality that exists beyond our realities. You can develop more worth and in turn more wealth. You can learn to Thank God for what is, as it is.

The stories in this book are real life experiences of people who have triumphed in the face of tragedy. They found appreciation for something that was in many cases downright torture. These are remarkable experiences of transcendence. The amount of real life "how to" present in these stories opened my heart wider, page after page.

My advice, flip through the book, and look for the stories that speak to you. What are you "struggling" with?

Thank God I...® is dedicated to sharing with you how human emotions work in connection to the universal principles that guide us all. Our authors share this through their unique stories.

Our mission is to inform you with accurate information that will serve you in mastering your mind, and in turn your life.

Yes, you will struggle. As you go through our books, our online community, our seminars and the Power of Perfection Education, we promise to share with you the world leading information on how to develop yourself, others and humanity.

Who knows, perhaps you will be inspired to share your "Thank God I..." story and help us develop minds while we touch the hearts of people all over the world.

Everyone of us is an expression of the divine. We all deserve to "thank God," and we all have a unique *Thank God I...*® story.

The more you embrace each part of yourself, (the positive and negative stories) the more fulfilled your life will be, and the more you become congruent in sharing the gift of what you are here to do.

In Loving Service,
John Castagnini

Introduction

IMPORTANT...

PLEASE READ THIS SECTION.

Why this book? What makes it so different? Not only are the answers important, they are integral to your understanding of the stories presented here. Thank you for not skipping over this brief introduction in your eagerness to get to the meat of the book itself.

When I first thought to include "Thank God I Was Raped" as one of the stories for the first anthology, the concept sent chills through my spine. Could anyone who's endured this brutal, horrifying experience really embrace these words? Over the years, I've counseled countless women during their rape recovery. I chose the title after witnessing what transpires for them when they come to this conclusion of gratitude.

What became quite apparent over the course of thousands of conversations is that we only evolve past the mental trauma from such an occurrence when we can hold the love for it in our hearts.

What does God mean?

God—certainly, the biggest three-letter word ever

created. Grand Organized Designer best describes the GOD used in Thank God I . . .™. The thousands of people sharing their stories in this series all perceive God in their own light. Thank God I . . . ™ is about this network of people willing to move beyond having the right "name" for God.

Even the word God itself cannot finite the infinite. Rather, God refers to a system governing the brilliance of what is and is not.

What this book series is not supposed to be

This series does not condone or promote any of the acts the writers have experienced, nor do we suggest in any way that anyone should either commit any of these acts or subject themselves to any of these acts. This series also does not promote or label any specific kind of behavior as "right" or "wrong"; the stories were not written and the book was not published for the purpose of anyone rationalizing these types of actions or behavior. In addition, the Thank God I . . . ™ series does not promote or deny any religion. Rather, it honors the existence of all things as part of a perfect creation.

What is Thank God I . . . ™ about?

Our intention with this series is to convey this one key principle: ***The Perfect Idea™***. Each time we fail to recognize this principle, the next lesson that comes our way will once again offer us the opportunity to see the perfection and breakthrough it into freedom. In fact, finding perfection in the pain and pleasure of our own personal tribulations is the only way we will ever liberate ourselves from the bondage of patterns. Whether it comes in a day, a year, or a lifetime, situations will come into our lives that will force us to become thankful for "what was" and joyfully to experience "what is."

What does Thanking God mean?

During the creation phase of this series, we were fortunate to have as our ever-efficient assistant, Cassandra—a beautiful 22-year-old writer and poet. Just prior to coming to work with us, Cassandra was diagnosed with cervical cancer. A little over a year-and-a-half later the cancer spread, and she left this world before the first book launched.

After Cassandra passed, my heart was struck by the words she put to the page as she endured this experience. She wrote of her "earth angels" and her explorations as she left her body to "dance with angels." She didn't write about her "passing"; she wrote about Thank God I . . . ™ living as she moved through her life's greatest test and her life's ending. She viewed each person, each moment as precious. How fortunate she was to see God in the now.

Imagine, this is what she wrote about her cancer:

Tears fill my eyes daily with gratitude for every moment and every breath. It has allowed me to go after my dreams, to live from my heart, and to be truly free. I thank God for my cancer, and for allowing me to reach a place in me that I don't think would have been possible without this experience. I am now 23 and feel that I have stepped into my skin proudly. I have felt an inner peace that many don't find until later in life. I am truly grateful for all my earth angels and want to thank them for sharing with me this wonderful journey.
. . . Cassandra

There are four million tasks to accomplish in order to bring the Thank God I . . . ™ network to the standard of our vision. Thank you, Cassandra, for reminding me why Thank God I . . . ™ was conceived in the first place.

Thanking God is about the above. Not just what is above this sentence; it is about what is above, guiding us at every moment. Beyond the pain, chaos, and confusion of our circumstances exists true perfection. Thanking God is about finding this perfection. This place of thanking God might seem nearly impossible to find, but it is the only place we will find ourselves.

Thank God I . . . ™ is true gratitude.

Sure we all hear the same old wonderful things that people are grateful for in their lives. But is this gratitude? Thank God I . . . ™ gratitude is about a state of being. It is about a state of inspiration, non-judgment, and presence. Thank God I . . . ™ gratitude is beyond the illusion of positive or negative. It is beyond the lies of "good" and "evil." Thank God I . . . ™ gratitude is about finding God in every word, thought and deed. In spirit we are beyond the illusion of pain or pleasure and we are present with spirit. Thank God I . . . ™ gratitude is about equal love for all that is, as it is, was, or ever shall become. Gratitude is loving what we don't "like" as much as loving what we do "like."

The diversity of authors and experiences

The intention of this series is to reach all of humanity, every single unique creation. We did not base the selection of contributions to this series upon any faith or religious orientation. Each selected author took a former challenge into his/her heart, and each share the goal of the universal understanding of love/gratitude in all. The diversity of authors spans religions, countries, professions, age, race, nationality, and experiences. They range from those with disease to doctors, from ex-convicts to stay-at-home moms, and whoever they are, gratitude rules. From alcoholism to molestation or rape, the law of gratitude prevails with each of our authors. Thankfulness for whatever is, or is not, ultimately rules every one of our kingdoms.

The vision of Thank God I . . . ™

Little did I imagine how lightning-fast Thank God I . . . ™ would circle the world. Reaching diverse people, this network includes thousands of contributors sharing not only their stories but also their answers. Beyond the books, and the online community, we offer worldwide conference calls, workshops and seminars. This series provides all within specific communities information in order to evolve past the emotions that are holding them back. The people and the project are evolutionary. "All things in nature proceed from certain necessity and with the utmost perfection."
. . . Baruch Spinoza

Making Love with Words

Too often it is common to interchange synonymous words and use them incorrectly. The Thank God I . . . ™ authors and editing team have done their best to clarify many distinctions that have confused humanity in the Personal Development field.

Because the Thank God I . . . ™ brand has so many authors, the alignment of words, terms, and expressions has become an important focus for the "continuity" of meaning.

The distinctions in the expression of language are extraordinarily important—especially with written material.

Our intent is to use terms clearly and correctly.

The following are important word distinctions that can assist the reader in getting a more comprehensive understanding of the Thank God I . . . ™ "state of mind." For making these distinctions, we give special thanks to Dr. John Demartini.

1) Passion & Inspiration
Passion is an endorphin "high" eventually attracting the opposite "low." It is not heart centered. Inspiration is a state of being, love, and presence. It has no opposite and is heart centered.

2) Happiness & Fulfillment
Happiness is an endorphin "high" eventually attracting a sadness "low." It is not heart centered. Fulfillment is a state that encompasses happiness and sadness equally. It is heart centered.

3) Peace & Inner Peace
Peace is balanced by its opposite: war. It is an illusion that is not heart centered. Inner peace is a state of fulfillment, being, presence, inspiration, gratitude or love. It is heart centered and has no opposite.

4) Forgiveness & Appreciation

Forgiveness implies a right and wrong—and a judgment.
In the world of perfection—past, present and future—nothing needs an apology. Appreciation honors the perfection of what has been, is, and will be—in whatever form. It reserves no judgment.

5) Always & Never

These two terms have been almost completely edited out of this text. The Actual Existence of always and never in a relative universe is almost non-existent. In fact, by listening to where one uses the term always or never, one can become clear of the internal charges (misperceptions) that exist. The over-use of these terms can be indicative of stubborn positioning that can inhibit one's growth.

6) Positive / Negative & Equilibration

If you cut a magnet in half, you will still get a positive and negative "half." Each side of the magnet attracts its opposite. Equilibration. Thank God I . . . ™ fosters a state of Gratitude. It is an equilibrated state beyond the illusion of positive or negative. An equilibrated state is also expressed as inspiration, love, being, gratitude, presence, and fulfillment.

7) Reality & Actuality

Any emotional experience has an opposite emotion. Emotional realities are illusive perceptions with opposites. Actuality transcends the illusion of realities. Actuality is an equilibrated state. Actuality transcends two complementary opposite realities upon their unification.

8) Emotions & Feelings

Emotions are charged realities that are illusions and have opposites. They are not heart centered. Feelings are equilibrated actualities. They have no opposites. They are heart centered.

Honoring these distinctions can greatly assist the reader in understanding some of the key messages that Thank God I . . . ™ is sharing with humanity. Honoring them can greatly increase one's experience of ACTUALITY.

Thank you,
John Castagnini

Thank God
I Found My Orgasm!!

ANGELICA OSBOURNE

I was twenty-nine when I had my first orgasm. Before then, I did not believe that sex was for a woman's well-being. I believed it was just for men to use against us and upon us. I thought sex was a means to an end. Sex was just a way to have a man treat a woman nicely, to be given as an exchange for a few strong hugs, or to get a new ______ (fill in the blank: sweater, lip gloss, transmission).

Early in my marriage, I remember thinking: "I wish he'd fix the dishwasher." The solution: "I'll put out tonight and ask him in the morning." I did not stop to think, "I need to feel good; I should have sex in order to feel good." These thoughts did not occur to me. "Love" and "Sex" did not fit in the same space for me; together they were a foreign concept.

When I was a little girl, I lived in various small country towns in Alabama. My daddy was a Methodist minister; I grew up living and breathing church. My grandfather was a Baptist minister who sexually abused me for much of my childhood. My idea of God and sexuality became all tangled up, like a box of fishing tackle that has been sitting in the basement long neglected. In order to free the hooks, you have to tear through those beautiful, squishy, glittery rubber worms.

I went through a stage where I was obsessed with remembering every sordid detail of the sexual abuse I'd experienced. I thought that would help me get better. It was as if I needed more proof of how far gone I had really been in order to come back. I went to visit the apartment building in which my grandfather lived. I watched old television shows like Hee Haw and Lawrence Welk because I remembered sitting in his lap watching them. I would rejoice gladly with each new flashback, reliving the terror, and then giving myself permission to go full-blown crazy. I already felt like madness; I just needed the reason. When I first started having bits and pieces of memories from those years, I was relieved, "Yup, I was full-blown crazy, but I had a reason!"

It helped make sense of me, to me. There were many side effects to remembering. I suffered from three bleeding ulcers, deep depression, insomnia, twenty-six stitches in my wrists, and the tainting of my newly wedded sex life. I had to rip each of the demon's fingers from its icy grip around my spirit, look the demon in the face, and then send each one back to Hell before they damn near ate me alive.

In college, I had a superstar therapist named Ted. He not only counseled survivors of pedophilia, but he also counseled pedophiles serving time in prison. One day, I worked up the courage to tell him my deepest, darkest secret. A secret so disturbing I couldn't believe I was sharing it, a secret so horrific that no sane person could imagine this happening to any child. I almost felt bad for dirtying Ted's mind. To my surprise, after I managed to tell him, he calmly said, "You wouldn't believe how many women have told me the same thing."

Women? Plural? As in, more than one? How could that be? I wasn't the only one! In one way it was worse. If what he said was true, there were more "abusers" out there than I could fathom. On the flip side, knowing this was sheer bliss. Ted's words healed something in me. Those words were an armful of light to throw into the dark hole.

There was light through a crack over the door that I fixated on when I was in "my cellar." God's presence here saved me. I knew He was there. I thought He was pissed off at me and He was still there. Here is the thing about omnipresence though: What about when you want a little privacy?

When I was three, I began to enjoy touching myself a lot. And liking it. A lot. I had already been told that touching myself was wrong. Imagine my dismay at the realization that God was watching that, too! I thought He might close His eyes or just focus a little more on that sparrow outside my window.

"Just for a minute—I wouldn't need long," I thought, "He's God! He must be ten times madder about it than my mama!" I believed not only was He watching, but also He had a mad face on. As I got older, my guilt complex had a much greater capacity, and I felt even worse. I questioned why, if I wasn't supposed to do it, and God made my body, my body ached for it?

During puberty, I got a little out of control. I had a perfume bottle. Windsong perfume. It smelled like crap, but was perfectly shaped for...you guessed it...fitting right up my private space that I affectionately called "tootie." The commercial for Windsong crooned, "He just can't seem to forget you. Your Windsong stays on his mind..." as a dark-haired beauty walked on the beach, the wind rushing her good smells all over the ocean. She was so serene and confident. She looked like she had had a few intimate moments with the bottle herself. It made me laugh, and I swore I could feel another's laugh. Was that just a figment of my imagination, created by my dirty little mind? On the other hand, was it possible that God thought I was funny? Could it be? Was He in on my joke? My daddy always said, "I know God has a sense of humor—just look at the duck-billed platypus." But what if the duck billed platypus is humping a rock and gettin' off, all moaning and stuff? Does God think that's funny?

If you saw that at the zoo, wouldn't you laugh? I sure as hell would. I have this sneaking suspicion that there might be a whole host of angels watching and snickering too. I was taught masturbation was wrong. I let what I was taught override how I felt. I said goodbye to the perfume bottle (although it "stayed on my mind..."), gone was the jump rope handle, the left leg of my bunny rabbit, and the days of humping my pillow, pretending it was Luke Duke, or occasionally Bo Duke.

As I got older, I completely neglected my nether regions. I lived an active sex life in complete frigidity, never climaxing and never enjoying myself. I enjoyed what came before and sometimes after, which was the attention. The sex was just the show I thought I had to put on to get the rest of it. This didn't seem right either. Would God want his daughter to feel this way, to go through these motions?

I read in a medical magazine that there are over two thousand nerve endings in the clitoris. Two thousand! If all good things come from the Lord, and the clitoris is a very, very good thing, then surely He didn't make it to coexist with misery. Surely He wants us to enjoy the blessings bestowed upon us. When I came to this conclusion a few years ago, I became experimental—I had been liberated! I used toys, and lots of them. I prayed, asking God to help me use the two thousand gifts He had so generously granted me. It was still a process for me, but I can happily say that rediscovering masturbation helped me to find my orgasm after years of denying myself. I know God is delighted when I feel pleasure. He is happy to see me happy! That makes sense to me.

Imagine you gave a child a super-duper present, such as a bubble machine, for her birthday. You can hardly wait for her to play with it. Then, when you see her take that bubble machine outside and she has a good ol' time, just laughing, running, and beaming with pleasure, it makes you feel good. What, then if you saw her barely look at it and set the toy aside, without a response?

What if she just let it sit, put it in the closet and never even opened the box? You would be so bummed. I wonder if God feels that way when we let others abuse the bubble machine, not even play with it right, or use it for other stuff, like holding GI Joes while we refused to play with them. I want to encourage my fellow sisters (and brothers, even though I think my brothers out there mostly get this already) to open up the box! Get out your bubble machine! Make you some bubbles like never before. Of course, don't forget your manners; always thank your Creator for such a cool gift.

♥ ♥ ♥

Angelica Osbourne is a preacher's daughter form Alabama. She is a mommy, screenwriter, columnist for Rage monthly magazine, youth director, tranny trainer and avid animal lover. She is Inspired by survivors, dreamers and anyone that dares to be their authentic self. Her goal is to spread God's love by empowering woman to celebrate their sexuality while embracing their spirituality.

Angelica has been married 18 years to her wonderful husband Spence and is grateful for her 14 year old daughter Aurora Epiphany.

Thank God I Was Molested, Raped, Lived in a Car with My Daughter and Lost Everything Only to Find My True Inspiration for Life!

LISA CHRISTINE CHRISTIANSEN

Gi-Dee-Thlo-Ah-EE.

This is the name given to me by my mother Sosti (Mary Ann Groundhog) at the time of my birth. Today my name is Lisa, I am from the Blue People Clan and I will Break the Silence! I am only one of two living direct descendants of Sequoyah the inventor of the Cherokee alphabet; that is bi-lingual in Cherokee and English as well as is my daughter.

There have been many moments in my life when I have been brought to my knees praying to God in desperation for an answer, moments it took every ounce of inner strength to overcome the unbearable only to leave me emotionally drained and being reminded that God is the only answer... Always!

Fortunately, I have come to appreciate the challenges and gifts God has shared with me.

While at this moment that may be slightly cryptic, my autobiography – to be released next year – will reveal every hidden detail.

When my mother found herself pregnant, she tried to get an abortion. That was the first – but not the last – time my will for life would not be denied. Despite her intentions, I entered this world with a scream—a scream that went silent, yet would remain in my head, for most of my early life.

When I was only six months old, my father left. He didn't want a girl. He didn't want me. That was only the beginning of a pattern of being "not wanted" that would continue for way too long. At three years old, I was almost killed by my mother again. My aunt - who we lived with - gave it a shot when I was six.

Even though my whole family all lived together as I was growing up, we were very poor. Our home had dirt floors and most of our food was comprised of what my uncle was able to hunt.

Eventually, slowly, my mother did come to accept me as she did some "growing up" of her own. Yet, almost as quickly she became a true "part of my life", she was gone. She died when I was eight but I do remember a few key pearls of wisdom she was (finally) able to share with me in that short time. I treasure these things she told me because I know it took her a long time to get to this point. This is what I carry with me, from her personal journey to growth, that has impacted me - and my growth - through today:

• I can do, be, and have anything I want.

• If I didn't get it, I didn't want it bad enough.

• You are only "in love" once; you can love many people, but only be in love once.

• 80% of achieving your dreams is knowing what you want; 20% is the how—and the how will come!!!

Once my mother passed on my aunt was charged with the daunting task to take care of me. She would tell me "get off of me" when I would hug her or kiss her; she would push me away when I would say "I LOVE YOU". She would repeatedly say, "Don't expect to hear that from me or anyone else." She kept her promise and never said it. She often told me if I was not her sister's daughter she would not have me in her home.

Throughout the duration of my childhood I was not called by any name other than "the girl", "that girl", or "the child". (Now they just call me "woman".) I was not allowed to sit on the furniture because I was a girl.

I was raped at fifteen and forced to marry my abuser. My family blamed the rape – as all else – on me. They said if I didn't look the way I did I would not have been raped. This was "God's punishment" to me. They also said I must have done something to invite this molestation even though I was only 6 the first time. They also said that I would never amount to anything.

I didn't stay married that first time for long and soon after, met the father of my oldest daughter. To maintain the brevity of a "short story", I will skip ahead some now. However, I will say there were many more difficult – yet lesson-teaching – years I would face throughout my twenties. Yet, again, each of those lessons weaves and interweaves to create the fabric of the design which makes me the magnificent creature I know I am today.

I have risen above all knowing the true value of me. Even through what seemed to be a tragic childhood, I knew something was different about me. I knew I was capable of being equally as successful as any man, equally as intelligent as any man, have the same respect as a man and it is empowering to know that I can still embrace my femininity. At one point my six year old daughter and I lived in a car for six months and then later sold that car for $10,000.00 and spent every penny to put together bibles, roaster pans, vegetables, turkeys, toys, and fed over 119 low-income families in Lawton, Oklahoma.

I have constantly been successful at everything I have explored. In Mary Kay, I was Queen of Sales in my first quarter of starting my business, something it took others a year to accomplish in sales. In ARBONNE, my first two weeks I made $94,000.00 in sales and recruiting which earned me enough to purchase my brand new Mercedes Benz R350. I was recognized in the top income earners on stage and shortly after I earned $500,000.00 to buy my new home in Grayson's Mountain: one of the most elite neighborhoods with the former senator and local celebrities as my neighbors. I paid for my home...in cash! Thank you God!

Shortly after these magnificent professional successes, I met and married the man of my dreams—my one true love. At this time, I was expanding my business and enjoying even more success. Of course, this was attributable to my education but also largely due to the skills (emotional and practical) I had acquired through my life journey up to this point. I couldn't believe I was finally enjoying the amazing good fortune I deserved! I had it all! This life partnership was icing on the cake and I made it an "official" partnership by signing over everything I owned to my new husband.

Yet, life wasn't finished teaching me. Within a year, he too was rejecting me...he didn't want me either... and he was leaving me. His parting words - the day I was scheduled for a medical procedure - were: You are worthless. You are a waste of my time and nothing more than equity. You are damaged goods and I want nothing more to do with you.

My pain grew deeper but my resolve grew stronger. Didn't he know that he couldn't really hurt me? No one person could really hurt me anymore. Friends, the story goes so deep.

Interesting that I saw a pattern emerging in my life through this incident. You see, it was about this time that the patterns in my life really became crystal clear. I realized I could not escape them by avoiding them and pretending the events that created them didn't happen. My grandmother killed her brother when they were children. My aunt killed her other sister (my mom's other sister) before she was three. My mother was assaulted by her ex-boyfriend and sliced his back wide open with the same butcher knife my aunt assaulted me with when I was six. We were Cherokee and this kind of anger and violence is not really uncommon. But do you see the other pattern? I did and I realized I had spent most of my life submissive to an extent in avoid becoming like these people!

There was so much violence and pain in my family, in my life. Everyone was so angry with someone else for the things they felt that person had done to them. They didn't see, didn't understand, they were masters of their own fate. I am not sure I truly understood it either until this point. Yes, I had obtained "riches". Yet, I had lost them too. I had finally received (what I mistook for) "love" but I lost it too. I was not owning my emotions - not being selfish enough - because I was afraid that would make me like "them"—the others in my family. On the other hand, I needn't have worried because I would never be like them.

They hated me because they feared me; I was not like them and they knew it. I wouldn't fully conform to their world and I made a decision early on to put God - and my faith in his teachings - first in my spiritual makeup. Don't get me wrong, I have made decisions that others would not agree with, decisions that have made me who I am today. I was constantly living a battle between my heritage, what they expected me to be (a subservient failure), and what I expected from myself (to be a blessing in the eyes of God).

Thank you God for challenging me to grow.

In 2001, I was diagnosed with sinus tachycardia (fast heart beat) and from that I allowed fear to take over. I had challenges with the thought of even driving from one city to another, even though it might be a mere twenty minute drive. I found myself experiencing cardiac awareness which would cause mild panic attacks in the form of PVC'S. I was my own worst enemy which was disappointing as I had become a doctor of exercise and nutritional sciences. I had lived a healthy lifestyle: never smoked, drank, nor had done drugs of any kind. So you can imagine my confusion.

Two short years later my daughter was diagnosed with supra-ventricular tachycardia (fast and irregular heartbeat), with heart rates up to 260 BPM. The average person's BPM is around 100. As a mother this was very painful to watch knowing you can do nothing. Well, not this mother! I started her on a live food diet and proper exercise which was against her physician's wishes. She did show remarkable progress although she did not enjoy the exercise options I made available to her.

In May 2008, I bought my first trek bicycle. Two weeks later, I decided I enjoyed the sport so much that I bought a more expensive model with artwork portraying the most beautiful angel wings. In August 2008, my daughter and I completed the 50 miles together. In August 2009, I rode the "Hotter'n Hell 100" and finished all 100 miles in less than 4 hours!

I live free more than ever before and I do this as an example to my daughter. I believe you don't have to set the rule if you set the example. She has followed this example and found her passion in her bicycle - she has not been to the emergency room in eight months, her heart is stronger than ever and she is my hero! I have grown closer to my daughter through our passion for riding, we have both grown stronger physically, mentally, and emotionally, but most of all spiritually. We live in gratitude and embrace life with a fervent passion which is where we live! I am proud of my daughter riding with me in this fight for her life!

What I am saying here is important so if I leave nothing else with you, I wish to leave this...

No one is defined by their past or an upbringing that dictates their future. You are not defined by what other people say you will – or will not – become has any part in who (or what) you actually do become. I believe you are in control of your own actions, beliefs, and values. Consequently, you are also responsible for your own actions, beliefs, morals, and values and you cannot control anyone or anything else. it is wise to make your decisions with the end in mind and as you are guaranteed some sort of outcome, be wise in your choices for they will be your fruits.

I continue my growth exponentially and serve others more effectively. I continue my growth to serve the needs of others and serve the greater good of all.

I have the love of those who deserve my love, and I love everyone for their unique qualities as I love without prejudice and those who are nurturing and know the meaning of stay.

Love...... It is more than a gift. It is much more than an opportunity and far more than just a moment in time. It is a part of our obligation to live life fully. To find something in living that gives us such fulfillment and satisfaction that we leave with it a piece of who we are and take from it the essence of ever being near. To love is a gift you give without expectation, to be loved in return means he/she has discovered in you the part that was missing in her/him. Completeness is the goal. To love is a glimpse of heaven; it is a gift you give with no expectation of its return. I do not need permission to love nor do I need reciprocation.

The tenderness of a woman's spirit, the gentleness of a man's strength, the fragrance of two souls that have become one must be what lies ahead in the promise of eternal happiness...aaahhh, heaven indeed! To be loved is an honor. I am not looking for the ordinary. Life is playful, adventurous, and yet a comfort a place of safety, full of surprises and stability.

Even through all of the experiences of my life, I believe everyone is good at the core level and I trust more often than not. I know that somehow everything works itself out. I believe love will find a way to triumph over tragedy.

I am certain that I am a child of God. I acknowledge His blessings and am certain that I am life, strength, power, and love. I am passion, energy, and my gifts are faith and contribution. I am successful at whatever I decide through God's amazing grace and I am fulfilled each day that I awake.

I surrender no power to be held over me other than that of which I give to God which is all of me and what He has in his plans I am not certain only that it is for the greater good of all. My uncertainties do not rule me nor do I allow them to control me. I live my life well and plan as best as possible, I do not dwell on uncertainties.

Today life is great! This morning I woke up and have accepted my blessing from God just to have this day. I choose to share it in his name with all of this world and his children. I am excited about my life, my career, my success, my strength, my energy, and my optimism. I am proud of me and my influence to help others achieve their outcome and own their future. I am excited to enrich the lives of others. I believe everything happens for a reason.

I have found that the one thing that separates us from animals is the ability to have emotions. I have experienced a broad range of emotions and make it a choice to find the hidden blessings that make me happy.

To be successful one must live in gratitude and appreciation, to live in gratitude one must appreciate unconditionally; appreciation will set you free. Who will you appreciate to live in abundance? Maybe it's yourself that you haven't appreciated? Once you realize God's universal law of perfection you will see everything is, was, and will forever be perfect even what is perceived as imperfect therefore leaving nothing to forgive.

I did meet with my father recently who apologized for not being there for me. I replied to him, "Don't ever apologize for walking out that door. That was the greatest blessing you ever gave to me. The day you walked out that door, because you didn't want me, you gave me four brothers that I love dearly, the determination to succeed, the uncanny ability to love without conditions and a heart full of joy."

I now choose to live my life with excitement, happiness, joy and love. I now feel safe and protected, and I know all that I need is within me. I now feel I can be vulnerable and strong and remain all woman and a provider to my family, a mentor for other women to succeed, and inspiration to others.

Of all the roads traveled there is no right or wrong path to cut as they all lead you to where you are meant to be. I have traveled many roads and I have cut many paths —some unorthodox but most conventional. I will not try to fit in when I know in my heart God has meant for me to stand out! I will not apologize for my decisions or the events in my life, as they have made me a woman of integrity with the gift to accept others for who they are now and love them without prejudice.

Will you choose to follow the road of others or will you cut your own path – This is the question I leave you with...

Thank God I was told I was never wanted!

♥ ♥ ♥

Creator of extraordinary lives, Lisa Christiansen has served as an advisor to leaders around the world for the last two decades. A recognized authority on the psychology of leadership, organizational turnaround and peak performance, Lisa has consulted Olympic athletes, world renowned musicians, Fortune 500 CEOs, psychologists, and world-class entertainers.

Lisa's strategies for achieving lasting results and fulfillment are regarded as the platinum standard in the coaching industry. Lisa captured the attention of heads of state and the U.S. Army, all of whom became clients. Christiansen has impacted the lives of millions of people from 30 countries. Lisa has been honored by Cambridge Society of Who's Who as one of the "Top Business Intellectuals in the World."

Lisa has helped millions of people create extraordinary lives globally. Her expertise and guidance has enriched the lives of icons such as pop superstar Kelly Clarkson, Olympian Dara Torres, and the members of the rock band Journey.

Thank God
My Mom Died; Shattered Resilience

BETHANNE WANAMAKER

My sister said to me in a panic-stricken, shaky voice, "Oh God, Bethanne, I thought that was her last breath" ... and we looked at each other with a slight smirk and light sigh of relief, which lightened the mood for just a second, because it wasn't. In what must have been just a few short minutes until the next breath, a lifetime of thoughts came over me. I was about to take on another life that was so unknown, with so much uncertainty. My perceived stability would be taken away, and with no motherly support. In that time, I had an overwhelming feeling that I had to pull it all together as if to keep my sister and grandma, the only two remaining in my family, from falling apart. It was as if when I took that sigh of relief I swallowed all the emotions that were unraveling before me.

Overcome with fear and grief, a proud sense of composure swept over me. I kept telling myself to just power through it and I would have all the time in the world to deal with it. My head was spinning, body entirely physically empty and numb, my breathing constricted. I held my breath thinking if I released it that the inevitable would happen... so I held on, and held on.. however, for me, life continued.

It was the next breath that was her last. Right there I felt completely defeated – just a few seconds earlier I had managed to somewhat convince myself in that forced sense of calm that my mom was not taking her very last breaths of life. How could this be happening to us—to me? Would her breathing somehow return to normal and life would be miraculously better? It was as if time had stopped for me to sit there and seriously consider this. Yet, within just a couple of minutes, my life changed forever, and I would not be the same. This moment in time was irreversible, and I was now on a new path. Fortunately, I believe everything happens for a reason; of course, I didn't know then that this moment and this experience would eventually give me the power and belief in myself to do exceptional things for both others and myself.

I used to think people could see right through me when I talked out loud. It seemed as though this life-altering event could not be escaped and that others could see the sadness in my eyes, the deep hurt, and indescribable pain. There was a sense of shame in the cards I was dealt.

My world changed on March 6, 2001. It is the date that stays in my mind because it was the new beginning of a life that I came here to live. Had I not had this experience with hidden blessings, I doubt that I would have been put on my life's path with the intense purpose and beauty that flows so naturally now.

To say that day changed me doesn't even come close — it completely twisted me into a different direction. It all happened in a way that I can hardly express. I have tried to pull from beneath the shattered glass as careful as I could so I could tell you my story the way it was. I describe it as being shattered because everything I knew was gone in a heartbeat, while I just watched, out of control.

I was standing on this blue planet when suddenly the ground dropped ... what happened? How did this become my reality? Why was life continuing in that moment while I was dying inside? I spent the next two years in a foggy haze with a heavy shadow of sadness and such pain that not only did I refuse to look at the reality, but I couldn't - it literally was too much to handle. I felt there was absolutely no way to face this truth. In my entire lost being, there was just one little seed of hope that radiated so bright, an inner knowing that I would persevere. Yet then, I had still lost my will to live, and that is not said lightly. As I write this, I sigh in relief of not being in that space any longer. It's such a blessing to have crawled my way out of what I perceived to be the end of my own life. Nothing will ever compare in its simultaneous devastation and beauty.

My mom's greatest lesson that was impressed upon me was to believe in myself. This, along with appreciation, was the greatest gift I learned in the last few days of her life. I had the chance within days of her passing to appreciate who she was to me, and for the first time ever feel the weight-lifting relief that appreciation delivered.

She couldn't talk and was in a coma, motionless; I was intoxicated with heaviness and grief and completely childlike with a deep feeling of insecurity. I just had this one night to make the amends that would complete our relationship, and from there on, I had to be comfortable with the words I shared and make peace with myself.

My sister and grandma had already gone to sleep, and I managed to find the courage to go kneel at her bedside and open my heart without another soul knowing a word of what was said. What do I say? Would she even hear me? This conversation would bridge us together until we saw each other again. To have this conversation with my mom was impossibly difficult, much needed, and overdue, and provided the only sense of peace I had in that entire two years—from the time, she was diagnosed until at least one year later after her transition. There were several times that she squeezed my hand in acknowledgment, while I cried beside her. I could already feel her as an angel guiding me through, as she told me she would. I know that she was truly with me in that moment, could hear me, and that I would be okay in time – the comfort only your mom could give.

I felt shattered because my world shifted dramatically and the pieces of my life seemingly fell apart while I stood there helpless and in great awe.

These pieces lay everywhere, and I was surrounded by an insatiable anger. Where do you go from here? How do you get yourself together when you haven't even learned how to really be a grown-up? I was twenty-three years young and without parents, no plan for the future, and unsure of my life's passion.

The love from your mother, for a good majority of us, despite what reckless and argumentative years lie behind us, is unconditional. If there is absolutely no one else in your corner and you are in dire straits, mom is there on your side and full of support. I looked around and saw so many people, yet felt desperately alone with a quiet melancholy looming. I used to say I wasn't ready to deal with facing the grief of losing my mom and that it was just too painful—I would literally break apart if I faced it. I could feel the lump in my throat in conversations where I'd have to lie to shield myself from other's negative opinions of my embarrassing truths.

Five years after her transition, I went on a juice fasting retreat with the school I was attending for nutrition (Bauman College of Holistic Nutrition). Every morning we sat in a large group circle and passed this ball from one to another, each speaking our truth in that moment and talking about what was coming up emotionally as a result of fasting. Each of us was breaking through the nervousness and barriers that come with exposing your real self in front of dozens of others.

Each morning, I thought I was making real progress internally. I gradually began feeling a deeper desire to scream my story at the top of my lungs so I could finally release what I had kept to myself in silent shame for those five and a half years. On the second-to-last day of the retreat (and about twenty fresh juices later), the ball came to me in slow motion. Was the Universe showing me that I was ready to break free?

I began to slowly speak in front of my new friends, although complete strangers, and over the next fifteen minutes I let everything that had built up inside pour out. I was sobbing hysterically, unable to catch my breath, while everyone remained silent and listened with support, sharing tears in shock of my major breakdown.

I had spoken the words out loud: my mom had died several years previous, and I was ashamed of having no mom, an official orphan without parents — I was heartbroken, devastated, empty, alone, and slowly dying inside.

This dramatic release was the best thing that could have happened that week. From that moment forward, I gained an acceptance of my past and owned my current truth. I was no longer the sad victim. I had complete control of my life, and it was part of my journey to impress this lesson upon others.

As I've come to learn since the healing began, facing your fears is actually what moves you forward. It's quite a journey, one that is often difficult and can take a long while, but as time passes, I've found that healing will occur. There are great life lessons to be learned from the most traumatic times in our lives – it's all a matter of perspective. Instead of continuing to deny my past, I could now face who I was both to myself and to others and actually be proud of the profound wisdom I've gained as a result. It was this release and acceptance of who I was going to be from then on that triggered an impromptu decision to go by my given birth name, Bethanne, instead of my childhood nickname of Beth. This was a seemingly small change, but very meaningful to me and my angel.

Now I have a sense of peace around my mom's transition. I was meant to experience the 'loss' of my mom so that I can share this story with you and leap into the kind of life she and I always wanted me to live. I am a woman of resilience.

I have an indestructible strength inside me and have learned the character of a true survivor. I trust that the challenges that lie ahead will not hold me back as I once thought, but instead continue to strengthen the woman I am becoming. I know that I would not be the extremely grateful and empowered woman I am today had my mom not died when I was just twenty-three years young. I now understand and consciously think about how every other person has his or her own story that has made that person who he or she is today.

I believe life should be lived without regret and with deep appreciation. My heart knows that everything happens as it's supposed to, and that nothing is put in front of you that you cannot handle. Each experience, uplifting or tragic, sets the stage for the next phase of your life and allows you to build upon who you are until the next challenge is present. To me, this is the meaning of life - we are here to grow, evolve, and continually renew ourselves with bright new beginnings.

♥ ♥ ♥

Bethanne Wanamaker is a passionate certified nutrition educator and Superfood herbal skincare formulator, who is devoted to empowering both men and women to take control of their own health and become responsible and accountable for their actions and results regarding nutrition. She was introduced to Superfoods and the raw food lifestyle in the fall of 2001 and has been in love with Superfoods ever since. (Raw food passion came later.) Superfoods radically shifted her health status for the better and launched her own journey into conscious eating and living. Bethanne works with HealthForce Nutritionals as their national nutrition educator. Her work includes doing demos, sales, trainings, events, nutrition consultations, teaching classes, and leading the free weekly Superfood Education teleseminars. She is also the creator and writer for the Edible Goddess blog, www.EdibleGoddess.com, a resource dedicated to sharing cutting edge strategies to achieve everything you've always wanted for yourself: superior internal health and flawless external beauty!

Thank God Mercury Poisoning Changed My Life Forever!

NANCY SEAGAL

By the age of thirty-three, I found myself too exhausted to get out of bed most days. The last seven out of eight years, during which time I lived in Hawaii, there had been a growing problem with my health. I had gone from a healthy, energetic person to a person who had been zapped of every ounce of energy, and riddled with pain and a multitude of symptoms. My business as a massage therapist and hypnotherapist was slowly growing, while my health was rapidly declining. What had been sporadic unexplained symptoms throughout those years had now turned and spiraled into an out-of-control nightmare. I found myself desperate for answers.

In the fall of 1997, I was diagnosed with fibromyalgia. The diagnosis gave me hope that I would get better, yet I continued to feel worse. My symptoms started with unexplained nausea, dizziness, dry heaves, exhaustion, weakness, muscle twitching, stiffness, lack of coordination, widespread pain that was sharp, pins and needles, and feeling dull and achy. My legs especially felt this way including weakness, heaviness, hypersensitivity, burning, tingling, and constriction. I had needle-like pain in my pelvic and throat areas, IBS (irritable bowel syndrome), headaches, dehydration, rashes and hives, hypoglycemia, shortness of breath, visual disturbances including hallucinations, hypersensitivity to sound, temperature and touch, loss of hair, low body temp, low-grade fevers, tremors, insomnia, night sweats, atrophy, bladder problems, Candida, hormonal imbalance, outbursts of anger, irritability, anxiety, jitters, mild depression, impatience, brain fog, confusion, severely slow thought process, long-term and short-term memory loss, difficulty comprehending, and stopping mid-sentence with my mind completely blank.

Then, after a couple months, I additionally had paralysis, severe muscle spasms, rigidity, and seizures. Over the later years, before finding the true diagnosis, my symptoms were extreme and intermittent; I found myself often using a wheelchair and a walker. Many times I was afraid to drive, for fear my legs would become paralyzed; often I would have muscle spasms and lose control of the car. The paralysis would not only affect my legs but it would spread throughout my entire body. My muscle spasms were so severe that it would take the full strength of someone to get my leg or arm to bend so that it would break the spasm. Seizures left me unable to move, with bubbles of saliva coming out of my mouth.

These episodes left me completely exhausted and isolated. There were many times when I lay in bed feeling my body shutting down. I would surrender to God and ask him to take me. I was unafraid and ready to go; I had had enough. Yet, just at the moment of surrender, it was as if I were plugged back into the wall, and a slight surge of energy would rush through me. I would lie there confused and bewildered, trying to figure out what was happening. Eventually, I figured out there was much more in store for me.

I had learned years before from my past traumas, that for everything that seems bad, something great comes from it.

There were many times when my symptoms were exacerbated while I was alone. I would lie there sometimes for hours, paralyzed, unable to move...unable to call someone to help me. At times I went into full body spasms to the point where I couldn't move anything. I had been able to call for help in time but was unable to get to the door. The paramedics would have to break down the door and would find me lying on the floor, unable to talk, because every muscle would seize up.

In a matter of a couple years, I went from an extremely strong, independent person to someone emotionally and physically as fragile as dangerously thin ice over water, about to crack at any moment. I held onto my belief that I would eventually find an answer and prove the doctors wrong. I knew myself too well, and I knew they were wrong. The doctors were wrong!

Shortly after my diagnosis of fibromyalgia, I visited Japan. It was there I had my first episode of paralysis in my legs while lying in bed reading. I chose to ignore it, thinking that it was my imagination. A few days after I came back from Japan, I found myself in the ER...again... with my legs paralyzed. I was hospitalized, and after eight days of a myriad of tests, I was released. I had believed the doctors would discover what was wrong with me. Yet this was the start of another five years of not knowing what was making me so ill.

A few weeks later, I was back in the hospital again, this time with not only paralysis but severe spasms and full body rigidity. I spent another week of being poked and prodded. Because all the tests came back negative, the doctors concluded that the problem was in my head, otherwise known as a conversion reaction psychosomatic disorder. I had been very honest about my traumatic past with the doctors. This only gave them more reason to diagnose me with this label.

As a hypnotherapist, I understood that this could be a possibility. I didn't believe it to be the case, even though my childhood and young adult life had been full of traumatic events. My father passed away when I was four years old, leaving my mother to raise nine children. Much of my childhood was spent without supervision, guidance, structure, or support, which led me to become an extremely self-sufficient and independent person as an adult. My mother worked full-time as a cook and left my older siblings to look out for the younger ones.

As kids, we were out of control. Verbal and physical abuse among the siblings was commonplace, while my mother tried to keep order in the house. We were dirt poor and often had to rely on charity or state assistance to live. I remember many times we went without food in the fridge or having only mayonnaise and lettuce with which to make a sandwich, and nothing more. Growing up on a farm, we lived in an isolated area; our animals were my friends, and I would spend hours playing with them or riding the horses. On two separate occasions we had barn fires, and dozens of our animals perished. It was a terrible thing to witness, and for years I was left with a fear of fire.

Throughout my younger years, I had been sexually molested, and as a young adult I was date raped. It often felt as if I had a neon sign over my head that attracted these types of people to me. At the age of sixteen, I worried about everything and was very depressed and later attempted suicide.

Into my adulthood, though not without incident, I continually worked on myself throughout the years, reading self-help books, developing my spirituality, continuously learning new things, and searching for a better life. Had I believed the doctors who told me that it was 'in my head," I would not be here to tell my story in order to help others. I was focused and determined to find an answer, and I succeeded.

I decided to do several hypnotherapy processes to see if I would get any answers or clues. I worked on my fear, anger, resentment, and the physical aspects of my unknown illness, as well as several other related issues. I received some clues in a few of the sessions. When asked what was causing the symptoms, the answer was there was something there and the doctors hadn't found it yet. In addition to that, I got that my illness started with the letter "M."

These clues, along with the information from other sessions, were enough for me to know it wasn't a psychosomatic disorder and not to buy into the doctors' misdiagnosis. Knowing how powerful our minds are, and the infinite possibilities we hold within ourselves fed my determination to find an answer. Until I found the correct diagnosis, I knew I had to direct my focus on positive empowering thoughts rather than drowning in anger, self-pity, fear, and negativity. I had no clue to what my future held, but I constantly searched for what I could do to help heal myself.

Before I left Hawaii, I couldn't work any longer, and I closed my business. I exhausted my credit cards and resorted to living on food stamps. I relied on the help of close friends and family for a place to live when I returned to the mainland.

In Wisconsin, I was passed from doctor to doctor with no answers other than "it was in my head." I had another doctor who had good intentions of helping me, and finding an answer for me, but he misdiagnosed me as well, with stiff person's syndrome. Finally, I was sent to the renowned clinic in Rockford, MN and was hospitalized. Once again, one of the last doctors who I saw was a doctor of neurology and psychiatry, who labeled me with a conversion reaction psychosomatic disorder. I still refused to believe it.

About eight months later, I decided to move to Las Vegas. I still had a myriad of the symptoms plaguing me, but the worst seemed to be over until about a year and a half later. One day the spasms and paralysis came back full force. My friend gave me the name of a doctor, who saved my life. On my first visit with the doctor, after spending two hours with him, he told me to get my dental amalgams removed and then he would test me for mercury poisoning. I returned two weeks later to get tested. The results came back. The levels of mercury were off the chart, and that wasn't even at my worst. I can't even imagine what the levels were when I was at my worst.

Finally, I had found the answer. I had twelve years of heavy metal poisoning building up in my body. In hindsight, the major contributor to the mercury poisoning was my eating small to moderate amounts of fish. In addition, I believe that my dental amalgams contributed. Many years ago, I had broken a glass thermometer while in Hawaii, using my hands and a paper towel to wipe it up. I was unaware that mercury goes directly through your skin, into your cells, and settles predominantly in your brain and intestines. Mercury separates into beads and is very difficult to handle so I didn't remove it all. This happened in my bedroom, where I spent most of my time, and therefore I was exposing myself to it every day, all day long.

It was two years before I rid myself of the mercury poisoning. The first couple of months, my symptoms came back full force, and then gradually I felt better and better. The mercury poisoning caused the fibromyalgia, which disappeared after five months of detoxing. I couldn't tell how greatly this affected me until the poison was completely eliminated from my body.

It's amazing, the amount of energy I have now and how good I feel. I discovered later I have some residual problems, but now I know what I'm dealing with for healing. I had been to seven different hospitals and saw well over a hundred doctors from 1997 to 2000. After the 2003 diagnosis of mercury poisoning, I discovered that I had been tested for heavy metals on my second hospital stay in Hawaii. It showed that the levels were within the normal range. I believe these tests were not performed properly, or the lab screwed up, or both.

The answer was there all along; I just had to find the right doctor. The belief in and knowing of myself, the focus and determination with powerful inspirational thoughts, and trusting in a higher power was how I overcame this enormous adversity. I'm sure I would be dead right now had I believed it was "in my head."

No matter what happens in life, there will be challenges to face. The positive and negative have made me who I am today and created my purpose in life. What I do with it is my choice. From the trauma of my childhood to the discovery of and healing from mercury poisoning, my life has turned in a new direction. I am exactly where I am supposed to be. I am now living in the light; the darkness of the past is in the past.

♥ ♥ ♥

Nancy Seagal is a certified consulting hypnotist, hypno-coach, best--selling author, certified trainer, and speaker. Being a highly sought expert of overcoming adversity, Nancy is committed to being the catalyst for others to let go of their past that stifles them, take hold of their present circumstances, and achieve their greatest potential. Nancy's unique ability to use the power of determination and transformational thought processes is the reason her message is changing lives around the world. For more information please go to: www.RisingAboveIt.com

Thank God I Fell into Debt

MARK SOLDO

So here you are. The warm blanket of financial security is gone, and you've fallen into the dark depths of unbearable debt. You wake up every morning, with heavy shame in your heart, and spend the day hiding from relentless creditors. Your home is littered with bills, late notices, and eviction or foreclosure warnings. You keep telling yourself you're not a criminal, but it doesn't feel that way. In trying to make a better future for yourself and your family, you only brought failure and pain.

I know these things because I experienced it first-hand. But it wasn't always that way. There once was a golden time when life, like an old friend, brought smiles, gifts, and fond memories. And of all the gifts, the one I treasured most was a blue-eyed little boy named Andrew. As he grew, I often watched him play in his pretend kingdom, dashing here and there, occasionally bursting through the castle gates so I could arm him with a sword for defeating his foes. Hiking over unexplored mountain peaks with an emergency reserve of frozen Otter Pops, or running from giant Geese-monsters in the park, our life was one happy adventure after another.

Soaking in those moments, I didn't worry about bills, debt collectors, or attorneys. I was forty-three, single, in a successful career, and in complete control over my finances and my future. Many years of hard work had provided me a home in a pleasant neighborhood and a condo for my mother. I worked for the same aerospace company for twenty-three years, had perfect credit, and had a few hundred thousand dollars of equity at my disposal.

However, as time went by, dissatisfaction began growing within me. Although I didn't recognize it at first, it was a long-forgotten childhood dream beginning to stir, and it changed everything around me. A promising relationship failed, my career didn't feel right, and I no longer knew who I was as a man. I needed a major course correction, and like the friend it is, life was happy to oblige.

Suddenly, entering my life was a woman named Cyndi, and a city in the desert named Palm Springs. Although we just met, Cyndi and I found an immediate trust and familiarity, as if we had known each other for years. Without once questioning this odd chance of meeting, we quickly became investment partners, searching for real estate, and soon after that we purchased a run-down and ugly house. The plan was to refurbish and sell it for profit, At that time there was no better place to do this than Palm Springs, California.

The first house went like clockwork. That is, if the clock was built in 1950, was grossly deteriorated, and the people repairing it all came from Mars. The first two months of our investment journey were nothing but a bizarre parade of characters and events.

But with a sense of humor and an invincible vision of success, we finished the first house. When the home appraisal came in, I couldn't believe it: $35,000 and eight weeks of hard work had increased the value by $135,000! The feeling was amazing, and we didn't want it to end. Instead of selling the house, we refinanced it, pulling equity out for more investing. The house was prepared for vacation rentals, and we went on to the next.

We bought a second house, and although our initial plan was to work one at a time, we immediately found two others we had to have. Since getting a loan was about as hard as signing a form, we proceeded. Now we had four houses in progress, eight mortgages, over

$20,000 in credit card debt, and all in my name alone. Cyndi provided some initial cash and her own two hands for labor, but her credit rating was low, so I signed for everything.

We quickly finished the second home and listed it for sale. Its proceeds would finish the third and fourth homes, but instead of the quick sale we anticipated, we noticed something odd: Many "for sale" signs started appearing in the neighborhood, and our agent reported open houses with no visitors.

In October of 2005, the hot real estate market in Palm Springs froze. Everyone said it was due to the holidays, but the holidays came and went with no change. The rental demand was also down. Feeling desperate, we were the first house on the street, and perhaps all of Palm Springs, to make a drastic drop in our asking price. We expected a bidding war, but once again, no response, and no buyers.

During the next year, I borrowed large sums of money against my primary house and the condo, and pulled money out of my retirement plan. I used every resource I had to save those homes, but it was all in vain. One by one they were foreclosed and taken by the banks. I estimated over $200,000 of my personal money was lost; my credit card debt peaked at $70,000, and my debt to the banks was well over $3,000,000. Cyndi was also wiped out. In addition to her initial investment, she lost her primary house to the bank when she moved into the last remaining Palm Springs home to try and save it.

My head was spinning with despair. I couldn't sleep, and my physical health started to suffer. When I looked in my son's eyes, I felt ashamed. I didn't care what happened to me, but to bring harm to this innocent boy broke my heart. He was so positive and loving, and trusted that no matter what, his dad would always provide. The same feelings came when I saw my mother and my brother. Cyndi's health suffered far worse as she developed a life-threatening illness.

I risked everything for my family, and lost it all. My house was littered with late notices and lawsuits, and every phone call was a collector. While people around me were talking about vacations, new cars, and laughing, I had to hold back my pain and pretend I was still in their company. But I wasn't. I was in ruins.

These feelings came to a head during a business trip that spanned the weekend. On Friday night I had time to think about what I did, and my debt. Hours of painful reflection turned into emotional turmoil. At two o'clock in the morning I was on my knees crying and pounding the bed in anger. By three o'clock I was literally striking myself in the stomach, and in the face. With one last punch, a hard one, I finally gave up. I took a deep breath and admitted defeat. At that moment, something happened. I looked up from my tears and saw my laptop.

I sat down, wiped my eyes, and began typing. By six o'clock I had written ten pages. All the real estate lessons I had learned the hard way, the funny stories, and the life realizations all started to flood my mind. My fingers could barely keep up. At eight o'clock I made coffee and hung a "do not disturb" on the door. This went on all day and into the next night. It all came pouring out, and for the first time since my financial problems had started, I felt good inside. I was standing on top of a mountain, and before me was a new and refreshing life. I was finally able to see the blessing. That is when the warm glow of gratitude came, and in an instant, I was cleansed. All the grief and heartache was simply gone.

I began to recall the stories I had written during my childhood. I remembered the pleasure it brought me to create, and how I dreamt of being a novelist. I thought of my first year of college, when a friend saw me enrolling in literature and creative writing courses, and groaned, "Get a degree that makes money, like Engineering." The seed he planted misdirected me. From that point forward, I was simply too busy in my career to ever create another story, but life would not allow such an unbalance to exist forever. In the wake of my perceived disaster, a treasure-trove of blessings appeared!

The first came in the form of priceless investment knowledge gained. Books and television shows on "house flipping" didn't come close to preparing me for the true risks and challenges. But by falling in debt, I learned the full cycle of investing, including the vital practice of managing risk, and the unfortunate but critical process of negotiating and settling debt.

In the following weeks, other dimensions of my blessing unfolded as my creative energy was ignited. Incredible stories came to me, and capturing them became an obsession. If I had not experienced the loss brought by my extreme debt, I would not have found this creative force within me.

By equilibrating this perceived bad thing in my life with the many gifts that resulted, I fell into a state of thankfulness, and it transformed me. I gained new perspectives on work, family, and friendship. People around me knew something was different. My career blossomed, romance developed, and incredible news began rolling in. I gained the courage to negotiate with my creditors, and accounts started to settle. New opportunities such as this book appeared, and the true value of friendship became abundantly clear, as Cyndi remained a constant presence, coaching me through my debt settlement. Her blessings also came as her health improved, and her art, which became equally inspired, started to sell.

In the end, I realized that refurbishing life is like refurbishing a home. Sometimes the "old" has to be cleared out before the renovation can occur. So when the time is right, elements and people will enter your life that will create change.

For me, it came in the form of debt—extreme and fast. It was gut-wrenching and painful, but I am forever grateful for it. I'm happy now, writing several novels, and savoring every moment with my family. Although at one time I regretted they entered my life, I now thank God for Palm Springs, and for Cyndi.

If you have fallen into extreme debt, then congratulations are in order. You're now among the honorable and the bold. You don't observe life, study, and debate options; you act, you take risks, and you've received your battle scars in the process. In time you will see these scars as badges of honor, not shame, and you will wear them with pride. More importantly, falling in debt can be your first step on your true spiritual path in life.

When I agonized over my own financial losses, I asked the heavens if this happened for a reason. I know many people are asking the same question at this very moment. The answer is yes! You have reached this place for a reason.

Ahead lay two notorious paths: One leading to darkness, regret, and anger – the other to enlightenment, love, and gratitude. Don't take this moment lightly, as your decisions at this point will shape the rest of your life. Your task right now is to stand up and educate yourself. Study the "Thank God I" process of equilibrating your perceived positives and negatives. At the same time, learn all you can about negotiating and settling debt, and simply get started. It's not as bad as you may think. As you proceed, find the blessings your debt has brought, no matter how insignificant. The more your heart feels gratitude, the more negative energy is dissipated, and the more your world will respond.

I promise, by doing this, you will not only survive, you will be enriched beyond all imagination!

♥ ♥ ♥

Mark currently lives in Southern California with his son and four dogs. His experience in real estate taught him the true value of family, friends, and loved ones, and ignited a passion to entertain and educate through story. He writes his novels with his dog by his side, and swims in the cool waters of Laguna Beach with his son. He went searching for the perfect wave, but found his life instead.

Thank God I Lost My Job

JUDITH T. EVANS

"It's time to practice what you preach," I thought to myself walking away after being told that I no longer had a full-time position. I am a career consultant who was being released as part of a major downsizing at an international corporation. No longer a senior vice president, now I was unemployed like so many of the people I counseled.

For over fifteen years I had coached executives and professionals about finding new career options – another job, a consulting practice, a franchise, or even buying or starting a business. Euphemistically I told friends, "It's time to chart a new course."

The company that let me go offered part-time work. However, the same work would be with significantly less pay and no benefits. With a second income known as a husband or a trust fund, I would have walked away. But without such a safety net, I reluctantly said, "Sure."

Loss of income creates a struggle. Over the next few years, my savings would be tapped and my home refinanced. I didn't realize at the time that the situation had hidden benefits: namely, time to explore opportunities and gain additional skills and insights.

Early in my career when I was learning motivational techniques for selling, I was told that the "FUD" factor is what gets people to buy something new. That's Fear, Uncertainty and Doubt...FUD. I've rechristened this to a more motivational "FUD" factor for moving forward—it's Faith, Understanding and Direction. First, comes Faith in ourselves. This is confidence, optimism or self-esteem. Second, Understanding is the combination of learning along with critical analysis. It's a practical feasibility study that asks, "What are the odds of success?" Third is Direction. It's the action...the testing of whatever one wants to accomplish.

In charting a new course, the FUD factor is the compass that provides supportive guidance. For Faith, spiritual courses beckoned; for Understanding, innovative business seminars surfaced; and for Direction, numerous opportunities gave seductive clues for reaching the center of a career maze.

Initially, negative feelings needed to be released. Cumulative losses – a divorce, the long-term position, financial setbacks – held me captive. Losses fed an invisible enemy holding restraining ropes made of anger and fear. Tightly held, knotted ropes of negative feelings create a real handicap. These negative cords would be released gradually, but at this time, I was stuck. A personal recovery program was definitely in order.

Taking courses in the spiritual realm started the recovery process, beginning with an intensive program using spiritual principles for emotional healing. Training centered upon abandoning stories that no longer served a useful purpose and, instead, focused on negative feelings, releasing them and moving on. "Don't tell a story. Tell me how you feel," was the recurrent refrain.

A breakthrough came in one exercise while I was working with a top executive from a well-known European company. Initially, he couldn't start the process. Instead, as I gave him the instructions, he began slowly shaking, and then his whole body began moving violently. Finally he began to relax and finished the exercise. Smiling, he told me that, while going through this exercise, he discovered spiritual messages for himself that he needed to hear.

I learned something, too. I often hesitate to look at the dark side of life...the abyss or pain. One of my colleagues used to be annoyed with me and called me a Pollyanna. "Get real, " she would chide. "You want to splash sunshine on what is bad and sad."

Yes, I do prefer to look on the bright side and deny negative feelings. But a room with crying, shouting, and profoundly enraged individuals dealing with and clearing their pain has no room for my Pollyanna optimism. Fears, anger, and depression must be acknowledged... and, most importantly, facing these emotions can lead to a state of peace, empowerment, and creativity with the releasing of difficult stories.

Spiritual exercises tap into what is known as 'soul' or 'source' or 'higher power.'

This is the hidden wizard in each of us that protects and opens doors to personal freedom.

By studying spiritual healing methods and practicing processes with many people, I am no longer afraid to deal with my own issues or with clients who are stuck and troubled. The Pollyanna in me still wants to be in positive places, but negative areas are no longer off-limits.

Faith and Understanding joined together in an intensive series of financial prosperity seminars had me flying to different cities and sitting in crowded ballrooms listening to men and women give practical tips on how to succeed with a range of entrepreneurial ventures. Thank God that I had the resources to support this educational excursion because it introduced a new set of business skills, knowledge, and motivational techniques.

Selling and marketing approaches using venues such as the Internet, TV, and radio were center-stage topics. Multiple streams of income became a mantra for achieving passive, residual income. Speakers who are part of "The Secret" and early practitioners of "The Law of Attraction" shared what they knew. These business courses were echoing the earlier work from the spiritual courses. Affirmations, declarations, and visualizations were used for retraining our brains and revising mental financial blueprints to welcome and enter a higher level of prosperity and personal growth.

While pursuing this adult educational journey,

an unexpected challenge arose: I had carbon monoxide poisoning. One day my chimney backed up, releasing black smoke with toxic fumes. The firefighters came to my home shouting "Get out of this house! Our registers show high levels of carbon monoxide." I left home and went straight to a hospital emergency room.

In the days that followed, I was alive but so tired. The main effect physically was chronic fatigue, and there was lung damage. I could not walk for more than one block without getting winded. I went to bed tired and woke up tired.

A part-time position was all I could handle. I slept on the weekends and days off to have enough energy to coach people and to do seminars. One day after I taught two classes in New York City and started walking toward Grand Central Station to catch a train, I felt very weak. As a young man went by, I stopped him. "Would you carry my heavy briefcase?" He looked at me oddly, perhaps wondering why this stranger was asking for help. "I'm sick. I can't carry this another block."

"No problem, " he replied. He ended up walking me to the train. I still think of him with gratitude and mark this event as a litmus test of how truly ill I was because of the poisoning. Ultimately, I recovered, but it took three years to do so.

In the meantime, the spiritual and business courses were enabling me to tell my own story.

As a spiritual seeker for many years, I tried to keep this part of life a secret. After all, I worked with top executives in New York City, who might view me as flaky or too 'woo woo.' (Now I know that I can come out of the spiritual closet and share all that I have learned and continue to learn.)

Financial business seminars reinforced the knowledge that I was not alone in feeling badly about losses. Everyone at some point had a story of loss and overcoming. Instructors on the ballroom stages shared their own stories. There was the hedge fund manager and trader who lost $10 million of his own money. A business maven and real estate investor told of losing $400 million and entertaining thoughts of suicide. A business tycoon's company went bankrupt; and he faced a judicial system charging him with fraud. Although acquitted, he still had to start over.

Inspirational stories came from people without college degrees who were generating million-dollar annual incomes using their basic intelligence, hard work, and keen awareness of market opportunities ranging from car washes to selling 'how-to-do-its' on the Internet, using financial options and foreign currency trading, to vending machines, and on and on. A leader in the multi-level marketing industry shared that as a teenager he'd been arrested for armed robbery and was a felon.

Wow! Everyone had a story, and every story led to overcoming and, finally, to financial success and serving the world as a benefactor.

I spent over five years reestablishing my own career and found that Faith, Understanding, and Direction served as true guides in the personal recovery program. The Direction part was a times almost a trial and error process of being in a maze with dead ends. I tried many options that did not work. However, persistence won. I kept on trying and, finally, created a business with multiple streams of income that works.

Would I have learned all of this if I hadn't lost a full-time position? Yes, but the loss accelerated the process. Carbon monoxide poisoning revealed that working a full-time position at this time was impossible. Furthermore, the rewards from this loss are many, including coming out of the spiritual closet and learning a new set of business skills. Hearing so many gifted people share their stories of loss and overcoming was a powerful lesson about resilience.

In creating a new direction, I know that if my heart is inspired, I am on the right track! I've even changed how I introduce myself professionally. Instead of announcing, "I'm a career coach. I now say, "I'm a career crisis expert"...and thank God that I am.

♥ ♥ ♥

Dr. Judith T. Evans is an author, lecturer, and coach on issues related to career management and life transformations. She combines a corporate background with a lifelong study of spiritual practices.

Educational credentials include a Masters and Doctorate in developmental psychology from the School of Education at Harvard University and a Bachelor's degree from Michigan State University. She is a founding member of the Career Counselor's Consortium in New York City.

Her website is www.newcareerventures.com and email is judith@newcareerventures.com

Thank God I Got Divorced

PATTI HANDY

When we first met, it was instant attraction. We were introduced by a mutual friend; we were young and in college. We started dating immediately and exclusively. We talked forever and became best of friends. I had found the love of my life. After dating for eighteen months and graduating from college, we got married. We started our "corporate, grown-up" jobs, bought our first home, and started down a path of new beginnings. I started my career in the financial arena, first in the Investment Banking world, and then into working at large banks in the investment divisions. He was a sales rep for an industrial company. We traveled some, enjoyed boating, camping, and just being together.

After years of "playing," we decided it was time for a family. We both loved children and wanted some of our own. Unfortunately, becoming pregnant was not easy for us. We struggled for a couple of years without any success. Finally, we sought help from a fertility specialist, who put me on various drugs to help us along. A few more years had gone by, but no baby. I tried to stay positive, but with the drugs wreaking havoc on my hormones and the possibility of never having children, I was overwhelmed and extremely sad. I found it difficult to go to my friends' baby showers without coming home and breaking down.

After five years of trying we opted for in vitro fertilization. It was a very expensive procedure, not covered by insurance, and without guarantees. I just had to try. I, once again, had to endure shots and procedures as part of this process. After coming home and waiting for weeks to feel signs of pregnancy, I was disappointed that I was feeling so good. No signs of nausea, no tiredness. No nothing.

It was time for the doctor's follow-up visit and pregnancy test. I could almost hear my doctor telling me I was not pregnant because I felt no signs. As I waited for the results, I was heavy-hearted and anxious. Then the nurse walked in with a smile on her face, announcing I was pregnant! I screamed so loud the entire waiting room heard me!! Actually, I think the entire floor heard me. Words cannot describe how happy and elated we were. God had blessed us with a miracle baby!

When my son was born, it was truly amazing. The love that radiated from this child was God speaking to us. It was God's plan that we wait until the time was right. Our son was healthy, beautiful, and had a full head of hair. I remember the nurses would bring him to me after they had spiked his hair into a Mohawk. To this day, he loves spiking his hair! Sans the Mohawk, of course. Coincidence? Perhaps.

Life after my son was born was like most. Sleepless nights, altered routines, and compromises. I loved every minute of it, despite being exhausted. It was our dream.

I had just put my son to sleep and sat down for a little quiet time with my husband. He turned to me and said we needed to talk. Nothing could have prepared me for what was coming next. He announced that he wasn't happy, he wasn't sure if he had ever loved me, and that he wanted a divorce. It took me a minute to realize that I had stopped breathing.

Was he kidding with me? The look on his face told me otherwise. My son was eighteen months old at the time, and we had been married for nearly thirteen years. Thoughts of my son and the effect this would have on him consumed me. What went so terribly wrong? Why didn't I see this coming? My body shook from fear while I cried beyond control. I felt completely overwhelmed with not knowing what to do next. I was terrified of being alone, gripped with fear and not knowing what lay ahead for my son and me. How could he do this to me and our son? So many questions, very few answers. But, the answers came in time—God's time.

It was agreed that my ex-husband would take our son every other weekend for an overnight stay. This was more painful to experience than the divorce itself. My baby was being taken away from me, and I couldn't do anything about it. I knew he was in good hands with his father, but nevertheless, it was so hard to let him go. The minute I closed the door, I cried for what seemed forever. I had to close my son's bedroom door when he was gone, as I couldn't stand it being empty.

The first year that followed certainly had its challenges. My son was a toddler, and I essentially was raising him on my own. At that tender age, I couldn't bring myself to take my son to a daycare facility, so I found a profession that allowed me to work from home. It was a 100% commission position, which meant no stability, no security, and no benefits. I struggled financially and found myself going into debt. I was exhausted emotionally and physically, which scared me. I wanted, and needed, to be my best for my son's sake.

With the first year of being alone comes the "firsts" of everything. The first holidays, birthdays, and anniversaries. Memories made those days especially tough. Some days were better than others. It seemed as though I would take two steps forward and then one step back. There were days where I just focused on getting past the next hour, let alone the next day. I had to allow that experience to flow through me in order to move forward. Family and friends were amazing in their love and support. Never underestimate the power of love!

I tried my hand at various jobs that allowed me to work from home. If something didn't work out the way I had hoped, I tried something else. My priority was flexibility with my schedule, but I also needed an income. I persevered and kept moving forward. I had gotten certified as a personal trainer many years prior, and decided to pursue personal training, as I loved working with people and working out myself. I tried my hand at network marketing, was a Realtor for a few years, then went into the mortgage-lending world. As a mortgage broker, I was able to "marry" my financial background, my real estate background, and my love of working with people. It also allowed me to work from home and gave me flexibility with my hours. Much of my work was done once my son was in bed, or before he woke up. It was at this time that I was finally able to get out of debt and build my bank account back up.

The growth and transformation happened gradually. I came to realize that an emotional wound heals much like a physical wound. Nature needs to take its course, but how we take care of ourselves during that critical time can make or break our end result. I continued my exercise routine, whether I felt like it or not. I leaned on my family and friends for support. I did my best to eat healthy and was gentle with myself. I took care of myself the way I would take care of my best friend—something we women can have a very difficult time doing! I envisioned the life I wanted and asked God for faith and courage. I read books that inspired me and gave me hope. My son was also my strength as I continued on my journey.

With each passing day and challenge, I experienced an amazing transformation. It was ever so slight, but over time, life-altering. With God's guidance, I realized the strength and wisdom that I had within myself. I became stronger and wiser. I found hope, clarity, and direction. I learned to trust myself again, which allowed me to open my heart once more. I took control over my finances, my home, and in time, my life. I got out of debt completely and actually bought some rental property, in addition to owning my own home.

Today, my son is thirteen years old and a fulfilled, well-balanced, well-adjusted little guy. He loves to play drums, to skateboard, and to play with friends. He became a Black Belt in Hapkido and will continue into the junior level. His teachers confirm what I already know: he is compassionate and sweet, with a inspired attitude. As I write this, he is dancing around the room while trying to read what I am writing. Needless to say, he keeps me on my toes. As the teen years are just around the corner, I am in the market for a good helmet! For both of us.

Today, I am a money coach for teens. My inspiration is to educate and empower teens and young adults with money smarts, so they can create their own wealth. I feel I have found my life's purpose, God's purpose for me. I have written a book, dedicated to my son, which is a "wealth-building toolbox for teens." My company http://www.teenscashcoach.com has helped me touch many people, and I pray it allows me to reach many more. God does have a plan, whether we understand it at the time or not.

It is only after looking back that I realized I "lost myself" in my marriage. I would truly not be who I am today without having experienced my divorce. I came to a place of appreciation for my ex-husband and gratitude to him for letting me go. I not only survived the divorce, I thrived as a result of it. I found myself again. My divorce was a gift in so many aspects. Thank God I got divorced!

♥ ♥ ♥

As a speaker, author and founder of Teens Cash Coach™, Patti Handy teaches teens about entrepreneurship and money smarts. From school assemblies to bootcamps, she engages, entertains and empowers teens to create the life they deserve. Patti's quick wit and sense of humor make all her presentations interesting and fun experiences for teens.

She is the author of How to Ditch your Allowance and be Richer than your Parents® and the creator of A Millionaire in the Making-The Biz Building Bootcamp for Teens™. Visit www.teenscashcoach.com to learn more.

Thank God I was Depressed

RICK FISCHER

It was a beautiful day in July when the pain began. It came upon me slowly, and for the first few weeks it was just an annoying pain in the buttocks. It was summer though and so I ignorantly and stubbornly continued my intense gym workouts, speed-boating across choppy waters, and playing competitive tennis. It was a beautiful summer, and by the time it came to an end, I could no longer walk.

Thinking at first I had just strained a muscle, I ignored it. With each day though the pain became more intense, and soon I was fighting through it with every tennis stroke. My physiotherapist hypothesized it might be a disk problem, but my mind wouldn't accept that verdict. By the time I eventually had my CT scan, even before the results came back, it was very clear. I had herniated both my L4/L5 and L5/S1 disks. According to the words of the report, the L5/S1 disk was "obliterating the S1 root sheathe", and I now had severe sciatic nerve pain all down my left leg.

I was 32, at the prime of my life and physical condition, highly active and athletic with a life revolving around fitness. To be told that I was now faced with a life of chronic pain and would have to give up the physical hobbies I so love was devastating. This was not a case of a broken bone that would heal in six weeks. Oh how I wished it was just a broken bone. Instead I was faced with an injury that would change the rest of my life and the way in which I would live it. I cursed life and felt betrayed by it.

Before long, I was confined to the floor of my living room, lying flat on my back to lessen the pain, day and night. If I had to, I could stand up and walk, but the pain was excruciating. It felt like a dagger piercing my lower back and 100,000 volts of electric current shooting all the way down my left leg. For weeks I was forced to lay on the floor, doing nothing but reading books, thinking about life, reading some more, and sleeping.

It was hell.

I became extremely depressed. Outside, the sun glistened off the distant snow-capped summit of Mt. Baker (which I had been planning to climb the following year), and the sounds of late-summer laughter filled the air. Inside I was stuck on the floor, confined to a lonely, darkened room. My hopes of climbing Mt. Baker were shattered, and my love of surfing and tennis were now just a painful memory. I was told my life would never be the same. Hearing all about my friends' adventures didn't help me either. I wanted to be out there with them - the most beautiful time of the year, yet I was imprisoned inside. At times I'd be tempted to go out in the sun and do paperwork on my patio table. But then reality kicked in – I couldn't even sit in a chair. The truth is, I had to move my home office (computer, papers, everything) to the floor. My home looked like a hurricane had passed through – I wasn't able to do any cleaning since I couldn't bend over to pick things up. I could barely even put my own shorts or socks on. I felt useless, alone, an invalid. I saw very little hope. And I felt as if my life, at least the fun times, had ended.

Ironically, this is where my story would begin.

In the two years prior, my father had tragically passed away, I'd been through a painful break-up, my mother was in a car accident and was subsequently involved in a long legal battle. I was just resettling to life in Canada after spending five years in Asia, and I was trying to readjust and find my purpose. I was busy, successful at what I was doing, but I was lacking a clear direction.

As I laid on the floor reading, I was inspired by Lance Armstrong's recovery from cancer. I also remembered, from previous injuries I've had, that I was capable of recovering better than any doctors thought I would. Though this injury was different, I still knew I was capable of making a comeback, and at that moment I decided to make this the greatest comeback of my life. I could visualize it, like a scene from a heroic movie playing in my mind, and it lit a fire within me. I'd hit the lowest point of my life, and I knew this wasn't a place I wanted to be. This person wasn't me. In the way that a valley creates a mountain, or a rubber band shoots further the more it's stretched, I'd hit my lowest, and I was now determined more than ever to bounce back that much higher, stronger, and better!

My recovery began slowly. I started with very basic core strengthening movements at home. As the swelling around my spine slowly began to decrease, I was able to get out more to various treatments. I went to physiotherapy nearly every day doing traction and core exercises combined with massage. I hired a Grandmaster of medical Qigong to come to Vancouver to treat me privately. I tried acupressure. I learned and practiced meditation and visualization. I began acupuncture once a week (although first I had to undergo hypnotherapy treatments to help overcome a very real and terrifying phobia of needles). Little did I know that soon I'd also be getting weekly injections similar to an epidural that went deep into the nerves and muscles around the spinal cord. These injections (administered by a doctor of TCM) were a mixture of procaine, saline and B12 (to detoxify the area, increase local circulation and stimulate regeneration of damaged nerve cells), as well as dextrose injections (to recreate a controlled inflammation that would re-stimulate the body's healing ability). These three inch needles were painful, especially when they hit the nerves or vertebrae bone. I received four to eight injections per treatment. And I grunted and yelled through every single one of them! But I was committed to doing whatever it took to get better. These injections, in the end I truly believe, were one of the greatest aids in my recovery.

Recovering became a second full-time job. I was spending 30 to 40 hours a week commuting to, or in, treatments. And being self employed, none of my expenses were covered by a medical plan! There were set-backs.

I remember my eyes filled with tears once during a physiotherapy session when I was seeing no improvements and the situation again looked completely hopeless. I stuck with it though, and slowly but surely the combination of all these treatments started having a healing effect, and over the course of the next four or five months I was back on my feet. Being able to walk normally is a far cry from bodybuilding and playing competitive tennis though, and I was determined to continue improving.

It's now been exactly a year since the injury. I still have physiotherapy once a week, occasional soft-touch Chiropractic treatments, and occasional injections. I also regularly do rehabilitative Pilates and exercises in the pool. As of the past month, I'm finally back in the gym lifting light to moderate weights. As recently as three months ago the neurosurgeon was still trying to convince me that I'd need surgery! I knew I'd prove him wrong and I did. I'm well on the road to recovery, the natural way, my way.

I had just begun working with a life coach shortly before the injury. After finding out I had two herniated disks, I remember talking to her, almost in tears, afraid and devastated that my life would never be the same. She told me to search inside for the reason why this happened, and to also find a way to not only accept it, but also become grateful for it. At the time I couldn't comprehend that concept at all, and felt she didn't "understand my situation." How the hell could I be grateful for something that has destroyed my life?!

Perhaps that right there was the greatest lesson for me to learn – my way of thinking. We as humans are often too busy looking at the door that has closed on us to see the new one that has opened.

It took some time for me to shift my vision, but ironically, time was now the one thing I was blessed with.

As I laid on the floor, I thought about the brevity of life - how it can be snuffed out so fast. I thought about my father - all he had accomplished and taught me; and all the things he didn't have the chance to do. I thought about all the things that I want to accomplish and have in my life. I created a vision board so I could visually see those dreams. I suddenly felt a sense of urgency that I'd never felt before. Life is short. Why wait until I'm retired to start making those dreams reality, I thought. I'm alive. Right here. Right now. This is my chance! Right NOW! Live and love to the fullest! I suddenly felt a deep compassion for people around the world also suffering, and a burning need to contribute and help in some way. More specifically I discovered that I want to help children in third world countries not only get an education, but also give them the seeds to dream and help make those dreams reality. This was the beginning of a foundation which I've since started called 'Rising Horizons', the first project of which will be the construction of a school in South East Asia. I also realized that real estate, which I've dabbled in for years, is a bigger passion of mine than I had thought, and I vowed to pursue it more fully. I could now see clearly how real estate would help me achieve my dreams. I began taking courses and surrounding myself with inspiring people who have the same inspirations and goals as I do. My entire world began opening up, and I knew then that I was on the right path. From those dark moments lying alone on the floor, the map of my future emerged and I could finally (after 30+ years of searching) see where I was going.

Today, my body is healing tremendously. I have for it a renewed respect, love and understanding. There will be certain movements that I'll always have to be cautious with, but regardless I can see myself returning to a state of superb physical fitness. Spiritually I'm transformed. I feel more enlightened, wiser, and I see and understand life with more clarity. I exist on a deeper, more profound level than before, and I feel almost elevated by an inexplicable sense of joy and gratitude for being allowed this experience. Emotionally, I'm content and grateful, and I'm a stronger person.

I believe the key to my recovery was simple. Once I had come to grips with my condition, I then outright refused to let this pain and darkness ruin the rest of my life. The thought of recovering to the point where I could simply walk again and lead a relatively normal lifestyle was not an option. I had a picture in my mind of the person I wished to be both physically and mentally, and this became my reason for recovering. The answer to the 'Why bother?'. With unwavering commitment I was going to make that picture reality, NO MATTER WHAT IT TOOK! The body is capable of doing amazing things if you believe in it. Once you make that commitment to yourself and feel that burning fire inside, and if your 'Why' is big enough, nothing can stop you.

Now, would I want to go through this whole experience again? Probably not. Nobody wishes for tragedy. I believe though that this whole experience happened for a profound reason. Thank God I was depressed! Thank God I was knocked down that low, for nothing less would have opened my eyes! It was the wake-up call I needed to catapult me to a greater, more fulfilling life. It taught me an invaluable lesson which I needed to learn, slowed me down just long enough to evaluate and make necessary changes in my life. It strengthened me. I've grown so much in the past year. The opportunities I see now are endless. Everything happens for a reason and everything is now falling into place as a result. I now see all the doors that have since opened, and they lead to a more beautiful life than I had imagined before. I am grateful, and I have no regrets.

♥ ♥ ♥

I am honored and excited to be part of this ground-breaking project! The inspiration for me in writing this story is the hope that it will help others going through similar experiences. At the age of 32 I was diagnosed with 2 herniated discs in my lower back, causing severe sciatica and nerve damage in my left leg, and the prognosis was slim that I'd ever recover enough to play the sports I so much loved the way I used to. Surgery was the recommendation. The pain excruciating. Depression sunk in. My active life was destroyed. Through sheer determination, hard work, and a belief in the natural healing ability of my body, I was not only able to avoid surgery, I'm also well on the road to recovery, 95% pain free, and back in the gym again lifting weights exactly one year later. At the beginning I could only see the door that had closed on me. Now I see all the new ones that have opened. I see this past year's journey, as painful and dark as it was at times, as a blessing, and I'm grateful for it.

Rick Fischer
Thank God I Had Chronic Pain
Thank God I Was Depressed
Vancouver, BC
www.HowToHealMyBack.com

Thank God I Am a Survivor of Incest

TERI LYNN

Sometimes, don't you just think to yourself, why me? Why was I the one chosen for all of this to happen to? Couldn't I have had a normal childhood? Couldn't I have grown up in a "normal functioning" household?

My life, from as far back as I can remember, was consistently a struggle. I was the fat girl, the outcast. I was the girl who was told, "If you just lose a little more weight, then you can get that nice hairstyle you wanted." Or the time when I was going to get my shoes for Catholic school, and the woman who was helping me, said to my mother and me, "Oh my! Don't you have chubby feet?" Then there were the endless days of the boys, and even worse, the girls who would taunt me to sheer embarrassment in the school yard. The taunting got so bad one day that I ran out of class to the bathroom. The teacher made me share how each of the other kids had harassed me.

As much as it felt like a relief or payback in ways, it was also another embarrassing moment to add to the collection.

Now, don't be confused—this is not a story of "Thank God I Was a Fat Kid," although I could surely write one of those as well! But I wanted to provide some background because it relates to the rest of my story.

I don't recall how old I was—or how young—when it first happened. I don't recall exactly what happened, the specific number of years it went on for, nor do I recall many of the details. Even to this day, the majority of what happened to me and of my entire childhood is a blur to me. What I do recall is that it did happen. I know I cannot wish away my past, as hard as I try. So I have finally learned to accept my truth. And here it is, my truth: Incest is a part of me. It is a part of my life that won't be deleted, reversed, or forgotten. It is like my ten fingers and ten toes. I can't remove it from my life and go back in time; therefore, it is up to me to determine how I let it lead the course of my life. And for this reason I felt compelled to share my story.

I described the issue with my weight because, as you can imagine, I tried to be accepted, to fit in, and to be liked. It was not easy to live a life of constant torment and scrutiny for being overweight. No boy would ever even give me the time of day. I would have crushes on boys with the highest hopes of them magically liking me back—but those ideas were only in my wildest dreams. And so it happened that the only boy who would give me attention, of all the boys, turned out to be my brother. My brother and I had an incestuous relationship from the time I was a little girl until I was out of high school. I do remember the first time it all started. My brother came across some "adult" tapes that our parents had in their bedroom, and he brought me into their room when they were not home, to show me. I don't remember exactly what took place at this initial moment, and whether or not he encouraged me to mimic some of the moves. This would mark the first of many times that we shared this type of encounter.

It's interesting that I didn't blame my brother for initiating anything with me. I knew I was young, but I also knew I was aware of my sexuality and was curious to discover more. On top of all of that, I was aching for love and affection and attention in my life. And here I'd finally found it. Or so I thought in some distorted way.

So the cycle began. Many of the events that occurred are so distant from my memory that I cannot remember the sequence. What I know is that these encounters happened again and again.. and again... and again. At a time when I was so desperate for love and affection, the pleasure of instant gratification far outweighed "right" versus "wrong." Deep down, we both knew that the activities we were participating in were not healthy. Each time we would engage in an act, I was caught up in receiving pleasure, but as soon as we would finish, the wave of guilt rode over my body like hot sun on asphalt. Sometimes there was a mutual agreement to engaging in sexual behavior. But many other times, I would be lying in my bed and would feel a hand come underneath my sheets on the opposite side of the bed.

At first, I would feel anger and disgust. I would think to myself, "What is he doing here? Why is he coming in here again?" Then he would touch a certain spot that would feel good, and I would get turned on and forget about those initial feelings.

I remember the times when I would make bargains. I would say to him: "OK, if I do this for you, will you tell so-and-so that I like him?" During the act, I thought that my wonderful idea of offering to meet his needs at that moment would actually be fulfilling my needs of love and acceptance from the boys at school whom I liked. However, my bargaining did not gain the love and acceptance I was longing for from others. It only led me to feel guilt and shame as soon as we finished. I would turn over afterwards and say to myself, "Never again, Teri! Never, ever again will this happen." Each time, I swore I was going to run upstairs and tell my parents what had been going on for years and years right underneath their own roof. But the embarrassment of what we were doing and the fear of their reaction stopped me each time. And so it would continue for years to follow.

There was one time that is marked in my mind forever. We were in high school, and our family was on our yearly winter vacation in the Islands. This one afternoon, my younger sisters were at the pool with my mother, and my father went for a ride around the island. It was only my brother and I who were left in the bedroom playing UNO on the bed, in our bathing suits, with the shades drawn—a perfect opportunity to engage in a pleasurable activity. My father's suspicious inclination was correct as he left the condo, because not soon after he left, he quietly slipped back inside and upstairs, only to find my brother and me on the bed as he'd suspected. The recollection of this moment still causes me to shudder. I was mortified. There we were—caught red-handed. I was let off the hook as my father went after my brother and whipped his backside in the bathroom. I felt guilty and relieved at the same time. I felt guilty because I knew I wasn't innocent. I felt relieved because I wasn't getting in trouble. The shame and guilt crept throughout my entire body, and this time I was sure the behavior would stop.

My parents had no clue that this was going on for years prior to this incident. They didn't know how to handle the situation. We were told to go to confession. Go to confession? Is that what you think we need to do? I couldn't believe it.

I sat in front of the priest trying to confess to something that I couldn't really say because I felt such shame and embarrassment. Why am I confessing for something like this? Do they really think confession would clear up all of these years and make me feel better for what was happening? This was the chance to stop this cycle. This was the opportunity to scream out loud: "Hello?! Is anyone home? Does anyone know what I have been going through?" Instead, I completed the assignment for my punishment—I went to confession.

Now I thought, OK, so we were discovered, we confessed, and now it will definitely stop. I forget if I made a pact with just myself, or if my brother and I made it with each other. We knew this had to stop. We knew our behavior was inappropriate. But it didn't. It continued for the next few years, until finally I went away to college. But even when I returned for winter break, my brother snuck into my room and wanted to start something. I tossed and turned and made enough grunting noises for him to realize that I was not interested in this act of incest anymore. He left my room.

Even though my brother had girlfriends, things

were happening between us. I just couldn't understand why he would still come to me for satisfaction. I was the one who didn't have the boyfriends and wanted the attention. I kept wondering why this happened in the first place and why it continued for so long

After my first year of college, I returned home from school—another day permanently marked in my memory. I sat down on my father's bed and, with a lot of courage, showed my father a term paper I wrote during Freshman Composition class entitled The Patchwork Quilt. It was a story about interracial and non-traditional relationships. Although I was nervous for his response, I was very proud of my work. This really shook up my very traditional father. It caused him to recall the event back in high school. He asked me if my brother ever did something after that. I was completely silent, yet I knew I couldn't hold it in any longer. I felt that this was my second opportunity for help. This time my father was much more receptive to the situation. My parents finally realized that confession was not the answer, nor could we alone handle this skeleton in our closet. We finally sought the help of professionals. Since then, I have been so grateful for the help of our therapist.

I knew, though, there was more that I needed to do to heal. The first experience was in August 2008, I attended a camp that pushed me physically, yet because I was mentally frozen, I faced many demons. With the help of an amazing support system, I worked my way through the activities and the fears. I stood on stage on the last day and shared with the crowd what I'd learned that week, "I am OK with who I am and where I am. I don't have to be afraid or ashamed of my past." Not only did this release help me, but I had my teammates come up and say, "Wow! When you said you don't feel ashamed, I said to myself I can let go too of the things I carry shame for." My journey of my truth, and my acceptance and gratitude for my truth, was beginning.

In January of 2009, I stood up in front of over six hundred people and shared the mission that I created for my life. With my voice trembling, my hand shaking holding the microphone, but with the deepest conviction coming from my toes, I knew I had to do this, and so I stated the following: "My mission is to relate to survivors of incest through vocalizing my experience and to inspire and enlighten their lives to a level of healing, restored self-worth, and renewed appreciation of their sensual being."

I just about looked up from reading my mission statement, and all around me, there was a crowd of over six hundred people on their feet, giving me the loudest, most astonishing standing ovation I have ever received. (Actually, it was the only standing ovation I have ever received!). And to think that for something for which I carried so much shame, guilt, and embarrassment for so long, I was now being applauded and commended for. Unbelievable!

I realized this happened to me for a brilliant and ingenious reason. This happened for me to stop burying it, ignoring it, and pretending that it did not happen. This happened to me so I would stand up, open my mouth, and start doing something about it—for myself, for my family, for my generations past and those to come—for all of those who have been affected by it or know someone who has—bottom line: for the world. I must do something to raise the awareness and ultimately end this plague on a dynamic global scale. God has chosen me to be his vehicle—and for this I am grateful.

Although, there is still healing that needs to be done in my family, I have also learned that everything happens on God's course—not mine. Through my continual healing process, I will open the door in the Universe for other people's healing to take place. I now realize that accepting this truth as part of me can set me free. But what is even more awesome is that setting it free by sharing it in writing and in spoken voice allows the shame to be released.

After I shared my story, I had many people over the next two days standing by me, waiting to share their stories and to thank me for my courage and my openness. I even had a fourteen-year old girl gather the strength to ask me to come up to the stage to talk to me. It was at this moment that I said, "Thank God I am a survivor of incest." I am not alone. I realized that so many people have their stories to share. If I can just create that space of understanding and compassion for someone to tell their truth, I have made my mark. I can and will create a movement to pass on to others. Even if I only bring comfort and healing to just one person—whether it is one small child, one teenager, one adult, or even one aged individual—I will have accomplished my mission. But while I am here, I will be that voice, and I will invite all those affected directly or indirectly to join me on my journey to heal themselves, heal their loved ones, and to pass on the message that incest must stop once and for all. And that mission has just begun...

♥ ♥ ♥

Teri Lynn feels honored and privileged to make her story available to all those who have also walked in her steps or know someone who has so that they know they are not alone. If your voice is hidden now, know you can use hers in the meantime, until yours shines. For those that feel ashamed (including her own family and circle) of sharing this (or your own) story, please know that it is serving a Higher Purpose. Teri resides in Northern New Jersey and enjoys dancing, watching cooking shows, and feels deep gratification serving as a Trained Volunteer on the RAINN Online Hotline. Wishing all readers Inner Peace and Self-Love. Feel free to contact Teri at PutIncest2Rest@gmail.com

Thank God I Saw My Son's Drowning

ANNIE ROSE

Wow! What a gorgeous western Colorado day! The morning brought a tremendous summer thunderstorm with lightning bouncing from the Colorado National Monument to the Bookcliff Mountains. Then, as is typical here, the clouds broke and disappeared, leaving a crystal clear Colorado blue sky and sun-drenched day warming to 85°.

My fourteen and a half-year-old twins, Marty and Annie, had just finished Missoula Theater play practice and had a three-hour break until their next practice. They were to perform for the country club the following day in Pinocchio. Annie had been cast as the Blue Fairy, and Marty as Jiminy Cricket (Pinocchio's conscience). They took their theatrical endeavor seriously. I had left them at the country club pool to swim and do teenage things like hang out for a while.

I was sitting at my computer in my office cottage, a mere half mile up the street, when Annie called: "Mom, I forgot my lunch. Will you please bring it to me?" Moving slowly, I ambled towards the house to retrieve the car keys, admiring our brilliant flower and vegetable garden along the way. Then, keys in hand, I got another call from Annie. This time, her voice was more frantic: "Mom, call 911! Come right away. Marty's hurt!" My heart began to pound as I yelled to my seventeen-year-old, Lainey, and we ran to the car. I drove as fast as I possibly could on a rural road with my flashers on. It seemed like the longest five minutes of my life.

When we arrived at the pool, my son was lying on the side, "dead," with the lifeguard screaming, "Call 911! He's not breathing!"

My M.O. is cool, calm, and collected under stress. I have been to hell and back several times in my life. I am a survivor. Yeah, right! I lost it and began crying and shaking uncontrollably; I was losing my only son, my "sunshine," "Marty Marts"!

I became pregnant with twins at the age of forty. I was diagnosed with a rare genetic blood disease and required three blood transfusions to get us through an extremely high-risk pregnancy. There were no twins in our families and I had not taken fertility drugs. God wanted me to have twins. When I found out they were a girl and a boy, I agonized. I was terrified of raising a boy. Well, we all made it, and I was blessed with the sweetest son a mother could ever wish for! He was the clown as an infant, bringing us laughter and joy. As a young boy, and now a teenager, he was always giving me big, unsolicited hugs. How would I survive without him?

As this all flashed through my mind, Marty suddenly gasped for breath, then water and blood spewed from his mouth. He was alive!

On our way to the emergency room, my son told me that he was swimming with fifteen-pound ankle weights. "All of the kids, even the eight year old kids, do it, Mom," he said. "All of a sudden I got really tired. I sank to the bottom of the deep end, and I couldn't swim up. Every time I reached for the side of the pool, my fingers slipped. I tried to get the weights off, but the Velcro wouldn't loosen. Then I saw people above me and thought, 'Why doesn't somebody help me?' I saw the play and my part as Jiminy Cricket flash across my mind. It seemed like hours, and then I thought, I am going to die. I don't want my mom to be sad, and then I passed out. I was in a really bright place...."

After returning home from the hospital, that evening, Marty endured lots of teasing from my husband and his sisters: "So Marts... why didn't you just tie yourself to a cement block or anchor, then jump in the deep end, huh?" We all had a good laugh. However, we were all also visibly shaken and aware that we had almost lost him.

Later, after midnight, I asked my son to go lie on our new hammock with me. My husband had hung it between two perfect "hammock trees" out at the far end of our one-acre, park-like lawn. Marty said, "Mom, the hammock is wet." We had had a brief rain shower earlier.

I replied, "So what's a little more water?"

"Mom!"

Marty and I lay on the damp hammock and looked up at the stars together. We talked of his near death experience and felt closer to each other than we ever had during his fourteen and one-half years here. He was a baby again in my arms: a toddler teasing us with goofy faces to make us laugh; a ten-year-old plunging through deep powder and trees on double black diamond ski slopes; a teenager blow-drying his long hair Jonas Brothers-style and asking me if it was sticking up anywhere; sneaking up behind me to grab me for a bear hug. Marty smelled of chlorine and suntan lotion and he was here—and very much alive.

The next day it finally hit me! My only son had come so very close to leaving this earth!

My heart raced all day long as I frantically emailed all of my friends and business partners of my son's near death experience. I attached two photos of him and the email read:

Our fourteen and a half-year-old son Marty died and came back yesterday 6/26/09, unconscious at the bottom of the country club pool; he was stiff, with his eyes rolled back in his head by the time a little girl saw him and told a lifeguard. He was saved by angels within seconds of brain damage OR death! He said that his last thought was "I am going to die, and I don't want my mom to be sad!"

But those who trust in the Lord will find new strength. They will soar high on wings like eagles. They will run and not grow weary... Isaiah 40:31

Praise God!

Annie

The response was unexpected and overwhelming. So many emails from those who wanted to tell me how they were touched, and some wrote of their own experiences. Some talked of how they were "inspired" by this event. Several were contacts whom I had not spoken to in years.

I have been in network marketing for nineteen years and have been on a mission to help reverse Type 2 diabetes. I am inspired on a daily basis from those whom I speak with who are dealing with life-threatening illness. Now Marty's near drowning has inspired me not only to continue on my mission to help adults but now to also help children suffering from lifestyle diseases as well as to teach single moms how to create income from home. Our time is brief and valuable with our precious children!

Teenage years are often a time of separation for children as they begin the search for their individuality and disassociating from their parents. As a result of Marty almost transitioning, all three of our kids have bonded with each other, and with us, in a deeper way than ever before.

I am grateful and inspired for my only son's near death. I thank God for showing me His power and faithfulness and for the even deeper connection that my son and I have today.

♥ ♥ ♥

Annie Rose is president & CEO of her company, Diabetic Health Solutions, Inc. She is a successful entrepreneur and network marketer of FoodMatrix health products from Sportron International www.Rose.Sportron.com including The Blood Sugar Pack www.WeStopDiabetes.com. For eight years Annie has hosted a weekly diabetes support call on Thursdays at 8:30 Eastern. Call 1-212-990-8000, pass code 9902#. As well she has a popular radio show www.blogtalkradio.com/Bio-Med-Buyline

She lives in Grand Junction, CO. with her three children, Lainey, seventeen, and twins Marty and Annie, fourteen and a half, and her loving husband, Bobby.

Thank God
I Was Mentally and Physically Abused

ALIDA FEHILY

"You're no good. You'll never amount to anything." These were the thoughts that have haunted my mind for most of my life, and yet I have continued my journey in search of who I am.

I walked happily outside my grade 1 classroom to meet my brother for the walk home. He was walking towards me with another boy. As soon as I was within arm's reach, he punched me as hard as he could on my arm without ever saying a word. They both stood there laughing at me as I cried. I ran home, crossing the busy roads alone to get to the comfort of my mother's arms.

We lived above a convenience store that my parents owned. I ran through the store, up the stairs, and I ran into… him. I stood there terrified – I knew what was coming. With his teeth clenched, he screamed at me, "Stop your crying! Where is your brother?"

I did not answer him; I was scared to talk to him.

I cried hysterically while my father grabbed me by the hair and dragged me up the long staircase. My head hurt as my hair was being pulled out. We went up the staircase step by step. He opened the door to my bedroom and flung me across the floor.

"Take your clothes off!" he screamed as I watched him undo his belt. I lay there, shaking, too frightened to move. Not doing what I was told to do only made him angrier. He threw his belt over his shoulder and whacked it across my arm, yelling at me, "Take your clothes off! Take your clothes off!"

Fearful, I started to take my clothes off, and as I took each piece of clothing off I got another strap. I stood humiliated, naked, and sobbing uncontrollably. He whipped me until I fell onto the floor. As I lay down on the floor, he kicked me in the stomach and head. He started waving his finger at me, saying, "You're no good; you'll never amount to anything".

He walked out of the room while I lay sobbing on the floor, looking at the little strands of my hair. I was covered with red, puffy, raised marks all over my body. I crawled naked up to my favorite place, which was inside the cupboard, and I closed the door.

In the dark, I slipped into my own world of imagination, where I could experience peace. That night, at the age of five, I questioned, "Why am I here?" I wanted to go far away, but the only safe place I had been was in my imagination in the depths of my mind.

I sat on the floor with my legs crossed and my eyes closed. I could see and feel the warm, soft grass under my feet. To the right of me was a forest of trees, and in front of me was a magnificent waterfall with birds flying in the sky. Like a caged bird, I longed for freedom. I felt as if I were flying. I felt the breeze on my face as I flew up into the sky. I flew higher and higher until I landed on a beautiful white cloud. I was happy, jumping up and down each time, going higher and higher.

It was getting dark now, though the stars were still shining brightly, and then I felt someone was taking my hand. I could not see a face or a body, but I felt safe. We flew through the galaxy to different universes. Almost every night, I would meet my friend, my only friend, to guide me in my exploration of the Grand Universe.

My mother sneaked my dinner into my room. She hugged and kissed me and got me dressed, and then she left quickly so my father would not catch her.

A short while later I heard the screaming, yelling, and banging. I tiptoed out of my room onto the top of the landing, where I could look down into the living room. From up there I watched him as he punched her in the face. I really wished I could kill him.

I grew up feeling that I was very different from everyone else. I felt alone, and I did not have many friends. I did not fit into my own family; even they thought I was weird. The only time I felt love was with my guide, my friend, exploring the universe, or at the summer cottage, when I would sneak off with the gypsies by the side of the road.

No matter what I did in life, my father never approved. I was no good and destined not to be good at anything. Every time I was just about to achieve something, I myself would sabotage it. All I could hear were the words 'You're no good' ringing like bells in my ear.

A turning point in my life came when I was seventeen years old. I had a dream that a relative had died in Ireland. The next morning, I found out that he had died. This was the beginning of my search into the mysteries of life and beyond. I was further intrigued when I went to see a clairvoyant for the first time at age twenty-one. That is when I started to read extensively about metaphysical matters.

My everyday life was a torture, and the only solace I had was from my own imagination. I had no self-esteem, and I did not feel I fit anywhere. I had to find who I was. I started to read as much as I could and found my way to personal development and intuitive courses. That kept me happy for a while, until I outgrew them as well.

The magic in my reality happened when I found my way to Dr. John Demartini's work and discovered his methodology in collapsing belief systems to raise one's awareness to a higher frequency. My awareness was already vibrating on a high frequency, but I was still very unbalanced in the physical world. At that time, I was giving consultations using tarot cards and studying to become a Demartini Method facilitator. I was truly amazed at the impact it had on me and on my life. Everything started to make sense to me.

Once I was looking through a photo album of my childhood pictures, and I came across a photograph of me laughing. I remember my dad taking that picture. In that moment I felt grateful to my father because he helped me look within and experience my relationship with GOD, and that I was not alone and was loved. The love I wanted from my father was actually in the form of GOD, and in me.

'Emotions are illusions created by our minds. There is no separation between self, other, and GOD; all is a reflection of our infinite and abundant selves'.

I thank God I was mentally and physically abused; this is my perception of the stories I created into my life. Everything is an illusion – nothing is real except the unconditional love that resides in my heart, the gateway to the wisdom of my soul.

Thank you to my loving dad, my best teacher in life. He gave me the greatest gift that anyone could give... he got me to listen to my inner voice, which always guides me on my purpose in life.

'love and wisdom give you meaning in life'

Alida Fehily

♥ ♥ ♥

Alida Fehily is an International Wisdom Consultant, Australian Psychics Association award-winning "Psychic of the Year (WA) 2005," a Demartini Method Trained Facilitator, an intuitive healer, and author of the WIZ-cARDs ®, which are a wonderful tool to help people find the pathway within and to discover your own reality. It could help create the life of your dreams and inspire you to live according to your highest potential. She has helped thousands of people see their futures more vividly and clearly through face-to-face consultations, public speaking, radio talks, workshops, and internet social media. She consults for people from all walks of life including business owners, celebrities, and entrepreneurs. She doesn't need a magic wand; she just is magic! Visit her at www.alidafehily.com

Thank God I am a Doctor of Chiropractic

DR. RANDY ROMAN

Before I stumbled onto this path taking responsibility for my thoughts, words and actions, I grew up in a house where neither one of my parents graduated high school. I can remember coming home in third grade with a vocabulary book and reading, to my Dad, the word humongous. He said, "That is not a word! You're bullshitting me!" I remember how his words stung me. I can still clearly see as if this occurred just this morning. I cried out, "Yes it is a word, Dad! I can use it in a sentence: The elephant is humongous."

You see, my Dad came to this country from Columbia in 1962 not speaking, reading or writing any English. What he did learn came from TV and working various jobs in factories in New Jersey. He married my mother in September 1968. He learned drywall finishing from my Mom's brother Dennis which he still does some fourty-two years later. He is a proud man, a very hard worker and he sacrificed much for his family.

My mother grew up in New Jersey with her German father who was a butcher and who died when I was six months old. Her mother was sweet and morbidly obese. My grandmother lived with us until she passed away from a stroke in April 1984. That was my first encounter with the death of someone who I loved and shared my every day with. This impacted me in such a way it that it unconsciously influenced my decisions about how I lived my life for many years to come.

I flunked out of college and was working at Delta Airlines not as a pilot but in cabin service. Cabin service role was cleaning the seat pockets, tray tables and inside lavatories. I remember that I was nineteen years old and people telling me, "WOW! You have a great job. You get to fly for free!" I would respond, "Yeah it sure is." Then I would cleaning up warm vomit from the person who became air sick in seat 15 C. That's when I discovered a great desire in my life to do something different. I can recall cleaning aircraft arriving from and traveling off to distant exotic destinations. Saying to myself and fellow coworkers, "How can people afford to take these trips? I can fly for free and still cannot go to these places!"

Then one night I was watching TV... really late... you know when the infomercials come on. I watched a segment that Tony Robbins had on Unlimited Power book for $39.95. I did not have $39.95 and all I had was the desire to have that book. As it turned out, within a few short weeks while cleaning the rows of an aircraft, I found a copy of Unlimited Power. It was amazing! The book was thick like a bible. I remember thinking to myself I'm nineteen years old and cannot recall every reading a complete book cover to cover.

I went to my chiropractor in Pembroke Pines, Florida, Dr. Barry Goldberg. I was sharing with him that I just found this book Unlimited Power on an airplane that I was cleaning. I shared with Dr. Goldberg a section in one of the chapters that read, "Turn your hobby into your profession and you will never have to work a day in your life." The book challenged me to think about my hobbies and what made me happy. Dr. Goldberg encouraged me to really think about this.

At that time in my life, I spent nearly three hours, in the gym, per day lifting weights and another two hours preparing meals, then carrying all my meals neatly stored in Tupperware™ containers. I asked myself,

"How can I make a living eating healthy, exercising and helping people?" Dr. Goldberg said, "Randy, you would make a great chiropractor." I told him that he was crazy! "C'mon, I flunked out of Broward Community College and I am living with my parents."

He said, "Come with me into my office, Randy. I want to call Life College and have them send you an application and information packet." He spoke so matter of fact that I followed him, dialed the number and he handed me the receiver of the phone. I shared all my contact information with the registrar office. Dr. Goldberg reiterated to me, "Randy, you will make a great chiropractor!" As I still sat in shock of what just happened, I looked at him and thought to myself, "This guy is serious. He sees something in me that I haven't seen myself."

After that conversation, I walked down the hall to use the restroom at his office. I finished washing my hands and I saw a quote in a picture frame on the back of the bathroom door. It read "The doctor of the future will give no medicine but will interest his patients in the human frame, nutrition and the cause of disease. Thomas Edison." That quote spoke to the deepest part of my soul. Those words came to life and I soaked them in like sunshine on a cold winter's day.

What brought me to Dr. Barry Goldberg's office, originally, was a motor vehicle accident.

Being involved in motor vehicle accident brought great pain and I held resentment, as if something was stolen from me. I was having a pity party: I lost my car; did not have insurance; and had no other form of transportation. I felt like I had to start all over and I did not know which way to go.

My neck and back were hurting more than they had in my entire life. I went to the chiropractor more frequently, not only for correction but for connection to my purpose.

After telling Dr. Goldberg all the reasons I felt so bad one day, he said, "It was perfect, because God has a bigger plan for you. I examined what he shared with me and it was in alignment with what I enjoyed: meeting and helping people, eating healthy, and exercising. That is when it finally clicked for me that there was a lot more going on, for me, than meets the eye

Ghandi says, "We are not punished for our unforgiveness; we are punished by it." Not only was I discovering my purpose, but also, I was working through forgiving myself and the circumstances surrounding the accident. Through this process, I applied for, got accepted to, and began my education to become a Chiropractor. I really started to see and feel myself stepping in to the role of "Dr. Roman, Chiropractor" and the wise words of Dr. Goldberg.

In June of 1998, I drove from Florida to Atlanta, GA to attend my graduation at Life University. After graduation we went to a Mexican restaurant. It had just finished raining outside and I could see the reflections of the restaurant in the puddles. It felt cool outside and my wife, Tricia, as well as my mom and my dad were walking to the car after dinner. My dad put his arm around me and told me he was proud of me. That was one of the first times he had expressed pride in me like that. At that moment I realized all the events that had unfolded over the past eight years of my life and that all of them were perfect.

I would not be a doctor of chiropractic today if it had not been for the accident and meeting Dr. Goldberg. It enabled me to connect the dots of my experience of life to reveal a hidden order of divine perfection. This empowered me to tie my "current situation" into my purpose. By doing so, I felt eager, excited and driven to tackle the challenges that lay ahead on my path. Ultimately, that I am personally responsible for the story I create for my life.

This experience enabled me to release the dormant forces of my soul and to have my dream become a reality. I am open to learning lessons without having to have pain, struggle and uncertainty. I realized that I can learn through repetition or emotional involvement. The more intense the emotional involvement the less the repetition is necessary. In other words, I can read and study hot stoves or touch a hot stove and experience a hot stove that gets wired and fired into my system forever.

Things are not as they appear. Inside of every blessing there is a curse, and inside of every curse there is a blessing. Things are not as they appear. William James wrote "Nothing of the senses will satisfy the soul". This life is a blink of the eye, there is nothing wrong with accumulating things but "more, better and different" will never satisfy the soul. It has been my experience that gratitude and contribution are the qualities that enrich one's life to the fullest.

No matter the situation there are always two sides to a story. One story will hold you back the other will move you forward. Choose the one that will move you forward on your life's path. Thank you for reading my story. Know you are worthy to be loved just as you are today.

♥ ♥ ♥

I have an incredible passion for practicing chiropractic. That passion stems from my commitment I have in allowing each person I adjust to express their own inborn potential of health and vitality. I received my Doctorate in Chiropractic in 1999. I've empowered thousands of families each year to express their gifts and talents. 2005 Chiropractor of the year for the state of Colorado. I live and play in Western Colorado with my beautiful wife and children. To contact Dr. Roman please visit romanfamilychiro.com or thankgodi.com

Thank God
I Am Thriving After Breast Cancer

ANNABELLE BONDAR

Today is the beginning of spring, the leaves are in bloom, and the days are glowing with the sounds of birds chirping, squirrels scampering along, and the longer, sunny days. Here in Calgary, we receive more sunshine than most places around the world.

I am honored to have been asked to share stories of inspiration in the Thank God I book series, Volumes One, Two, and Three. Thriving after breast cancer is a blessing, and I am sharing stories with you from my heart, messages about wellness, trust, surrender, nature, and love. Today, after years of listening, asking important questions, and living a life of gratitude after cancer, I am delighted to share what I have learned.

Every day as I enjoy spending time with my little granddaughter, Lily, it reminds me of the journey to wellness. Two months ago today, Lily was born. In just two months, she has grown, she knows when she is hungry, she loves to go for walks and car rides, and she adores the movement of her swing. She recognizes me with smiles, and she is so precious. Coming into the world is the beginning of an amazing journey, and Lily takes in every moment.

I made a promise to myself many years ago to live a life of meaning and deep purpose. I love to work with women whose lives have been touched by cancer, empowering and inspiring them along their healing journey. It was in fact my cancer experience that I feel so grateful for because I know I am destined to be doing the very things I love to do today; write, speak, coach, and connect with others whose lives have been touched by cancer.

My story and transformation from cancer truly began almost ten years ago, eating well and looking at a new paradigm in health. Cancer, such a life-altering experience, truly shifted my view of life. From the time of diagnosis, my top value quickly shifted to one of health and wellness. There is a shift in mindset, to go that extra mile in certain situations.

The health consumer today is looking deeper for answers, and over the last nine years I have searched and talked to so many wonderful people in the health industry: practitioners of energy medicine, holistic medicine, eastern and western medicine, and functional medicine. Today I know that cancer is a state of being that, along with so many other conditions, can be prevented and also reversed.

My secrets of well-being are simple:

Journaling: A wonderful healing tool when used to look at the progress towards wellness. Journaling keeps you in the moment, not focusing on the past and the future. It is important to heal and celebrate the results.

Meditation: A quiet place to go deeper with your thoughts. When it is practiced regularly, you will feel relaxed, and your stress level will lessen. Stress is responsible for a large percentage of doctor visits today.

Daily protocols of loving yourself unconditionally and treating others like a friend: Go the extra mile for the things you believe in, be a part of your healing process. Find a doctor whom you resonate with, who spends time looking at your history and the changes in your journey to wellness.

Energy work: This looks at the flow of energy to the organs of the body. With wonderful soft music, a sauna, and plenty of water, this is very detoxifying and rejuvenating. There are many people trained in this medium of healing, and for me, for several years, it made all the difference.

Eating healthy: Adding more greens to your eating pattern, organic foods, and things that are ripe for the season are very beneficial for your health. Vitamins and minerals are key to vital health.

Drinking plenty of water and flushing out the toxins: This keeps your body healthy, boosts the immune system, and maintains the body in an alkaline state. Cancer cannot thrive in an alkaline environment.

Plenty of sleep: The hours of sleep you have before midnight can be very important. A good night's rest will reinvigorate the systems in your body to better cope with stress and stay healthy. Try for eight hours, and your body will be rested.

Exercise is one of the things that keeps the body toned and stimulates the mind and the spirit. Be sure to schedule exercise into your week; it is a great way to stay motivated, and you will see results over time. One hour a day of exercise that you love can reduce the onset of disease.

Disease can begin in the colon. Hydrating and cleansing the colon on a regular basis rids the body of toxins often built up over a long period of time. Colon hydrotherapy makes room for the intestine to absorb nutrients.

All these things are practices of the ages, and I find they seem to be working.

To be almost ten years cancer-free is a gift. Having met so many mentors, doctors, healers, and wonderful everyday people like you has helped me put all the pieces together for longevity, anti-aging, and optimum wellness.

Blending traditional medicine with functional medicine, looking at the body, the mind, and the spirit is the secret to thriving after breast cancer.

Treat your body, your mind, and your soul with respect and special care. Take responsibility for all areas of your life, and do what you love to do. Ask important questions, and feel gratitude in your heart every day.

Thank God I am thriving after breast cancer.
Live simply, expect little, give much.
Fill your life with love.
Think of others.
Scatter sunshine.

If you put some of these truths into practice, you will begin to experience a true breath of fresh air and successful living towards healing.

♥ ♥ ♥

Annabelle Bondar is an inspirational speaker and best-selling author. She was born and raised in Calgary, Alberta. Her diagnosis of breast cancer in 2001 led her on a journey of healing and transformation which she has boldly shared in her book Messages From The Heart: Learning To Love Cancer.

Annabelle is the founder of It's Me Annabelle Inc., an organization dedicated to raising awareness of complementary cancer care and optimum health and wellness.

Annabelle dedicates her life to inspiring those around the world to transform their lives and discover the beauty in healing. Annabelle is a Certified Trainer of the Demartini Methodtm since 2008, and a Certified Dream Coach since 2010. Annabelle is a second time nominee for the RBC Canadian Woman Entrepreneur of the Year Award and a 2010 nominee for the Woman of Vision Local Hero award.

I invite you to visit my website,
www.itsmeannabelle.com

Thank God(dess) I Am a Single Mom

AUDRYE SUSAN ARBE

There was a time I would have been terrified at the thought of being a single mother. I felt overwhelmed at the prospect of bringing up a child, a soul in human form, by myself. As it turns out, that is what I did. The result, for me, is enhanced self-confidence, vulnerability, an open heart, and plenty of strength. I am so pleased with and proud of my daughter, and I am absolutely honored to be her mom.

When I first held my tiny 3-pound 12-ounce daughter, born six weeks earlier than her official due date, I was ecstatic to finally have this tiny wonderful person in my life. With trembling hands, and despite all my preparation, I also wondered how I was going to be a great mother.

Who would ever dream I would give thanks for being a single mom? In my life with my daughter's father, I learned about life and myself in unparalleled ways. We had a deep, soulful, sensitive, and sensuous connection with a fabulous intensity and passion that fulfilled both of us positively and in other ways, including our then-needs for dramatic, full emotional expression. It was an immense opportunity for each of us to heal and transform psychological, energetic, and emotional patterns from our pasts so we could live and create our lives in a new mix of both deep connection and inner peace, which was what we both said we wanted.

Without going into the ramifications of the intricate and interconnected aspects of my relationship with my then-mate, we parted ways when our daughter was about two years young. My life immediately appeared much more peaceful.

How was I going to handle raising my daughter? I found out as I created it. The main challenge for me was the financial aspects of being a mom. I had taken myself out of the mainstream conventional manner of garnering finances--having a j-o-b--as I always liked to do my own thing. Though I lacked the confidence and self-esteem at the time to truly pursue my soul's purpose, I knew it was vital that I create a stable income for my child and myself. After my former mate and I went to court, I was awarded $30 a week in child support, for which I was grateful. Manhattan expenses required more, and life continued.

My former mate and I went through a seesaw with his visitation with our daughter, who often told me that after he picked her up, he would drop her off with other family members and leave. It was only when my daughter was older that she told me that she saw him only about half of the allotted times. For five or so years, we went through various court juggling and machinations, shifting visitation hours. I was doing it all and had gotten great at handling childcare, sleepovers, and a work schedule, and was able to have Saturdays nights for myself.

When my daughter was about six or seven, I picked her up from her dad and felt a vibe about his inner chest area. I told him that something was going on in his chest that needed attention and asked him if he felt okay. He sloughed it off, as though I were being an annoyance. I asked him two more times, recommending that he have it looked at medically, as I was clearly "getting" that something in there needed attention. He ignored me, and I chose to refrain from pushing him. Then about a year or so later, he called me and let me know he was going into the hospital, something he never did. It turns out he had lung cancer.

He had an operation. The cancer had metastasized beyond his lungs. This incredibly vibrant man with such a zeal for living died at the age of forty-seven while still in the hospital, several days after his operation. I felt and knew earlier that day that he was going to pass. I was mulling how to tell my beautiful, wonderful seven-year-young daughter that her daddy was going to die. I asked Source for a day to figure out how to do this. My daughter and I, along with other family members, had just seen my former spouse that day. His last words to her were, "Don't worry. I'm not going to die."

Then the phone rang in the middle of the night, about 2:30 am. I howled and shrieked. My screams woke my daughter. She knew immediately, without my having prepared her, that her dad was gone.

For a few days and nights afterward, my daughter and I slept together in my bed hugging each other, reassuring one another that we each were real, corporeal, and alive. The day after I was told my former mate had passed, I actually wondered if I had invented him, because the idea of his dying was so alien to me I could barely wrap myself around the concept, never mind the actuality of it. Then I looked at my daughter, and I was unable to figure out how I could have created her on my own. I knew this momentous "death" event was something real in the third-dimensional world, in my personal world, and in the world of my daughter.

I was now a single mother in the physical arena in every sense of the word. My daughter's father no longer existed in this realm. It was all up to me. As much as my daughter saw my grief, I actually withheld the extreme expressions of it for when I was alone, as I was concerned for her well-being if she would see the extent to which I screeched my grief over his death. Sounds ripped out of me that I never knew were in there. Then, as my daughter once put it, I picked myself up and raised her.

When I was birthing my daughter, I had a near-death experience, where I met with several Shiny Light Beings. This was a marvelous realm, filled with love, brilliance, color, and peace. These Beings let me know that it would be easier for me to die rather than to birth my daughter. I was adamant about birthing and mothering her. I had waited my whole life for this opportunity, and nothing -- N – O – T – H – I – N – G -- was going to stop me from having this child and being her mom. The Guides let me know that if I chose to live and have my daughter, there were three things that were either going to happen or that I had to agree to:

1. I would do it alone,
2. It would be difficult, and
3. I would have to take off my rose-colored glasses.

I readily agreed to all three conditions. I felt if I had chosen otherwise, I would have never left the glorious Light-filled realm I was visiting, and the physical me would never leave the hospital room where I was in the midst of having an emergency Caesarian section. Now, did I expect that in seven years my then-mate would die? No. That I would get the brunt of raising my daughter? Yes, I expected that.

In the raising of my daughter, I would receive spiritual guidance. When my daughter would ask me how I knew something, I would tell her it was in the mother's manual. She asked me where that was. I would open my left hand as though it were holding a book, bring my open hand up in front of her, and tell her it was right there.

"Where?" she would ask. "Right here," I would respond, bringing my hand close to her face. She would shrug, seemingly roll her eyes, and then nod.

Because of the experience of raising my daughter, other life influences, and my strong desire to facilitate other mothers, I created and wrote a book, The Mother's Manual, A Spiritual and Practical Guide to Child Rearing and Motherhood©. If I can be a great mom, anyone can—single, married, or what-have-you, with love and wisdom! I hold motherhood to be a sacred journey, special beyond description.

So, why do I thank Goddess for being a single mother? In some ways, I am the quintessential mom, being born under the astrological sign of Cancer, the nurturer of the Zodiac. I love being a mom, just adore it.

In raising my daughter, I have grown strong in a way that is indescribable. Being my precious daughter's mom, I am living out a specific part of some of the purpose of why I incarnated.

In being a single mother, I can let women everywhere know that it can be done, and it can be done well. Yes, it is wise to conceive, carry, and birth children consciously and be a conscious, aware person and mom, and anyone can be this. It is innate. We simply have to awaken this wisdom, and release-transform-transmute any of our individual and collective issues, from wherever, whenever, however.

Being a single mother helped me realize this. For me, to have had this life without my daughter is beyond comprehension. I have been a single mom, a single self-supporting mom, and it is miraculous.

Being a single mother, having Guidance given, and writing The Mother's Manual, A Spiritual and Practical Guide to Child Rearing and Motherhood ©, I give thanks for being a single mom, you can be sure. I have experienced single motherhood and succeeded! I raised a magnificent daughter, who is now immersed in her own life journey and a mom in her own right.

Being a single mother has afforded me the opportunity to stretch beyond what I felt I could be, do, and accomplish. It has strengthened me, softened me, and helped me further understand women globally. I have a living understanding of family and love that is tremendous. My compassion has had plenty of opportunity to operate, as has my innate drive for leadership.

My daughter also knows how powerful women can be, while also being feminine, attractive, and loving. We are the gentle genies of the world, filled with the power of the cosmos. I am also thankful for my former mate for happily creating my daughter with me. Being a single mother? Thank Goddess this has been my path!

The relationship I have with my daughter is ever evolving as we each develop. While life would have been great, certainly, had I been with a mate, I can attest with certainly that my daughter and I became incredibly close, and, yes, sometimes with challenge. We are both open to the glories and bounty of life in all ways. The adventure continues.

Know that wherever you are, whatever is occurring, you also can have a blessed life of beauty and bliss.

♥ ♥ ♥

Audrye is a mom of a great daughter and "Grammie" to two fabulous grand-daughters, as well as a spiritual therapist, healer, clairvoyant-astrologer, artist, and author, committed to causing transformation, sustainability, love, conscious evolution, and bliss with people here and now. This bundle of energy loves dancing to African and jazz drums under the stars and invites you to join her! To be an enlightened mom with evolved children, get her book, The Mother's Manual, A Spiritual and Practical Guide to Child Rearing and Motherhood©, plus her FREE ebook, The Mother's Manual Sampler ©, at www.TheMothersManual.com You may contact Audrye at Audrye@TheMothersManual.com and 1 888 75 PEACE (1 800 757 3223). Many blessings to you and all of us!!!

Thank God for My Son's Learning Disability

BRENDA MARTIN

My son was fifteen years old at the time we sat together on a plastic formed bed...no blankets, bare, aged white walls, the echo of our thoughts and the smell of an overused emergency room. We were waiting for him to be admitted to the hospital for "suicide ideologies." We sat with our shoulders and knees touching, hands folded, resting on our laps. At times he'd rest his head on my shoulder. I tried to be reassuring, but it was unknown territory for me, too. I held him, careful to be comforting but not overbearing. The door was a third of the way open. We could see two other rooms, inhabited by a young woman of about twenty years old and a man in his early forties. Two uniformed guards stood sentry over us.

I recall vividly looking back and wondering how this could be – the two of us sitting together somehow connected in a suicide ward? Carson was so gentle, sensitive, and bright. But early on he struggled in school and eventually became withdrawn.

It's a common pattern, I'd later learn, for families contending with learning disabilities. He came in at 7 pounds, 4.5 ounces. I dreamed of the white picket fence, one girl, one boy, married... We selected a quiet family neighborhood with a little house in a cul-de-sac.

At three days old, Carson and I returned home from the hospital. Sleepless nights grew from the normal first few months to an excruciating two years. He cried night and day, with intermittent periods of rest. Eventually, when he'd start to cry, I'd vomit.

I dragged him from doctor to doctor, only to be told there was nothing wrong with him and the problem was "my parenting." I would debate with family and friends, half believing it was true. Thankfully, my family was supportive, reminding me that my daughter was thriving and without any similar issues. I needed to hear that this wasn't my fault.

I'm not proud to say this, but I have walked the line between turning and walking away, barely avoiding the desire to stop the insanity by striking my young, helpless son in abuse. More than once I had to call a neighbor for help to rescue myself from my own impulse. I needed respite from the constant screaming and was horrified that I could not see how we could continue. A lengthy calm spell was forty-five minutes during those first two years.

Around his second birthday, I was introduced to an individual who suggested I try tissue salts to calm him down. I tried every doctor, including naturopaths, massage therapists, child specialists, and an iridologist. If I thought there was an answer behind a door, I would open it! Within three days his crying all but stopped! Finally, there was peace, laughter, and joy. He would run, play until exhausted, and scream with the unabandoned joy only children know how to release. I thought we had made it through the war and onto the other side.

Carson continued to grow and pick up on details that escaped my perception. As I drove, he would call out all the speed limits posted along the roadside. He excitedly described every color, size, and shape of vehicles surrounding us. He was also naturally gifted as an athlete and could run like the wind. His quick wit and sense of timing could put us all in fits of side-breaking laughter.

However, we could not get him to do anything he was uncomfortable trying. Living in a Canadian city, outdoor activities were a rite of passage. We tried to get strap skates, cross-country skis, and snowboards on Carson, but we would face a bizarre scene of uncontrolled limbs flaying each and every way. The scenes in other sports were just downright embarrassing for us. The saving grace occurred when I learned to have a third party teach him. Off he went on ski camps and learned to snowboard. Once he learned...look out!...he was not only proficient but a bit of a show-off daredevil even with the initial reluctance to start.

Another example of his physical abilities not matching his performance was bike riding. Oh dear, the hours and years I spent running behind him, holding onto the bike seat while he anxiously peddled! We would go for miles without progress. My husband finally got Carson to ride a bike. He showed Carson a $5 bill and told him it was his if he went to the end of the alley and back again. Apparently it was a hilarious situation, with Carson purposefully out of control and riding directly into fences or garbage cans. Over his screams of torture, Bob responded by waving the five dollars around! With quite the commotion he made it back to Bob, earned his monetary bribe, and went on to happily ride for years.

Carson's entry into preschool painted a bleak future. The morning was clear, and the air was filled with anticipation. He lined up to enter the school as the bell rang. Carson was the last child in line. As the other new students made their way to and through the door, Carson retreated to the corner of the play area. Sitting crossed-legged, holding his new football backpack over his face, he refused to move. To him it was a black abyss of unknown territory. My heart sank, seeing the expression of terror on his little face. Carson was destroyed, knowing he was different from the other kids; headed for trouble. He was anxious for what he knew would be a thirteen year jail sentence.

The years progressed, yet Carson did not. In grade three, he started acting out inappropriately: slashing curtains, hurting his sister, being dragged to school, and he was miserable. This was not his personality. Thankfully, I convinced the school to conduct a psycho-educational assessment to test for learning abilities. This would accommodate a scribe, or reader, during exams, allowing the school to perform better in city ratings. It was discovered that Carson had multiple different learning disabilities and AD/HD, hindering his ability to understand the work. His IQ was above average, yet he was two years behind his contemporaries.

Finally, an answer. Now what?

I am a strong believer in public education, but not for Carson. I knew the system did not have answers. Nothing was more frustrating than starting a new year excited about the possibilities only to experience a continued stream of "tried that, did that, nope, did not work." We finally heard about Foothills Academy Society. Our lives changed — it became our million dollar winning ticket.

Carson started Foothills Academy, in grade five, at a grade one reading, writing, and computing level. The staff pulled together to help him to read and learn how to learn. The administration, teachers, support staff, custodians, and other parents — all were partners in learning. It was a symbiotic relationship. We belonged. Before long, Carson was reading at grade level. Thank God!

This was not to be the end of our struggles. As a result of Carson's first five long and terrible years, he suffered a tremendous negative emotional impact. He developed issues with anxiety, depression, becoming withdrawn and sullen. I was certain he was headed for jail or would take his life. At the time, I was unaware of how accurate my assessment of Carson's future was.

Learning to read and write is only part of the solution, especially when a child has struggled failing for so many years. It takes a toll on self-perception, worth, and abilities. I even experienced a trip to the hospital with Carson, who was planning his own suicide. I learned that, left undiagnosed, persons with learning disabilities grow to be underemployed, depressed, and anxious. A large percentage of young offenders have undiagnosed or untreated learning disabilities.

With the constant companion "major road blocks," we continued under careful guidance to watch Carson compete and win his grade 12 certificate and entrance to university. The road was fraught with difficulties...and I would not change it for one minute.

I thank God every day that my son has learning disabilities, for in his struggle, I found my purpose, my reason for living. I now have the great fortune to have grown within my work, and direct my energies to influence a larger audience. My inspiration is to provide help and solutions to people with learning disabilities.

I receive daily phone calls from exasperated parents/guardians searching for answers to why their sixteen-year-old cannot read; is in trouble with the law; is withdrawn; is unable to be reached; and is mad as hell. "Why not?" We have not given him the existing tools to succeed. I will continue to be a voice as long as a young child is failing, unable to read or write, possessing the mental ability to learn.

My method to reach others is unorthodox. The World Summit 2008: Learning Disabilities, Fact or Fiction brought together one hundred eighty-six experts, ranging from scholars to advocates. The result was a surprising consensus on future directions. A well-read and received government white paper was produced; an award-winning, two-part television documentary created, and a free online resource guide produced.

I continued to search for methods to reach the public, knowing that in every home, someone is silently suffering with learning difficulties. This searching led to the partnership with Stampede Entertainment, creating the LOL Kids Comedy Night featuring Mr. Bill Cosby. We had a riot selecting five youths of Calgary to open for Mr. Cosby; all brilliant and funny, all in support of learning disabilities. Mr. Cosby was generous; understanding firsthand, through his son Ennis, that learning differences bring both gifts and difficulties.

Because of our struggle and journey, there is freedom. Carson is free to live his life according to his values and the strength to live his convictions. My other children have the knowledge that you never give up. They have worked side by side as a unit, helping each move toward their goals. Our lives are an individual commitment to a group effort. I am so thankful my children understand their worth. I am grateful my husband and I have a relationship that is strengthened due to our joys and disappointments.

I am deeply and profoundly thankful that, because my son has learning disabilities, I am able to help hundreds. My life has made a difference, and I will continue to be an agent of change. I am the benefactor of the combination of trials and tribulations of those with learning disabilities. Because of the generosity of others, we have changed our story to one of hope and control. Call it what you will: "learning disabilities," "differences," "dyslexia," ... there is a war being waged, and I refuse to acknowledge defeat or surrender.

Every day, I wake up grateful for my son and thank God he has learning disabilities. I am encouraged in creating the next LOL 2011 and World Summit 2012. May there be change and progress.

♥ ♥ ♥

Brenda has professional experience as the manager of international corporations, as well as being an entrepreneur, owning and operating her own businesses. Brenda actively promotes the expertise of the Foothills Academy Society, specializing in Learning Disabilities, to the global community.

Brenda understands firsthand the value of research and instruction in the field of learning disabilities. Her fourth child experiences difficulties with short-term memory, organization, attention deficit, and anxiety—in short, learning disabilities.

Brenda's inspiration is self-evident when working with organizations engaged in research and advocacy of learning disabilities. Her personal goal is to halt the downward spirals and fragmentation of children experiencing learning disabilities.

Thank God I Went to Iraq

BRIAN LIPSKI

Remember those kids who made everything look so easy? They excelled in sports, in school, and with the girls. Life came easy and natural to them, and their heads were as big as balloons. That was me as a kid. I was a star athlete, popular, and breezed through school. I took all of those skills with me to the Marine Corps, thinking I would be the best officer the United States had ever seen. I figured I could go anywhere, do anything, and lead men into battle with no problem. Looking back it's easy to see that I was headed for a major reality check, one that would wake me up to the realization that life is not always as easy as it seems, and that a combat zone is not the place to learn this lesson.

It was the fall of 2007 when my unit left for a seven-month deployment to Iraq. I learned the ropes pretty quickly and had a good handle on our mission and what we needed to do. As the platoon commander, I was directly responsible for fifty enlisted Marines, whose mission was to provide security to one of the bases and all its surrounding areas. With each passing day, I was growing more and more confident in this environment, and my productivity as a platoon commander grew. The mission was being accomplished with complete success! After three months in Iraq I had become a cocky, overconfident Marine Corps officer in Iraq. I had my platoon literally on cruise control. Cruise control can be a good thing at home, but in a combat zone it can only mean one thing; a storm brewing on the horizon.

Half way through the deployment, my platoon was tasked with a two-day operation outside the base. We were to send two of my three squads to the outskirts of a nearby town for observation and to conduct a thorough search of the surrounding area for any weapons caches or contraband hidden by the insurgents. On Day One we left base under cover of darkness and set up to begin at first light. Once daylight struck, we began our initial search, and things were quiet until midday.

During a foot patrol through a Wadi, the Marines noticed a pickup truck racing directly towards them. This is usually a bad thing, so the armored vehicles providing perimeter security immediately began to intercept the vehicle. They used escalation of force procedures, which are used to prevent firing on innocent civilians or vehicles. While one Marine had his machine gun fixed on the vehicle, the other went through the proper procedures before finally shooting a flare at the vehicle. Luckily the vehicle stopped after that, or we would have had to fire warning shots. It turned out the driver and passenger were local residents in the town and were just not paying attention to us as they went home. Nothing serious came of this, as the incident was reported up the chain of command, and the two men were allowed to leave.

Later on that night I was picked up by another patrol and returned to base, while the rest of my Marines remained outside the wire to continue the mission. I was not leaving the mission because I wanted to; I was leaving because my platoon sergeant had the lead out there, while I had to get back to base and prepare for the next assignment. I went back assuming everything was good to go. When I returned that night, I informed my company commander of what had happened and assured him that all key personnel and the operations center were informed of the incident.

What happened the very next day seemed like an episode of the Twilight Zone.

It turned out that our report of the incident never made it to Operations Center, which tracks all missions.

Somehow the commanding officer found out about this incident and had a fit over the lack of reporting. The blasting my company commander received due to this wasn't pretty, and since shit rolls down hill, I then got an earful of not-so-nice things. I was basically accused of flat-out lying about the incident and for being incompetent in my duties.

This entire turn of events came as a complete surprise to me. I was totally caught off guard because in my mind I had followed proper protocol and done my job. I left my boss's office questioning my own actions with a deflated ego as I tried to put the pieces back together. One could only imagine the questions I was asking myself as I walked away. How did I go from being a successful platoon commander to being an incompetent liar overnight? If I had lost the confidence of my superiors, how could they trust me to lead Marines in Iraq?

That same night, my platoon returned from their mission. As they sat around smoking and joking, I noticed some Marines laughing hysterically. One of the Marines proclaimed, "Sir, you missed it." With my interest piqued, I asked what he was talking about.

Before he could utter a word, another Marine shouted out, "Don't tell him. He wasn't there—he left." It was like my own family had stuck a knife right through my heart. Because I left early, because I was not there, because in their eyes I didn't finish what I started, I was now being ostracized. I could have reprimanded that Marine for insubordination, but that would have accomplished nothing. So on top of being called an incompetent liar, I now became the butt of the joke for my Marines, too.

I went back to my room that night baffled by the events of the day. Failure and rejection were something new to me. I thought to myself, "I have been doing everything right. How am I all of a sudden screwing up?" And, "Why doesn't anyone see this the way I see it? It's just a simple miscommunication; it's not that big a deal." I knew I was not a liar and was telling the truth, but that wasn't the worst part about it. It was that I didn't know if my Marines had lost their trust in me as a leader or, worse, if they thought that I had abandoned them for no reason. I knew this wasn't the case, but they wouldn't care how good a reason I had. It was now official—the balloon I'd had on my shoulders had burst, and I was having a tough time dealing with it. It was tough to accept the fact that I had screwed up, to accept that I failed. Losing confidence in the middle of a war zone is a dangerous thing. And that was the road I had just turned down.

The feeling of doubt and incompetence raging on inside began to eat at me. I labored extra hard the next few days in an attempt to show the world that I was better. I put in extra hours and triple-checked my work to make sure I made no mistakes. The little motor inside me was running at full speed, and to be honest it was exhausting. During the next few days, I would go back to my room drained from the extra work I had been doing, and the ironic thing is that I wasn't being any more productive, I was just keeping busy.

Three days had passed since the incident, and I was worn down. I wanted to keep pushing harder and harder, but the little voice inside convinced me otherwise. I listened to that voice and hit the gym to clear my thoughts. Exercise was my escape, a chance to stop thinking about work and have some fun. About halfway through the workout, as I was admiring my physique in the mirror, I noticed that I had really made some improvements over the past three months. In that exact moment, as I vainly checked myself out, I had my moment of clarity. My moment when the light bulb lights up, when lightning strikes, when everything just seems to make sense. I realized I was overreacting. One bad event or experience or decision doesn't make me a bad leader, bad officer, or even a bad person. I knew for a fact that I was no quitter, and the only reason I had been stressing over these things was because I couldn't let them go. But if just a little exercise each day improved my health and physique, a little more effort and attention to detail would help my work. I finished that workout with a new sense of purpose and a goal to choose quality over quantity.

The very next day, while on a patrol with my platoon, lightning struck again. The platoon had not lost confidence in me or thought me less of a leader. Of course they had some fun with it, but the fact of the matter was that they knew I was looking out for them and not just doing my own thing. The only person to feel any anxiety over what had happened was me. My company commander and commanding officer had not lost trust in my as a leader, or I would have been fired, and my platoon had not lost trust in me as their leader or they would have quit on me. At that moment I completely accepted my failure. It is our job to accept what happens and learn from it. When we returned from that patrol I had a newfound confidence in myself, in the fact that I could handle failure as long as I learn from it and move forward.

Looking back, I am grateful for having that lesson thrust onto me as it was. That experience was destined to happen, and thank God it did not come at the expense of others. A combat zone is not a place to be taken lightly, and with my ego as big as it was, I was bound to make a mistake. Having gone through a deflating experience, I learned that we all make mistakes and that all we can do is learn to accept them, learn from them, and move forward. Getting in trouble with your boss is not a bad thing as long as you don't repeat that mistake. I emerged from this experience a better leader and a better person. Thank God I went to Iraq. I am so grateful to have had the opportunity to serve with the finest men our country has to offer.

♥ ♥ ♥

Brian Lipski is a graduate of the United States Merchant Marine Academy. After graduation he served four years as an officer in the United States Marine Corps and completed one tour in Iraq. Brian is co-founder of the Adventure Travel Company, Ride Our World. They set out on adventures across the globe with a goal of inspiring others to live life in the present. www.rideourworld.com

Thank God
I Have a Son with ADHD

CARLA VAN WALSUM

Most people think "ADHD" refers to "Attention Deficit Hyperactivity Disorder," but my son is actually "Aligned to Dialing into a Higher Dimension."

Truly when observed with clinical psychological eyes, his seemingly uncontrollable impulsive behavior cried for a diagnosis. Why? To make life easier, to have him accepted by others; to rescue him from developing a damaged self-esteem. A painful realization, that I as his mom, who loves and works with the holistic approach of no 'deficit' or 'disorder' but apparently imbalance or an opportunity for learning and growth, became happy with a label.

There he was, September 1997, my baby boy Uriel, Hebrew for "Light and fire of God." His middle name, Amichai, means "my people live." The boy who I "knew" would be born exactly three years after my first child, Liora ("my light").

Although I was certain about his coming, I did not know that he would not sleep, would have eczema, suffer, and experience bronchitis and restlessness. As exhausted as I was, I "saw" a third child waiting to be born just two years later, Ophir (light of gold) Raphael who completed the family.

In the stroller, everyone looked at the chocolate-brown, sparkling-eyed, bright, smiling kid. As soon as

Uriel could walk, he jumped around with the speed of a flea. Everything he did was too wild... too fast... just too much! Fully present in the moment, he did not understand the concepts "future" and "later."

As, to him, everything should be now and here, I tried to teach him the nice feeling of longing for something. For his third birthday he got an airboat for the coming summer. It was an almost successful experiment. One day, walking in the first floor's hallway of our flat, I saw water running down from the stairs. Following the trail of water, I soon discovered Uriel in his bedroom. He apparently had blown up his boat partially and brought cups filled with water one by one to spread on the floor. "Want to sail, Mom?'

As a toddler, he was happy to cook with pots and pans on the kitchen floor, imitating my cooking activities. Real fun! The phone rang. Engrossed in my conversation, I vaguely heard running water coming from the kitchen. I ran to see what was happening. Uri was peeing in the pot! A great experiment! Four-year-old Uri watched on TV the innocent stories of Pippi Longstocking. The next day he tried to imitate her. If Pippi could jump from the roof, Uri certainly could do that too.

Soon the judgment and interpretation of his behavior by adults was perceived very clearly. Uriel knew how people were judging him. At age five, that happy and world-exploring kid was crying in his bed, "Mama, I want to die! I don't like life!"

In an angel channeling I received, it was explained that Uriel was not particularly welcomed in this physical world, and he knew that on a deep level. Children come into this world with their own agendas. A little sanding and shaving is the best we can do. We learn from them. Uriel was not a bad child; he was just a bundle of joy, full of life, and eager to discover anything. He was a child who required that his environment adapt to his needs, instead of vice versa. At a painful moment, I realized that I was the only one who still understood and supported my son. Sensing the bigger picture, I felt strongly compelled to contribute to this world in understanding children and treating them with love and kindness. I realized that this is all about awareness and consciousness. It's all about how we, as educators, perceive the world and digest our lives. It is even more important how much we spend healing our own wounds and intentionally become a love-filled personality.

Think love, be love, give love. Open your heart! As simple as it sounds, that's how simple it is. See the beauty in people rather than their "faults." See what happens energetically. See the joy and pleasure we sense in general when we see a happy toddler in action. The love we radiate then is not of the same quality or intensity we often express to older children.

We are products of generations and generations of passing on the same kind of education. When feeling powerless or not respected, many parents project their frustration back on the child, who might have had totally different intentions. Use of power, force, coercion, punishment, rejection, violation, violence, and abuse are the results. It is in our backpacks we carry with us. Systemic Family Constellations show that when wounds and scars of the past are not healed, the coming generations take over, out of loyalty, that which does not belong to them. And where is the real healing hidden from the intergenerational scars, simply from parents to children? Not in blaming them. Not in holding the child for years on a chair as a victim. That is a situation that creates powerlessness. Neither of these feelings provides or allows healing.

Compassion for suffering? Oh yes. Suffering allows the bystanders to develop more compassion and taking love-based actions. Understanding, detachment, honoring for that what just is and was, can have a big healing effect. "You gave me life, and that was the best you gave me. I can take care of the rest." Set aside here the presumptions of what made us decide to incarnate in a physical body prior to our birth. What is and was the path we choose to go? What is our life purpose, and are we in tune with it?

Again an insight for adults: Observe without judgment, criticism, or comparison. Judgment stems from fear. Oh yes, we love our children deeply, most of the time. We open our arms in gratitude for that wonder that comes into our lives. Then, after a little while, our inner voices start to work and influence our thinking. The wish for parenthood is often deeply rooted. Yet, we don't own our children but are allowed to care for them, to assist them in becoming their brightest self. That sounds great! But, how do we do that? Do we really unconditionally love? When our beloved kid behaves differently from how we want, feel, expect or wish...we send him or her away with punishment...That is really conditional.

As a child, I witnessed the consequences of being judged and interpreted, and the senselessness of punishment. I was determined to raise my children compassionately, with unlimited understanding and connected to their emotional needs without manipulation. I was dedicated to teaching them to be responsible for their own fulfillment. I recognized my thoughts in the powerful model of the crystal clear "Non-Violent Communication," from Marshall Rosenberg, which became a red line in my parenting visions, life, and work.

Living our happy life in Holland in the aftermath of World War II, balancing between Waldorf holistic school system (Antroposophy) and Montessori school choices, I was searching for a child-friendly nurturing environment, where creativity could freely flow. One day my children decided that they did not want to be Jewish anymore as a result of anti-Semitic eruptions. Another day, my family and I read in the newspaper that after the September 11th event, in the United States, our national three minutes of silence for the innocent dead was not honored and permitted in the high schools out of fear of eruptions from Islamic minorities. My husband and I soon decided to move to Florida, with our three children, all under the age of eleven, to allow the children to experience that it is normal to be Jewish.

The warm, spiritual Jewish school did not accept Uriel (age eight at the time) despite his brightness. He was disruptive. Public school became the answer. Uri hardly knew the English language and wanted so much to adapt and appear American. The second day of school, the teacher explained to Uri, "This is a whistle, and when I blow on it, recess is over. Do you understand?"

Of course, Uri said, "Yes," but he did not know what she meant.

The next day, hundreds of kids were playing at the playground, at recess. Uri did not know who belonged in his class. He heard a whistle, but he still saw many children playing. As children, one class by one class, started to go inside the school, Uri thought, "Maybe class started already?" Uri hurried back in to his classroom, and the teacher said, "Uri, you are too late! For the next week there will be no recess for you." He had to sit on a bench, not allowed to move. It was quite impossible to find and reach the teacher. It was even more impossible to explain to her that he really did not know what she said.

Then a small Jewish, friendly appearing school accepted Uri and his brother. The classroom held third and fourth graders and only had eight students. One day Uri, in the fourth grade, was put in the corner with a worksheet for the entire day because he was distracted by the lesson given to the third graders.

Uri absorbed everything he saw passionately and intentionally. Our new neighbors were very hospitable to my sons and allowed them to watch, unknown by me, a movie about a doll killing people. The next day, the whole kindergarten was told about the movie. We became suspect parents. A few days later, Uri played "knight" with the Kindergarten. They loved it. We became more suspect.

Tattling, in Holland, is allowed until five or six years of age. After that age, it is considered betrayal. This lovely school encouraged the students to "tell on" Uri. Subjective information was given and influenced all of the parents. Five girls were making fun of Uri and his penis. Uri would not tattle, so he decided to take it into his own hands. In his frustration and humiliation, he hit one of the girls with his forehead. The result: expelled. A desperately crying Uri came home with a paper in his hand with his writing: "I am Uri, I am a great kid." He consoled himself with the affirmations he had gotten from me in the past.

I was desperately asking for answers. I did not want to sacrifice my son. I asked the Universe for help and answers. I felt very drawn to go to a comforting bookstore and knew the answers would be shown.

A book fell on my feet: Angel Teachings."

My clinical background veiled what I knew intuitively. There were guidance and messages the angels had been giving me throughout my life, and the more I listened, the more I received.

So I tuned in to the path of meditation and channeling and received guidance, which helped me tremendously. This helped me in my understanding of Uri, my presence in Florida, and my divorce, which have all been supported by angelic help, and more importantly, I learned through them how to work with energies and intentions to help heal others.

I received valuable information from archangel Uriel on emotional healing for children and their families. I developed "Happy Children, Happy Home " workshops for parents who chose to be their brightest selves in mastering consciousness, awareness, joy and being a relaxed parent.

The Systemic Family Constellations, already practiced in Holland, became my expressed inspiration in work, a combination of traditional psychotherapy and intuition.

The gift my child gave me, carrying the name Uriel and connecting me later with Archangel Uriel, has enriched my life tremendously, which in turn, has greatly influenced healing for many others! Thank God my son has ADHD!

♥ ♥ ♥

Carla Van Walsum was born and educated in the Netherlands. She began her career as a concert flutist. Although music enlightens people, Carla's desire to contribute to the wellness of others resulted in her studies in Psychology (Open Universiteit Nederland 1986-2001) and Integrative Psychotherapy in Holland. In 2009 Carla received a Ph. D in Transpersonal Counseling from the University in Metaphysical Science, California. Carla is a Licensed Spiritual Health Counselor. As founder and owner of Transpersonal Counseling, LLC: a Holistic practice for families, couples and children, Carla practices currently in Boca Raton, Florida.

Thank God
My Brother Committed Suicide

CARMEN NOSEWORTHY

It was a spiritual tornado, its power equally commanding as Mother Nature's mayhem. But I did not hear the sound of a train coming, there was no warning signal, there was nowhere to seek shelter.

It's strange how God will present itself sometimes. I cannot recall a time when I have not believed in a higher power; however, my relationship with it was obtusely unconscious up to this point. It is said, "God will do for me what I cannot do for myself." But I didn't want help from God, even though I was at a point in my life where I absolutely knew something was missing. I had dreams, but no real direction. I was easily irritated with life, taking no responsibility for my part in creating it.

Toronto, Friday night, May 31, 2002: I was catching up with a friend, and we were laughing, relaxing and having fun. The calm before the storm.

10:30pm, my phone rings. It's a Montreal area code. I thought it was my brother, Danny. Instead, it was a stranger's voice identifying himself as a detective from the Montreal Police Department. Humorously I asked, "Oh my god, what's Danny done now?!" Danny had once chosen to go to jail instead of paying the hydro bill; he did weird things sometimes, so why would this be any different? The French man's voice was eerily glum as he confirmed that I was Danny's sister. Pin drop silence filled the air waves; a wave of anxiety consumed my body. With trepidation I said, "What is it, Detective? Just tell me!"

"I regret having to tell you that your brother Danny was found deceased this morning." The tornado struck ground.

This was a joke. Who would play such a cruel joke on me? Cynically I said, "Yeah, right. Who is this?" As he again identified himself, the joke turned into a nightmare. Struggling to get out of the way of this whirlwind, I asked for a return phone number, I wanted to find out who was behind this candid camera scene. I thought, "Who do I know in Montreal that would do something like this?" I even thought, "Danny this really isn't funny."

When I dialed the number and reached the Montreal Police Department, my heart sank and the tornado shredded it into pieces as I was patched through to the detective I had just been speaking with. Emotion poured out fast and furious as I heard: "He took his own life about ten days ago. He hanged himself in the closet." The tornado barreled into me. I left my body and was now watching this scene as if from the balcony of a theatre. I wanted to leave right away, go to Montreal and see the body for myself, still needing proof. The detective suggested against that, as after ten days his body was well decomposed. I asked about murder—no evidence of that. Drugs? No evidence. I asked why? There was no note.

Torment swirled inside me, and the tornado was about to go into warp speed. I couldn't control its power, and I had to direct it, full force, into the lives of people I loved. Why me? Why do I have to steer this tornado into other peoples' lives? Why was I the chosen one? I sure did question and have a few things to say to God then.

Feeling like the pointed end of a dagger, I started contacting family and friends. It took me all night and several Canadian Ryes to muster up enough courage to call home, 2000 miles away. I called my oldest brother first; he then delivered the news in person to Mom and Dad. That's when the tornado lacerated the remaining foundation.

A two-week journey began during which time ceased to exist inside me. A journey so surreal at times, I didn't know if I was witnessing, receiving, or observing. It was all three.

If you knew Danny, you loved Danny. He was a brilliant, passionate, well-respected jazz guitarist and composer, had just put out a CD, and was working on another one. Danny was the one who created homemade gifts for all occasions, who made sure we all remembered birthdays, anniversaries, etc., was so extraordinarily giving and caring, with a belly laugh from the heart. Always supportive, encouraging, and interested in what was going on. Intelligent, a genius, an inspiration to many people. Nobody saw this coming.

"What was going on inside your head, Danny? Why didn't you talk to me about it? Were you thinking of this six months ago, at Christmas, when you came to Toronto? Why didn't I give you the money you asked to borrow? God, I don't understand! Please give me some answers!"

The family had to make quick long distance decisions and arrangements. Seven days after "tornado touchdown," the five of us converged in Montreal. If it were not for Danny's community, I'm not sure we would have been able to achieve what we did in five days. His friends and colleagues quickly, respectfully, and compassionately arranged for our family: airport pickups, in-city travel, accommodation, cremation and funeral arrangements, landlord communication, entry into his apartment, announcements, food, community engagements, and a wake. It was remarkable how so many people in throbbing pain could give so much.

The five-hour drive to Montreal with my younger brother and family friend Sue was filled with uncertainty and nervousness. We tried to keep our minds off where we were going and why. My body was filled with anxiety and tension. I wasn't ready for this. It was weird to walk into a stranger's house as a family. It was the first time we had been together in about six years. Hugs, food, conversation, and drinks ensued. Nobody mentioned Danny. No one wanted to, or we just didn't know what to say.

I put on a brave face for Mom and Dad, but really I was scared, angry, and confused. As we all were. Because there was no note, huge strains of guilt ravaged everywhere, filling the air with lonely tension. Thankfully we still had our sense of humor, which managed to break up the angst from time to time. It was an emotional yo-yo. To this day we still do not know why. I started to learn that understanding others is one of the greatest gifts we can give to the world.

As we climbed the stairs to Danny's apartment, I felt a curdled knot of pain in my gut. The first thing that hit us when we walked in was the smell. I gagged from the reek of death that lingered. The place had an unsettling void. The stench of death combined with the wonderful memories. Walking around, looking at the job ahead of us, I was overwhelmed. How the heck are we going to pack up and sort through thirty-nine years in five days? Sue and I walked into the bedroom, the eye of the storm; there was blood on the floor in the bedroom closet. My breath panicked, I wanted to scream. "Why the hell didn't the police clean this up?" A picture of my brother flashed in my mind that broke my heart, and my soul cried. Maybe later, I'll scream.

Friday morning: Mom and I picked up Danny. There he was, an urn of ashes, dust. I wanted to open it up and slap it. Mom was dazed, clutching the urn like it was a lifeline that had been tossed to someone who had fallen through the ice. The funeral was bizarre; all of these people knew and loved Danny. We knew only two or three people. A fake casket was lowered at the end, and that was it...Gone.

I felt a great loss as the casket lowered its way into the tomb. It was a beautiful sunny day.

That was the easy part. The next five days were spent in an awkward stupor of subdued sadness, focused sorting, wondrous memories, bursts of various emotions, and dizziness from the lingering odor of his death (despite the open windows and constant burning of incense). Friends would stop by; some of them told us stories, helped us understand the significance of this or that. We cried, laughed, got mad, gave mementos away, and in the middle of it all were trying to find his cat.

Dad dealt with the office files, my oldest brother took care of his music, Sue and I bundled up memoir things and the kitchen, my younger brother sorted out the bedroom and clothes. Mom...well, she just walked around completely absent-minded with Danny's guitar on her back, in and out of the apartment, back and forth to the house. We never did find a note. That was, and still is the hardest part for my parents. Personally, inside me I knew there was a higher purpose for this. I was beginning to open up to God.

When Sue and I closed the bedroom door and scrubbed the remaining blood off the floor, all senses vanished, and our hearts howled willingly. I prayed to Danny, to God, to help me understand. Later, I realized that I had compassionately watched myself through this whole experience.

Monday night: A wake had been organized that hosted at least a hundred and fifty people during the evening. Jazz musicians from all over Canada came to play tribute to Danny. We shared stories, memories, and all I could think about was the six degrees of separation. I gathered up enough courage to speak, I didn't know what I was going to say, but I was compelled to say something. I stood there looking at all the people brought together from one person's love, generosity, and passion. Then it hit me. It was a phenomenal feeling to experience how much love one person could generate. It became crystal clear that love exponentially begets love. The love in that room, that night, burst open a seed within my own heart. So that's what I spoke about. My only regret was that I didn't get a chance to say thank you and good bye in person.

Wednesday: Everything was sorted, divided, packed up. Then we all departed. We were left to ponder, "What the hell just happened??" This was an exhaustively surreal, out-of-this-body experience.

I started asking myself, Am I happy? Am I doing

what makes me happy? At the time the answer was no, and NO! That's when I began doing more things that intrigued, fascinated, and inspired me. I indulged and engaged myself in universal principles, energy work, healing modalities, understanding who I truly am, living passionately.

Another crystal clear moment was seeing the polarity that exists in every moment. Through the intense pain and sadness, there was unconditional love and inspiration. According to human standards, this was a tragedy. The beauty lies underneath the status quo perception, where we allow ourselves to receive prolific life lessons, messages, and inspiration. Not only did I shift my vision and purpose of life, many friends and family members did as well. We have embraced our unique lives, each with its gifts and talents, and started nurturing them, following our bliss. Danny helped so many of us find and receive our own fulfillment. What, I ask you, is more important and beautiful than that?

I wish to say, "Thank you, Danny, for giving me a divine gift by taking one away. I love you dearly and know that you are with me. I hear your joyful laugh, see your terrific smile, and feel your encouragement ... just in a different way now."

I embrace him in spirit as I couldn't in form. His greatness and brilliance is also a part of me, and leading me through mine. I now live on purpose, following my bliss, and have an amazing relationship with my inner power and God. Thank God my brother committed suicide.

♥ ♥ ♥

Carmen Noseworthy is a sparkling energy unit. Her understanding and knowledge of energy, the universe, connecting with our inner power and divine guidance is brilliantly unique. Following her own bliss, Carmen is transforming lives by adding gobs of fun to spiritual concepts. She is also an actress and voice artist. For more information go to:

www.InnerPowerPlayGround.com

Thank God My Parents Died

CELESTE BARBIER

I came home one day in April of 1997 to my mother frantically telling me that my father had been rushed to a local hospital with possible pneumonia. I had just gotten back from a late night rehearsal for the musical I was in at my high school. I was rather surprised, I had never known my father to be ill. He had always been the healthy one.

As a result of earlier events in my life, I was a miserably depressed teenager, who often found relief from my psychological pain through cutting myself, and I experienced constant thoughts of death and suicide. I had become such a dark girl that the majority of my school believed I was into black magic or Satanic practices. Although I wasn't practicing any dark crafts, the reason I had become so dark is that I was angry at God. I was angry for all that had happened to me. I believed it would be better to die than take part in such an existence with people who I felt did not care for me. I reveled in the idea that people were fearful of me to the point where they ceased to make fun of me anymore for being smart, dorky, or weird. I did nothing to prevent the rumors and even perpetuated them by dressing and acting the part of the tragic and sullen girl.

Sitting in the hospital with my father, I listened to the doctors as they informed us that he was going to be just fine and they just needed to run some tests. The diagnosis had been pneumonia, but he wasn't responding to the treatment they were giving him. They told us a biopsy would be necessary to figure out a proper diagnosis and treatment. We sat on his hospital bed playing Monopoly and eating hamburgers, awaiting the next day's "routine procedure."

Things were finally starting to turn around for us as a family. When an opportunity to get his old job back at the University of Colorado in Boulder came up, my dad was reinvigorated. We moved back to the first "hometown" we remembered as a family in the small mountain community of Conifer, Colorado. During the past sixteen years, we had moved from California to Colorado to Florida, back to Colorado, to Hawaii, and to Washington. My parents had become financially and emotionally drained in Washington, longing for an escape. My father had fallen into a drunken depression due to his inability to find work that would support us. Everyone in our family had been living together, but separate in our own private worlds of pain and melancholy. Conifer was that special place where my family had its fondest memories. We thought we could easily return and be the happy family we had once been years ago. However, as the saying goes, you can never go back home. My sister and I were teenagers, still recovering from early traumatic incidents in our lives, and we constantly fought with one another. My mother had become angry and embittered, with an addiction to pain medications. She was far from the loving and kind woman she had been during our younger years, and my father was a sad and quiet alcoholic. We found that we only brought our misery along with us.

The next day, my father went in for his biopsy, and he was put into the post-operative critical care unit. The first day they said that he was going to be fine once he recovered. We stayed and watched over him, and my mother reassured us Dad was going to be all right and would be home in just a few days. To our dismay, his condition wasn't improving. The doctors started using terms such as "his chance of survival," which instilled fear in us. This wasn't the way it was supposed to go. There wasn't supposed to be a worry about a "chance." Something had gone terribly wrong.

Lately, my father had been on a mission to accomplish a few things he'd been putting off due to a lack of money. He bought a motorcycle and a comfortable new bed. My parents had been sleeping on the floor for a while at that point. He wanted to have a reunion with his six remaining sisters (out of nine), most of whom he had not seen in almost twenty years. We knew very little about our father's life and family. My dad had never taken us on a vacation, though we had traveled extensively with our mother, who was a flight attendant. He had always stayed behind to attend to our menagerie of animals. He made this trip very special with us, his daughters, to meet his family, hear their stories, and know him better for the first time.

As his condition worsened, my mother began to contact extended family members to inform them that there was a possibility that this could be the last time they would see Richard Barber, my father. I didn't want to believe it. I believed he was going to be fine. He was the glue of our family, made of pure and unconditional love, a quiet and strong pillar who held our family in place. As the family started arriving from out of state, we surrounded him with our love and support, each in his or her own way.

I held his hand steady while he wrote to us on a memo pad until he could no longer write. I gave him the chart used for spelling things out you want to say by pointing to letters with a pen. As his condition worsened, for unknown reasons he could communicate with us only in Spanish, although he had not spoken the language since he was six. He told my Mother he didn't want to die in a hospital, he wrote the words to us "no más," meaning "no more." I sang softly to him, since I knew that always brought him joy. We waited for his condition to improve, knowing that if it did not, we were to make sure that he was allowed to let his life take a natural course and to turn off the machines, if they were all that was keeping him alive. We didn't want it to come to that. We didn't expect it to have to.

He was my only friend and ally in my family. When my sister and mother went on rampages, he was there as my protector and confidant in his quiet, yet loving way. He was strong, even in his weakness and depression. He was a superhero to me when I was a little girl, and he was my biggest fan when I would sing or perform. He was always there with roses when he could afford them. He always embarrassed me with his uncouth way of hooting in the manner of Arsenio Hall after I'd perform, pointing and exclaiming, "That's my daughter!" He always had a tear and a twinkle in his eye. He admired my intelligence, bragging about my academic accomplishments to his colleagues. He made me feel important and truly special. One day when I was fifteen, after I'd done something that made both my parents quite angry with me. My father told me that no matter who I would become, and no matter what decisions I might make in life, he would always be proud of me and love me. This was, and continues to be, the most important and meaningful thing he ever said to me.

After only two weeks in the hospital, my father had slipped out of consciousness and was unresponsive. His lungs were failing, and he was on life support. The difficult decisions fell on my mother as to how the hospital should proceed. In wanting to keep her promise that he would not die in the hospital, she consulted with them about bringing him home, but they said he most likely would pass en route to the mountains. She made the choice to move him to the hospice floor. As soon as he was situated, my mother whispered in his ear that he was home. Forty-five minutes later, my mother came to retrieve us, saying that his breathing had slowed and we were losing him. We held his hands, calling him back to us with only the word "Papa" every time there was a delay in his breathing. Then, with his hand in mine, I felt the warmth leave it. He did not come back when we called out to him the last time. As this was happening, my father's older children from a previous marriage were returning from their lunch, and while walking into the hospital, they were knocked over by a gust so strong it toppled the eldest girl into her two brothers, yet the gust was not felt or experienced by anyone else standing in that vicinity. With that powerful breeze, he left an impression on all of us.

At that very moment, my life changed forever. All those selfish years of focusing so much of my time and effort on death, suicide, and self-loathing, I realized were a waste. Rather than focus on death, I realized I needed to make an immediate decision as to whether I was going to end my own life or live life to the fullest. I managed to escape those demons that had taken such a strong hold on me. I looked to God, spirituality, everything I could grasp onto that was the opposite of the dark pit that I had fallen into. I wanted to feel alive. I wanted to feel love. I wanted to feel and know beauty and joy. I wanted to change. In every way I began to describe my father's death as salvation.

I was shocked to find out that many of my classmates had pulled together in support of me. I found out I had won an award for my performance of "Unchained Melody." They asked for an encore. I performed the song and with tears streaming down my cheeks, I dedicated the last song I sang to my father and to his memory.

The incidents surrounding his death...the reunion... the motorcycle... and the bed only revealed to me the hand of God in all of this. I saw a real plan, a purpose, and a larger picture that encapsulated me, my family, and all the love my father had ever given us. Quite unexpectedly, I experienced renewal and rebirth as opposed to grief and despair. I felt, for the first time in my life, gratitude for life. This was the major pivotal point of my existence and growth. I was scared and excited with this new sensation. I had been numb for so many years to pain, happiness, fear, anger, and the full range of human emotions. I had been an emotional void up until that moment.

I suddenly felt free and grateful for everything. I was also scared because I thought people would think badly of me because I turned this death, which was nearly unbearable to me, into something of a miracle. The internal changes that took place over the course of the next three years were incredible. It was a daily challenge for me to tackle my own negative psychological patterns. I overcame them, without shame, and with total respect and admiration for my father. I thank God my father died.

Unfortunately, even with that great turning point within myself, my sister, mother, and I did not mend our relationships. Each of us slipped further apart. As I left for college, my mother was diagnosed with cancer, but due to a poor immune system developed a long-lasting staph infection after a radical double mastectomy was performed. My sister hated me because she felt abandoned and left with my mother, whom she felt an obligation to care for over the years. I heard that my mother's health had worsened; I attempted to contact my mother via phone and wrote numerous letters to her, but eventually my mother told me she did not wish to speak to me. My sister and I spoke perhaps three times in a matter of nine years. I had become estranged from them and knew nothing of their lives.

On New Year's Eve 2007, I found myself sitting at the funeral of my great-grandmother, a woman whom I had the great fortune to get to know as a live-in companion for two years after I left university. I casually decided to send a text message to my sister to let her know that our great-grandmother had passed away, not expecting a response...it had been so long since we had communicated. Yet she sent me a message back that she was now married and had two baby girls. My great-grandmother's death thus became a catalyst for my sister and me to rekindle our sisterhood. We began speaking regularly and started a new relationship, though we were now strangers as adults living very different lives.

As we became closer, speaking frequently, I learned much about my mother's failing health and mental condition. I found out that she had even been in a nursing home for a while. She had such a severe addiction to medication that she tended to be cruel to those close to her and alienated them.

It's funny how God works in such mysterious ways! The plan was ultimately so beautiful, none of us could predict the reason God brought people into our lives.

My sister and I had built a new trusting and mutually supportive relationship. Within weeks after my wedding to my life partner, Ren'e, the week of Thanksgiving 2008, I received a text message from my sister that our mother had died during her sleep

My sister and I didn't know what to say; we felt so many emotions at once because of the relationships we each had with her. We sat on the phone, softly crying, and not saying much to one another. We felt emotionally confused. I felt an overwhelming sadness, knowing that my mother had died alone because she had pushed all those who loved her out of her life. I told my sister that Ren'e and I would fly out there and be with her.

She told us to wait because the family planned to hold a memorial for my mother on her birthday, which was Valentine's Day. We flew out for the memorial despite my personal reservations about seeing my mother's family, who surely had heard only bad things about me and my abandonment of my mother over the years. After a few of my aunts and uncles had read scripture and said their bits, I looked over at my sister. Her eyes and my eyes locked, full of tears. I saw a longing in her face that I should speak for both of us. So I did.

I told the story of our life. About the dream my parents had of us, to our adoption, to happy years in Colorado and Hawaii, our trips abroad, our farm full of small animals, and all the adventures that shaped our lives. While speaking, I felt so much weight lift from my shoulders. I felt my mother's pride, joy, and love, which she could not express in the latter part of her lifetime. I felt my parents' elation to be united without pain, anger, or misery anymore. I felt I spoke for both my sister and myself, and that with each word I renewed and sealed our bond as sisters. I finally felt free from the guilt and pain I had carried with me. I felt complete and whole because I had no more hate or resentment lingering in my heart. The bitterness had been dissolved by love.

During that weekend, my sister and I cried together and shared stories with our spouses about our unusual life growing up and about our crazy mother. She gave me photos, scrapbooks, and even my father's naval hat for protection. My sister had saved everything. She even had her children dressed in our baby clothing, which was handmade by our mother. Her home was filled with nostalgia; she kept everything my mother had collected from around the world, and things we had in our home, growing up. I felt like I'd been put in a time warp, watching her children, the same number of years apart as we were, playing in our baby clothes, in a home full of things from our past.

I know my sister has an opportunity to give these two girls a beautiful life, and maybe they won't be as sad and angry as we were. Maybe they will love each other in a way we never did as sisters growing up. I love my new relationship with my sister, and for this reason I can now thank God my mother died, also because she brought us together and made my heart whole.

♥ ♥ ♥

Celeste Barbier was born as Sarah Barber. She has always had an artistic and musical soul, having studied vocal performance in college. Today, she is married to her wife, Ren'e Cosby, and they have their beloved parrot, Oiseau. Celeste is still pursuing music as well as voiceover work and has aspirations of helping people find their goals and move beyond obstacles to attain their dreams through healthy lifestyle changes. Celeste loves to travel as often as possible. Together, Celeste & Ren'e create a powerful and dynamic duo with energy that attracts people to them. They both have entrepreneurial spirits, running multiple businesses in an effort to create more time for leisure, travel, and philanthropy. Most importantly, Celeste loves to enjoy life to the fullest extent by seeing or creating the adventure that life is each day!

Thank God I Have Cancer

CHERI BAUGH-WOODS

I couldn't figure out why I was so tired all the time. For months, I came home from work exhausted. I started taking naps, but that didn't seem to help. I finally decided that I would go to the doctor and get checked out.

I made an appointment, and my doctor gave me a thorough checkup, including blood work at the lab. A few days later, while watching a movie, I received a phone call. It was my doctor. He gave me the results of the blood test I had taken, which showed that indeed, I was anemic. He then told me that he was a little concerned because my white blood cell count seemed to be very high. He told me not to be alarmed, but he was going to refer me to a Hematology and Oncology specialist. He wanted them to double-check the bloodwork findings. I thanked him for the information and went back to watching a movie. I wasn't too concerned because other than being tired I felt great. I wasn't really sure what an oncologist was, but I knew that hematology was the study of blood. I wasn't too worried.

My visit with this new doctor was not what I expected. I am usually a very happy, bubbly, gregarious person, but what I heard next sent me into shock. I was absolutely dumbfounded. She announced to me that I had CLL. As I was thinking to myself, "What is that?" the next words out of her mouth were that is Chronic Lymphocytic Leukemia.

I said, "What!" She repeated it, "Cheri, you have Chronic Lymphocytic Leukemia. Cancer." I was mortified. My thoughts where racing: How? When? Why me? As my thoughts raced, the doctor also informed me that I also had thalacemia—an inherited blood disorder in which the chains of the hemoglobin (a type of protein in red blood cells that carries oxygen to the tissues) molecule are decreased. I was numb from everything that was being said to me, but I knew I needed to focus and try to understand, because if this was indeed true, I knew my parents would ask me questions that I would need to try to answer.

She then asked me if there was any sickle cell in my family, to which I responded no. I shared with her that my uncle had leukemia, but I didn't know what kind. I asked her if it is a genetic thing. She told me that it was not genetic. They don't know why some people get it and others don't. She then pulled out a paper and began to diagram the CLL disease. She tried to put it into layman's terms, but I was still confused.

She told me that there are four stages: 1) lymph nodes are affected; 2) lymph nodes and spleen are affected; 3) a lower hemoglobin count and then, 4) platelets are low. At this stage, a bone marrow transplant has to take place.

I quickly asked what stage I was in. She said she thought that I was probably in stage 0, which meant that I didn't really have any symptoms other than a high white blood cell count. I asked her what we needed to do to get rid of this, and she said that there is no cure for leukemia. She continued to inform me that the mortality rate for people with my particular disease is between seven and fifteen years. I just about fainted when I heard this. This was not the kind of news I wanted to hear. The doctor then informed me that I was a rare case because this is usually a disease for elderly people and that they really don't have any information on the effects of this disease on people my age. She then said that chemo and radiation were the only ways to attack this disease, but at this time for me, no treatment would be the major treatment. She also stated that I would be taking iron for the anemia and that she wanted additional tests done to make sure that I indeed had CLL.

I left the appointment for the lab for one more blood test. Afterwards, I drove home, pulled into the driveway, went inside my house, and crawled into bed. All I wanted to do was sleep. I was totally drained from my experience at the doctor's office.

The next day, I awoke with a splitting headache, but I packed my bags in silence. I was getting ready to go on a women's retreat with my church. My mind began to race with when should I tell my parents, should I tell my friends, what should I do. My friend Barbara arrived, and we began our trip up to our annual women's retreat. As we drove, she noticed that I wasn't acting like my usual self and asked me what was wrong. I just blurted out that I had gone to the doctor and that they thought I might have Chronic Lymphocytic Leukemia. She was floored. We drove in silence for a while. I told her that I had just finished taking another blood test and that it was going to determine whether I had it for sure or not. I was hoping that by some miracle they had been mistaken. I told Barbara that I didn't want anyone else to know until I had confirmation. I wanted her to keep me in her prayers. I told her I just wanted to have a good time. I decided to pretend that I had never gone to the doctor at all. I tried not to look worried, and during the quiet times at the retreat, I went off by myself and just cried out to God with reflection and prayers.

I received the results of the blood test the following day, and my hopes were dashed when I heard the CLL had been confirmed. I plopped into a chair and thought to myself, "What do I do now?" I realized that I needed to tell my parents and my brothers. I gathered my thoughts and made the phone call to my parents. My dad answered the phone, and I told him I had something I needed to tell him and mom. I shared everything that had happened As I shared, they listened and were calm. They really didn't have a lot of questions for me. I guess I had done my research before talking with them. I shared all the information I had from not only the doctor but the Internet as well. Both of my parents were extremely supportive and let me know that they loved me and would help me any way that they could. I then called my brothers, who had a similar reaction.

I went back to work, teaching children, and decided I wasn't going to tell anyone what was going on with me. I didn't want anyone feeling sorry for me. I figured as long as I taught the children and gave it my all, I would be okay. I certainly didn't want my students and their parents finding out. After a couple of weeks, I realized I had to tell my principal because I needed to take off work for blood tests and doctor appointments, which often were scheduled on meeting days.

I began to isolate and pull away from people without even realizing it. I would put on a happy face around people and pretend that everything was hunky-dory, and yet inside I was distressed and depressed, I was upset with God, asking, "Why me?"

As time went on, I knew that I needed to change my attitude. Because of my faith in Jesus Christ, I believed very strongly in prayer. I knew from other experiences in my life that prayer works and that prayer could help me in my healing. Although I had been a Christian for years, I found that I had allowed myself to wallow in my self-pity. I needed to once again put my faith and trust in God and believe what His word says in the Bible. I began reading the Bible, praying, and combating my fears.

I began to exercise a little more and to change my eating habits. Extra activity has increased my circulation and, according to the research I have read, it even helps speed oxygen, nutrients, and water to my other cells. It purges my body of deadly toxins and helps to bolster my immune system. I also learned that food has a powerful impact on the human body.

I needed my thoughts and my feelings to be restored. I wanted to focus on the positive things in my life. God says In Psalms 56:3 that, "When I am afraid, I will trust in you." I reminded myself of this and many other truths that God promises in the Bible.

When people would ask, I would tell them about my faith in the healing power of God and let them know that I believed I was already healed. I was just waiting for the manifestation of my healing to occur. For me, it became important to visualize myself in a more positive manner. I remember hearing one time that what you think on is what you become. I didn't want to be bitter and afraid. I wanted to be happy and alive.

My friend Barbara and I began a music group and started singing and writing music that was God-inspired. Both Barbara and I believed that we would be able to use our music as an avenue to help others. We would be able to share our stories and perhaps reach others who were struggling in some way or another.

I made it a point to start living. I took time to smell the roses and see the beauty around me. I slowed my pace and stopped keeping my life filled with the busyness of nothing. I began to interact with others again. Isolation was not the answer. In 1 Thessalonians 5:16-18 it says, "Rejoice always, pray without ceasing, in everything give thanks; for this is the will of God in Christ Jesus for you." And thus I thank God I have cancer.

It has been six years since I was initially diagnosed with CLL. Since that time, my leukemia has progressed to a stage 2. Although it has progressed slowly, there still has been progression. My doctor tells me that at some point I will need to begin treatment. I still believe that I am healed and that I am just waiting for the manifestation of that healing. Just recently, my father and mother were both diagnosed with cancer. My mother, at the age of seventy-four, was diagnosed with breast cancer and has since undergone a mastectomy of her right breast. I am very happy to say that they were able to get all of the cancer, and she is in the process of going through reconstructive surgery. My father, at the age of seventy-seven, was diagnosed with CLL just like me. I thank God I have cancer because when my father was diagnosed with CLL, I was able to share with him the knowledge I had already gained for myself, including the different stages of the disease and what might be expected. I was able to help him formulate questions for his doctor. I was able to help ease my dad's mind. We are a big support for each other.

Another friend of mine who was diagnosed with prostate cancer came to me and shared that he had gained strength from me when he had to undergo surgery for his cancer. He said that I was an inspiration to him. He said that if I could have such a positive outlook and loving and giving attitude, he could too. He shared with me that positivity helped him to heal much faster.

I get such a joy when I am helping others. I am so grateful that I have the opportunity to share my story. It is my desire to help others, giving them strength and encouragement and the ability to develop acceptance when needed most. Having gratitude has helped me to be more positive about my own diagnosis. I plan to continue to share my inspired attitude with others. People comment that I always have a smile on my face, and that it in turn makes them smile.

Each of us has a path that we need to take, and many of us will walk through tribulations and trials. I believe that God guides us, by his Holy Spirit, along the unique way that leads not only to our restoration but also enhancing our ability to fulfill the great purpose that God has for an individual's life. God leads each of us in the path that is right for us. May He lead us through with love and gratitude for one another.

♥ ♥ ♥

Cheri Baugh-Woods is an educator and teacher. She is also the cofounder of Braided Chord, a contemporary Christian music group that ministers through music. Widowed at the young age of thirty-two, Cheri lives in San Diego, California where she has taught and influenced young elementary minds for the past eighteen years.

Thank God I Was Misdiagnosed as Mentally Ill and Suicidal, and Woke Up

DEBRA GATLIN TOWNLEY

In the late afternoon of June 4, 2004, I awakened from a self-inflicted coma. At the end of my bed sat the doctor who had led the team in saving my life. She asked me if I had meant to kill myself. I told her quite frankly that I had and I was livid that she and her staff had intervened.

For four years prior to this incident, I had attempted suicide ten other times, and no one was aware that it was the rare side effect of an anti-depressant medication that I'd been prescribed (initially for a mild ongoing depression) that had plummeted me to the depths of psychosis and severe suicidal ideation. I had been in and out of mental hospitals for four years because of this, and the final straw for me was that my husband and my psychologist had decided that I wasn't functioning well and needed to be placed in a group home.

Within a day after my waking up from the coma, my psychologist called to tell me that I was a liability. She needed to step away from being responsible for me and was no longer willing to be my therapist. She believed I was "failing to thrive" and speculated that maybe I'd been born without a desire for living. I spent the next few weeks coming off the medications with severe headaches, vomiting, mental confusion, trembling, and a desperate sense that I would have been better off dead. But the longer I went without medication, the more everyone could see that I was becoming clear headed. There was no longer any psychosis, and cognitively I was beginning to function as I had before ever taking the drugs. I realized that this mental illness that had taken four years of my life, peppered it with fear and paranoia, false beliefs about reality, and a depression that was so unbearable that I felt the need to end my life, had been medically induced. I was devastated.

How could this happen? How did the doctors whom I trusted miss this? How could they have kept me underwater with medications for four years? I had tried to tell them that I thought it was the medication that was causing my symptoms. The more I complained, the more they categorized me as non-compliant, and the more they pushed the medications. After all, how could an anti-depressant cause depression? The doctors considered themselves the authorities on this subject, and this as a real side effect had not yet been confirmed. At one point I had been told that if I didn't take the medication willingly, a court order could be obtained to force me to take it. My life had deteriorated to a simplified existence of smoking cigarettes and watching the clock to keep up with the next dose of anti-depressants, anti-psychotics, anti-anxiety drugs, mood stabilizers, and sleep aids. My spirit was being consistently whittled down, and after four years of this, my marriage ultimately fell apart and my entire life's worth bottomed out at zero.

After returning home from the hospital, I put in a call to Dr. Lynda Malavanya, a well respected dialectical behavioral therapist and Stanford psychiatrist. I asked her if she could please help me fix this train wreck, and she assured me that there was hope for me. Initially, I didn't believe she could help me, but I had nothing to lose. I was left emotionally raw after four years of psychosis. Trauma from the overdose had left my nervous system so easily overwhelmed by the slightest stimuli that even the softest t-shirt was like sandpaper upon my skin. I was desperate to end this pain but without psychosis, I no longer had the abandon to kill myself. I was forced to find a way to recover. Over the next year, Dr. Malavanya and Dr. Gerald Cohen, a classical homeopath, helped me to rebuild my life again. Dialectical behavioral therapy is known for teaching life skills that help to "create a life worth living," and homeopathic remedies promote healing. I began learning techniques for skillfully managing my emotions. I started slowly, trusting that somehow I could overcome what had happened to me. As I gained confidence and abilities and began healing physically, I realized that my marriage could not recover. We divorced, and I was forced for the first time in my life to be independent. I got a job and a place to live and began commanding some of my own authority over my life. This was something I had not done before, and after all I had endured, I was quite insecure about my abilities.

Shortly after I had just begun to put things back together again, Dr. Malavanya became very ill and was forced to close her practice. I felt disappointed by yet another doctor who was unable to help me and thought once again about giving up. Dr. Malavanya convinced me that I owed it to myself to keep going. I interviewed several therapists and, though I was still angry and unwilling, I began working with Michael J. Hutchinson, MFT. He worked hard to gain my trust, and together we picked up where Dr. Malavanya and I had left off. Michael and I continued down the path of putting things back together again.

While working with Michael, I started believing somewhere along the way that I might actually have an incredible opportunity to create a life for myself that could truly be worth living. Soon the choices that I made became so much more important. I began to understand that every minute that I spent doing anything at all or doing nothing at all belonged to me. I could create whatever I wanted. In this there was hope. And with this hope came a desire to be exactly who I am and not necessarily listen to the things that others had been telling me about myself. I then found my own inner voice and began trusting God. I was soon on my way to creating that life worth living.

Now as a successful teacher, entrepreneur, and dedicated mother and foster parent, I find people are astonished to think of me as someone who spent four years in and out of mental hospitals for attempting to take her own life. Today, I am inspired, healthy, and optimistic, and I am medication free. Before the "medicinal catastrophe," the moments of my life were going by and I wasn't taking notice. My daily routine was being lived out unsatisfactorily, and that's what led me to try anti-depressant medication in the first place. My marriage was based on tolerance, not love. My life was being haphazardly built by what happened to come along or what others were defining my life to be. But today, I'm living a new life that I purposefully create. By having had my life almost completely destroyed over the course of four years, I was given the opportunity to now create anything I wanted for my life. I understood that it was up to me how that life was going to wind up.

Through a medical mishap that kept me paralyzed by psychosis and depression for four years, I saw a depth of emotional devastation and a desperate sense of reality that many people never get to see. If they do, many times they don't return from it. I saw a truly terrifying perception of the world through psychosis and fear, depression and hopelessness. It is a place of despair so deep that even causing one's own death can seem a haven. I know a forfeit of life that I cannot ever erase from memory. And because I carry this memory with me now, I know that experiencing each day, each moment, each breath that I take is a choice. I look around and sometimes I see others going about their lives without this understanding, and I remember a time when I, too, didn't know it. I can no longer sit comfortably unaware while the moments of my life are passing. There is a loss of innocence when suddenly I am sensing the urgency of being awake in each moment. But I wouldn't have it any other way. It is a gift to be able to choose each moment as it comes. I am now thriving and continuing to create a life worth living, a life worth celebrating! The life I live now is more purposeful and meaningful than anything I could have created before coming to know that every moment that I live belongs to me. I thank God that I was mistakenly medicated, mentally ill, suicidal, and in a coma. And I thank God that I woke up.

♥ ♥ ♥

Debra Gatlin Townley lives in northern California and is the proud parent of two fabulous teenagers. She is the director of a preschool program that she created for her neighborhood church and is also a foster parent. She openly shares her life experiences with others hoping to inspire and teach that every moment, no matter what the experience, can be enthusiastically celebrated as part of a life worth living. She has great gratitude for Dr. Lynda Malavanya and Michael J. Hutchinson, MFT and would like to also thank Dr. Marsha Linehan for creating Dialectical Behavior Therapy and clearly defining many of the skills necessary to creating a life worth living.

Thank God I Was Let Go

DEBORAH BROWN-VOLKMAN, PCC

From the time I was a little girl, I just wanted to be happy. Although my parents were loving people, they married young and were immersed in child raising and paying the bills. At times I did not feel loved, and many times I felt lonely. I felt trapped, and these feelings carried into my career.

For over twelve years, I ran successful sales and marketing programs for Fortune 500 companies and dot. coms. Although I was good at what I did, I did not enjoy the politics and bureaucracy of the corporate world. It never made sense to me that we had to run around producing campaigns, budgets, and numerous reports, many of which never got used or read. I worked long hours. I was stressed, overweight, and always wishing for something more.

I hadn't always felt that way about work. When I was in college, I majored in Marketing and was amazed that you could ask consumers what they wanted in a product or service and then use that information to create spectacular marketing and advertising campaigns. Writing term papers came easily to me, and I relished the fact that someone wanted my opinion and enjoyed reading what I thought. I graduated from college with honors and could not wait to take the working world by storm.

I got my first marketing job in Manhattan. It was the early eighties, and Wall Street was booming. I loved the pace, the excitement of a big city environment, and the salary I was earning. In fact, I loved it all. I excelled at my job, but after a few years, the excitement started to fade. I wondered, "How could this be happening to me?" No one was more excited about work than I had been when I started. I was working in marketing and sales because I was people oriented, fascinated by how people behaved, and wanted to gain a deeper understanding of what motivates them to take action. Why was I so unhappy? I felt like I was caught in a world that made no sense to me, where making decisions made an eternity look short. Day after day I took my assigned place, to work by rules created by others, for endless hours that belonged to others, to achieve the goals of others. I was slowly becoming invisible.

Because I was so unhappy, I switched jobs a lot—every year or two. I started each job with good intentions and told myself, "This is it. I'm staying here forever!" But a month or two later, I would start experiencing unhappiness again. I felt trapped and unappreciated. I looked for support and affirmation from the people in my life. I wanted someone to "get" me and tell me I wasn't crazy. But instead, I heard questions such as "What's wrong with you?" Or, "Why can't you be happy?" And, "Why can't you stay in a job for an extended period of time?" I did not have the answers. I just knew I wanted more.

In my eighth year of working full-time in the corporate world, I was employed by a start-up company. There was a lot of change in the company, and I was on my fourth manager. I was reporting to the head of purchasing, and she did not care about the creativity that marketing needed to shine. Instead, she focused on cost-cutting and getting the most work done at the cheapest price. I was miserable. I remember burying my head in my hands and asking the universe for a way out. I got my answer three months later when I took a Learning Annex class on How to Become a Coach. The funny thing is that this Learning Annex catalog had been sitting on my living room table for three months.

When I got to the class, I did not know what to expect. But something happened inside me as the instructor spoke. The instructor talked about coaching, and I knew instantly that I had found my purpose in life. It hit me like a bolt of lightning. Coaching was a profession dedicated to helping people change their lives. Friends were always coming to me for advice. I listened well. I encouraged them to go for it, take chances, and live their dreams. I had always enjoyed inspiring people but never thought I could make a living at it. For the first time in a long time, my next career move made sense to me.

The next day I signed up for coaches' training. This was 1998, and no one knew what coaching was at the time. It was a brand new profession. Even though I was heading toward the unknown, I jumped in anyway. I had no idea where this journey was going to take me, but I was ready to find out. I chose Coach University as the place to help me. I opened my part-time coaching practice and began coaching people.

Transitioning into my second career took longer than I wanted. From the moment I found out about coaching, I wanted to do it as my full-time profession, but it didn't happen as quickly as I wanted. First of all, I had debts to pay. How could I possibly start a new venture without money to back it up? Second, people did not understand the purpose of a coach. Sure, they understood coaching in the world of sports, but in the context of life? It was a foreign concept. Last, I was scared. What happened if I wasn't good at coaching? What happened if I said the wrong thing to someone? Would someone pay me to help them? Even though I had doubt and real concerns to overcome, I pressed on. I made a decision to be debt free and paid back the money I owed to credit card companies. I began an educational campaign and told everyone I met about the benefits of coaching. As I coached people, my confidence grew. I was getting stronger as a coach but could not seem to make the leap and make it my full-time job. Not knowing if it would work, I continued to hold onto my marketing job for dear life.

Then, God stepped in. I was working for a technology company, and they weren't making money. One day, my boss called me into his office and said he had to let me go. The funny thing was I wasn't scared—I was delighted. I thanked him, packed my belongings, and headed home. I told my husband that night when he returned from work that I was not going back to the corporate world and was going to make my coaching practice work. To my amazement he said, "OK." I became a full-time coach that day and have been one ever since. Transitioning from working for someone else to working for myself was daunting for me in the beginning. I remember sitting at my desk at home the day after I was laid off, wondering what I was going to do next. Even though there was information on how to coach, it was spread out all over the place. And there was no concrete information on how to make money at it. I was determined to make it work and told myself that I would not give up until it did.

In my first year as a full-time coach, I learned self-discipline, organization, and time management techniques. I taught myself HTML and updated my website. I got focused, wrote articles like crazy, built a database of reporters for whom I could be an expert, started a coaches chapter, and coached my heart out. I made sure I learned something new every day. I also worked with a coach who taught me how to sell, which was key to growing my practice.

All my hard work has paid off. Today I have an amazing coaching practice that continues to get bigger. I get to help people. I feel appreciated, respected, and listened to. The interesting thing is that I don't think about switching jobs anymore. I love what I do and can't imagine doing anything else. As for the skills I learned while job-hopping: resume and cover letter writing, interviewing, networking, and salary negotiations, these became the coaching services I offered, and still offer, to my clients. Funny how things turn out!

I am living my purpose and am so grateful for it. Every day I get up and thank God for my life. I am finally inspired. I am very lucky. In addition, to a great career, I have a wonderful husband, who is my best friend and soul mate. We live in a beautiful home, and I have wonderful friends who no longer question who I am. Rather, they "get" me and embrace the person I have become.

I joined the Thank God I series so I could share with you my journey and how I took something that could have been a terrible chapter in my life and turned it into something I am grateful for. My wish is that reading my story will kick start yours. If I can make change possible in my life, then I know that you can too.

Thank God I was let go.

♥ ♥ ♥

Deborah Brown-Volkman is a Professional Certified Coach (PCC), author, and the president of Surpass Your Dreams, Inc., a successful career, life, and mentor coaching company that has been delivering a message of motivation, success, and personal fulfillment since 1998. She provides career coaching for senior executives, vice presidents, and managers who are looking for new career opportunities or seek to become more productive in their current role. Brown-Volkman has been featured in The Wall Street Journal, The New York Times, Fortune Magazine, and many other publications. She is the author of several best-selling books including Coach Yourself to a New Career, Don't Blow It! The Right Words for the Right Job, and How to Feel Great at Work Every Day. Deborah Brown-Volkman can be reached at http://www.surpassyourdreams.com info@surpassyourdreams.com.

Thank God I Went Bankrupt

FELICIA BROWN

"It's business. I'm just glad you are handling this so well," said my business banker, Michelle, after I told her I was closing my day spa and defaulting on my commercial loan. "I've had to talk a couple of my clients 'off the ledge' recently. They've been practically suicidal over their failing businesses and the likelihood of declaring bankruptcy."

Although I was putting on something of a brave face, I think Michelle and I were both pretty surprised by the overall level of optimism in my voice and attitude when we spoke that day. While I hated to hear other businesses were also struggling, I was glad to hear that I was handling things better than some of Michelle's other clients...and perhaps better than I realized.

It hasn't always been that way, though. Since the finances at the spa first began crashing down in early 2009, I've felt a lot of things: anger, rage, sadness, deep grief, betrayal, hopelessness, humility, disbelief, gratitude, hysteria (good and bad), disgust, amusement, contemplation, shock, bewilderment, love, overwhelm, drunkenness, awe, pride and even joy. But believe it or not, suicidal is one thing I haven't felt because of the "failure" of my company or the economic re-education it has given me. In fact by contrast, I can actually say here on the other side of the process that I am thankful I went bankrupt.

I don't want to mislead you into thinking this mindset came quickly or without effort. To be truthful, I've spent plenty of moments wondering why this happened to me and what I could have done to prevent it from occurring. But around and between those moments, I have had just as many experiences that made me see how lucky I am to be living the life I have right now...the same life in which I've lost so much and had to declare bankruptcy.

One of the times that was filled with both brilliantly light and deeply dark emotions happened about a month after I closed my business. I'd been in Columbia, South Carolina, visiting my friend Susan for a couple of days. We'd spent a lot of time talking, eating, drinking and just hanging out the way old friends do. For the first time in several weeks, I actually felt pretty relaxed and somewhat upbeat about my future.

As I was preparing to return home from the trip, I received a call from a woman who had previously rented my vacation home at the beach. After her rental, she had offered to purchase some of the furniture in the house should we ever decide to sell. With the recent turn of events, I'd let her know I was getting rid of a few things including the furniture she had asked about. She was calling to finalize her purchase and arrange a pick-up for the next day. As soon as I answered the phone, my relaxation evaporated almost immediately. I then reluctantly agreed to meet her husband at the house the following morning.

The beach house was my "happy place" and a reward for many years of hard work. I had purchased "Balance by the Sea" after selling my first successful business, another day spa. My husband and I had spent countless times there by ourselves and with our family, friends, and dogs. We even spent our honeymoon there. To me, it almost felt more like home than the house where we lived most of the time.

However, times had changed. Selling off the furniture was the first step in getting rid of a property I could no longer afford. The call forced me to face the reality that I would soon be giving up my "home away from home" and promptly sent me right back down to the depths of depression. With no other choices, I packed up and began the seven hour, tear-filled drive to the coast.

The next morning, after I'd gotten a fitful night's sleep, the woman's husband and son came to pick up my bedroom set and some other furniture from the beach house. Holding back tears, I watched as my bedroom was dismantled and moved piece by piece down the stairs and out the door. With each item they loaded up, I felt like another part of my life was being taken away. I closed the door and sobbed in the hallway as their moving van drove away.

A few minutes later, I went outside to gather my thoughts and prepare for the long drive back home. As I sat on my sunny deck, writing in my journal and mourning the loss of my vacation furnishings, I suddenly began to laugh at myself right through my tears. The silliness of weeping and grieving for bedroom furniture! While I sat there with the salty breeze blowing gently on my face, laughing and crying, I had a great epiphany: A bed is just a bed, a house is just a house...what makes these things special is the people you share them with and the memories you create in them.

Likewise, I came to the conclusion that by letting go of the property and everything in it I was finally facing all my worries about the house head-on. I was also letting go of all my "what if's" about it. Questions like "What if we can't pay the mortgage?" or "What if there is a hurricane?" and "What if we have a bad renter?" would no longer matter to me. That was a pretty awesome discovery and made the transition from current beach house owner to former beach house owner much easier.

A few months later, I moved into a place of peace and gratitude somewhat unexpectedly. Because of a heartfelt request from an old business acquaintance, I began providing massage therapy to a couple of patients with amyotrophic lateral sclerosis, or ALS, Brad and Norm.

Making the connection to these PALS (patient with ALS) was really a miracle! Had I not been in a place of financial desperation and been willing to do whatever was needed to get back on my feet, my PALS would not have become part of my life. Why? Because I would not have previously accepted the new clients or the home based appointments.

The moment that my attitude totally shifted was after my second appointment with Norm. In the span of just a few days between our appointments, I could see a big deterioration in Norm's mobility. On my first visit, he'd been able to change television channels with the remote control on his own. By my next visit with him five days later, Norm could no longer move his arm enough to change the channels or even scratch his nose. I left that appointment with a deep level of gratitude for all that was good in my own life and resolved not to feel sorry for myself or my situation any longer. Norm died several days later.

A couple of months after Norm passed away, I began working with Brad. Though his physical condition was actually much worse than Norm's had been – he had absolutely no movement ability anywhere in his body and could not speak without the assistance of a special computer – Brad always brightened my day with his smile and positive energy. Though I could sense the frustration he lived with being trapped inside his body, I felt better just being around Brad.

Most memorably, when I arrived for our third appointment, Brad had a surprise waiting for me. He had programmed, into his computer, a compliment about how my work helped him. This was something he could not have done alone; he must have thought about it quite a bit between our visits.

As I listened to the mechanical voice tell me how much "he" could tell I loved my work and taking care of people, tears streamed down my face. To know that I had made a difference in his life was unbelievably rewarding and touching. That someone with such a huge problem could take the time to make me feel good about myself was so incredibly meaningful and humbling.

After working with these two special PALS, I really felt empowered to take charge of my own life and health in a much more proactive way and to remember what matters most. Seeing Norm and Brad's struggles and frustrations, up close, made me see that my financial problems were actually quite manageable and gave me a new perspective on my own priorities.

Money is not at the top of the list. Making a difference in other people's lives and making each day count is what matters most.

My business failure and subsequent bankruptcy were the vehicles that brought Norm and Brad into my life. Their presence and impact was an incredible gift! My experience with them made me stop in my tracks to get a handle on defining what a real problem or crisis is for me. I am forever grateful for the time I spent with them before they left this world.

Neale Donald Walsh said in Conversations with God, "Words may allow you to understand something. Experience allows you to know." Throughout this journey, I have learned a lot about letting go of what isn't essential and holding on to what matters most to my life. I've learned to appreciate the "here and now" and remembered that, no matter how difficult my pain seems, I can still make a difference in others' lives. I've also learned that life goes on if you let it.

The day I signed the bankruptcy papers I felt a huge weight was lifted off my shoulders. I felt that one long chapter in my life had finally ended and that I could finally begin to explore new things and let myself move on. Happily, I also experienced the peace of mind of knowing that all the creditor calls were going to come to an end. Believe me, that's something to celebrate!

Going bankrupt and receiving my "economic re-education" was one of the best things that could have happened to me. It brought me greater rewards than I could have ever imagined. I hope you are able to find the gifts and rewards in whatever challenges you've been dealt and that someday you'll be able to say Thank God I __________.

♥ ♥ ♥

Felicia Brown is the owner of Spalutions!, (www.spalutions.com) a firm that provides marketing coaching, business consulting, training, and education to massage, spa, and wellness professionals. She has written for numerous local and trade publications including Skin Inc., Massage Therapy Journal, Massage Magazine, Massage & Bodywork, Spa Management Journal, Spa Business and Dermascope. Felicia is also the author of The Sunflower Princess, a healing fairy tale (eBook) and the audio CD Just Breathe: Guided Meditations for Inner Peace. A native of Greensboro, North Carolina, Felicia enjoys running, yoga, reading, cooking, travel, and adventures of most any sort. Felicia and her husband, David, have a houseful of pets—four dogs and one cat—all of whom are rescued.

Thank God I Had Breast Cancer

GINAT RICE

"It can't happen to me."

So I thought when I developed breast cancer in April, 1999. I had been practicing macrobiotics devotedly and guiding others in this way of life for over twenty years, advising people daily how to deal with the illness I now manifested. Imagine my shock when I felt a small lump on my breast. I instinctively felt that it might be a big lesson for me, but I didn't know how to make it happen.

I consulted with my macrobiotic advisor, who saw no reason for concern. When the area began to hurt, I arranged for a medical examination. Palpations and a mammogram proved inconclusive. So I continued with my macrobiotic lifestyle, thinking it enough to tighten up my practice to a more precise healing diet.

Nine months later a second medical checkup showed a whopping thirty-percent growth in my tumor! An alarmed examining surgeon performed a painful needle biopsy that sent me home in tears. I was surprised that my macrobiotic counselor concurred with his recommendation for immediate surgery. He further recommended chemotherapy for the initial shock it would give my body, but cautioned against the standard protocol of long-term drugs. I felt powerless in my slide toward the medical world. This was so foreign to my normal health perspective. I had never been ill before!

I could only be grateful for all the years I had enjoyed good health without medical intervention.

In holistic terms, cancer results from the stagnation of energy. Amelioration requires time, and the tumor growth was rapid. Shocked and tearful, I agreed to the surgery to help me open up physically until I had time to do so spiritually. I recognized that I was living my life with unresolved relationships, resistance to change, and the contradiction of desire.

My mastectomy revealed the cancer to be confined to my breast with no growth beyond the chest cavity. Two lymph nodes were found to be cancerous. I accepted a chemotherapy treatment of four sessions administered at three-week intervals. This procedure of slash and poison was a debilitating experience of dehydration and illness entailing emergency hospitalization with intravenous transfusions three times. The oncologist agreed that he might have administered too high a dosage of drugs, so he cut down the individual portion and added a fifth chemotherapy session. My opposition to the invasive medical treatment was strong; I was sicker than the horror stories I'd heard from so many well-meaning survivors. It was the lowest point of my life.

I hesitated to reveal my condition to the Jerusalem macrobiotic community, projecting their condemnation of me as if my illness proved macrobiotics a failure. I feared I had let them down. Contrary to my expectations, my illness actually united people. The phone rang constantly, locally and internationally. By week's end my bedroom looked like a flower shop. So many people who we had helped in the past were returning all that they had received and more. Despite the misery of my condition, these personal outpourings of love raised my hopes and frame of mind. Thoughts of gratitude filled my heart as the upside of my cancer became increasingly clear.

With deep self-reflection, I realized that there are no guarantees in life. I determined to take personal responsibility for my illness and focus on my emotional and mental needs. Even though I was awash in the world of hospitals and doctors, I considered medical intervention as adjunct to true healing. I actively sought programs that would help me release acknowledged anger, impatience, and guilt.

I worked with a superb healer between chemotherapy sessions, met with an osteopath specializing in mind-body therapy regularly, and began yoga classes with an inspiring teacher and friend. My stint with the hospital psychiatric services was seemingly less successful—I found the staff psychiatrist to be lacking compassion and personal warmth. I realized that saying no to him was actually a sign of inner strength. I frequently turned for reassurance to a clinical psychologist friend instead. I joined a prosperity workshop to repair my relationship with money, organized an anger workshop, and joined a meditation group. I learned healing visualizations to release resistance. These avenues of spiritual growth eased my anxiety about the cause and cure of my disease.

One of my most rewarding healing experiences involved a workshop based on the teachings of Louise Hay. This ten-session course coincided with my scheduled fourth chemotherapy session. I knew that I could only manage one or the other. The strength and support I garnered from these gatherings set me firmly on the path of recovery. I found it empowering and reassuring to be making changes that could affect my future. The value of my medical treatment and my ability to survive it was becoming doubtful in my mind. Still, I suffered great personal anxiety in the face of heavy medical and family pressure to continue.

Finally, I understood that it was up to me. Chemotherapy had jolted my system out of its chaotic growth pattern. Now it was up to me to initiate deeper healing. I made the brave decision to take charge of my own health regardless of protocol, pressure, or personal fear. As I discovered the power of my mind, I began to love myself more. Little by little the gifts of my illness were beginning to shine through. So many doors had been opened, and I knew now that I was in charge of my life.

In reviewing the story of my illness, for this anthology, I was delighted to realize the progression in my thinking. Before I got ill, I was caught in my belief that diet was the cause and cure of health. This thinking kept me a prisoner of my kitchen, fearful to eat what I wanted. Today I believe that my tumor was created from a place of emotional vulnerability. While food and sentiment are a single continuum, the greater imbalance was on the side of emotion. I had left unresolved a dysfunctional and emotionally abusive personal relationship several years before. Then I married into a family that was still healing its own divorce trauma, living as a bride with my husband and stepdaughter, whose role as Daddy's housemate I had usurped. With her, I re-created the emotional abuse I had just left behind.

In addition, I worked long hours advising people how to recover their health and solve personal issues. I remember a dream in which my students were pushing me up against a wall and I couldn't escape. My husband and I were realizing that our orthodox religious practice didn't satisfy our spiritual longing, and took the bold move of adopting a more universal expression of belief, risking both patronage and friendships. My older sister was recovering from breast cancer, still another spotlight on the big C. All of this added up to a sense of helplessness and lack of control. In fact, anger was my abiding issue—I would erupt with frustration at things that didn't go my way. It was a position of powerlessness.

I owe a great part of my recovery to Jerry and Esther Hicks and the teachings that they channel from Abraham concerning the law of attraction. I have learned to manifest my desires by allowing and letting in the well-being that abounds universally. With seminars and recordings, I have steadily retrained myself to seek positive aspects rather than dwell on the negative. I have been able to see my difficulties as wonderful avenues for joy and freedom.

I finally can understand my dis-ease as a reflection of my life choices and know with confidence that I can command my health. I surrender my arrogance about my invincibility and my magical thinking that "it can't happen to me." I realize that I am entitled to be unwell even to the point of serious illness. My empathy for sick people has deepened. Thanks to this experience, I have healed deep emotional trauma and resentment that I would never have admitted. I am so grateful for the supportive environment of my loving husband and wonderful friends. Best of all, I cherish the wonderful relationship with my new family, particularly the stepdaughter who was such a mirror for my growth. She and I share a closeness that provides me the joy of a mother-daughter relationship, something precious to me. The more I self-reflect, the more my spirits rise.

Today, seven years after my surgery, I have no symptoms of disease and abundant evidence of well-being. My energy is vibrant and my mood upbeat. I am happier than I have ever been and truly grateful for the opportunity to change life patterns. Knowing myself better than ever, I use food, thought, breath, and movement to fashion the experiences I desire. I affirm my ability to create my own personal health and happiness. These represent the most profound expression of life and the ones that I treasure most. To the degree that I can conceive health, I am well. To the degree that I can know God, I am whole. I have great gratitude for my experience of illness as a powerful new opening and for radiant health now. I am so grateful for the opportunity to expand my understanding of these issues in writing this story. I can truly say, "Thank God I had breast cancer!"

♥ ♥ ♥

Ginat Rice is a macrobiotic counselor in Israel, guiding people to health and fulfillment through principles of balanced living and thinking. She is the author of numerous magazine and Internet publications on these topics and focuses her life on three major arenas: Israel/Judaism, spirituality, and natural foods. After completing a master's degree in International Administration, she became co-owner and manager of Satori Natural Food Restaurant in Boston, MA. She studied extensively at the Kushi Institute for macrobiotic studies, becoming certified as a macrobiotic counselor and teacher.

In 1999 she overcame breast cancer, bringing clarity to a confused, discontented life. She married Sheldon Rice in 1995 and traveled extensively with him in a motor home across North America. Together they operate a Bed & Breakfast in Jerusalem along with macrobiotic and law of attraction educational groups.

Thank God I Was Laid Off

HEATHER VALE GOSS

The business world seems to be made up of two fairly distinct groups: employees and entrepreneurs. There are many grey areas between them, but if I had to boil it down into a black and white rule, I'd say if you get paid by a "boss," you're an employee; if you get paid by customers, you're an entrepreneur. I've been both, but I can say without reservation which one I prefer... Thank God I'm an entrepreneur.

I've heard that franchise sellers have certain criteria when looking for potential franchisees. They specifically do not want people who exhibit entrepreneurial tendencies, which seems counter-intuitive because running a franchise in essence means running your own business. However, franchises want the employee mindset to ensure people will do what they're told, how they're told, and when they're told in respect to presenting that franchise just like every other link in the chain rather than an individual business.

For me, being an individual is what drives me forward toward my goals and dreams. I have done well only in employee situations that welcomed my creative tendencies and allowed my individualism to shine; but usually it gets to a point where they just want me to pull back and be like everybody else. Eventually, that has resulted in my being fired more than once from jobs where everybody around me thought I was the best on the team.

Some people say you're meant to be either an employee or an entrepreneur, for life. I think a lot of us start out as employees and, through the laws of contrast and polarity, we are able to see why we're just not happy in that situation, and why we are destined to be entrepreneurs.

A lot of the people I've talked to about this feel you can be both an employee and an entrepreneur, at different times in your life, or even overlapping. If you really want to be an entrepreneur in your heart, you'll be one sooner or later, because working for someone else can only inspire and motivate you for a limited time.
But the employee experience, at least for me, is what proved to me that I wanted, and in fact needed, to be an entrepreneur. The employee experience stifled me. It tried to make me into a lemming and didn't allow much room for creativity. But as an entrepreneur, I have no one to answer to but my customers, and can be as creative as I want every day. In short, I can let the true me be revealed to the world instead of being identified by the title on my business card.

A few years ago I won several speech competitions in Toastmasters with a humorous speech titled "Do What You Love... and the Money Will Follow?"

It poked fun at the fact that I had been doing what I loved – working in media, hosting shows and becoming known as one of the best interviewers in Canada – for close to ten years, and yet still had not gotten to the point where the money was truly following.

Sure, I had had some paying gigs along the way... but not enough to pay the rent. I first made a splash on the media scene with a local cable show whose sponsors only gave me goods and prizes, and then with my own internet projects, which were about to pay off when the dot-com crash hit.

So in essence I had been volunteering much of my time doing what I loved for years, and bartending at night to make the real money. What did this mean in the big picture? I was a professional bartender and a struggling entrepreneur, and thankful for every moment I got to dedicate my energy to doing what I knew would one day take over my life.

After fifteen years of this, I promised myself that my current bartending job was my last, and then I got fired for something I didn't do. It wasn't the first time that had happened to me. Looking back on these experiences, I saw the pattern as a sign that being an employee was a temporary learning experience.

I decided to try working in my first love... radio. I had always been fascinated by the immediacy and intimacy of radio but hadn't liked my voice much. However, I took a shot at a traffic reporter job and got it, with no experience. The let down was that radio apparently paid much less than I had ever imagined, at least in entry-level positions that just happened to be guiding thousands of people safely home.

So in a need to escape the seeming inability to make a living doing what I loved, and the late nights and lack of opportunity for advancement as a bartender, I left the service and media industry at the same time to enter the corporate world.

I had been focusing for years on what my ideal job would look like: being paid a certain dollar figure that represented the perfect salary to me. I wanted to earn that money while talking to people, communicating, giving speeches and trainings, writing, and having a flexible schedule that allowed me to do my work on my own time. I had assumed that job was going to be an on-air position at a TV station, but it turned out to be as an Account Rep for a wireless phone giant.

Strangely enough, that "employee" position almost satisfied my entrepreneurial desires for several years. I loved every minute of it, and it seemed like the coolest job in the world. At the same time, I landed a much higher paying radio job as a news anchor on the weekends. I was flying high and loving every minute of it.

Then there were some organizational "realignments," and I got stuck on the "uncool" team. My territory suddenly grew, but the products I was training on were all basic entry-level handsets that few customers wanted to buy, and few sales reps needed training on. I had gone from being excited and challenged every day to feeling like I was almost useless. This restlessness paved the way for some new opportunities to enter my life.

I had found a fascination with the law of attraction and other metaphysical principles. I knew that I had manifested this job but couldn't understand at the time why I had manifested my current unsatisfactory position.

I had manifested the radio news anchor job on the side, and being a news anchor was one of my goals that I needed to achieve. But once I started doing this, I realized that my love was not reading the news... my love was interviewing people about what made them tick. Once I made that decision, the position suddenly ended. It had apparently been temporary from the start, but just as I started to excel, I suddenly didn't get called in anymore.

Right around that time, I was listening to a teleseminar with Jack Canfield, the co-creator of the Chicken Soup for the Soul empire. What stuck with me was the concept of inspired action: when you're tuned in to what you want, you'll get sudden overwhelming ideas and a strong inclination to take action, even though it may not make sense at the time.

He said it usually took thirty days, but two days later I was practically whacked on the head with a powerful flash of a thought: I was meant to take all my years of experience interviewing people, my media experience in TV, radio, and print, and combine that with my drive to discover what makes some people successful while others struggle. I was meant to interview the world's top success experts, and publish that as a book. It was suddenly clear: everything I had done to that point in my life was coming together into a perfect moment of synchronicity.

I pursued that dream through a year and a half while continuing to work the corporate job that I no longer loved. The book idea morphed into an online radio show at first. Every week I was interviewing personal development experts, and then successful entrepreneurs. I knew that my full-time entrepreneurial venture was in my future, but I was too addicted to the comfort zone to walk away from the job.

Guess what happened once again? I manifested myself out of another job, with a sudden layoff that came without warning! The way the events unfolded were so amazing that I found myself awestruck and incredibly grateful for the situation.

Along the way I partnered with several different people to make entrepreneurial ventures pay off. There was one partner I was working with who really made me see what life could be like going full-time on my own. That person was Barry Goss, originally my co-host and business partner on our Masters of the Secret project. (Barry later became my soul mate, life partner, and husband!)

One weekend, I attended a live seminar with Dr. John Demartini. I kept phoning Barry to fill him in on what was going on. And every time I did, he asked me what it would take to get me to not go back to work on Monday, and concentrate on Masters of the Secret instead. Of course every time he asked, I told him that although I'd love to, I just couldn't do it.

Then Monday morning rolled around and I got the fateful phone call: that I was no longer employed as a wireless representative — effective immediately due to additional restructuring. I smiled, knowing instantly that Barry and I had manifested that over the weekend.

Thank God I was laid off!

Since that Monday morning I have never looked back, and I don't foresee the need to ever go back to being an employee again. Now for the first time in my life, I feel like I enjoy everything I do. I'm travelling more - and not mundane road trips for work, but real trips, fun trips, even when they're for business! I'm seeing different parts of the world, meeting other incredible entrepreneurs who have uncovered their dreams, and loving every minute of it.

But most importantly, every day I awaken knowing that I'm going to love and be grateful for every moment of the day. When I'm working, I feel like I'm playing. When I'm playing, I'm thinking about working. Because, in all honesty, it's the exact same thing to me now.

When you start doing what you love and finally truly trusting that the money will follow - allowing it to follow – things just snowball and you'll attract more opportunities than you could ever imagine. I know, because I've lived the journey. The secret is to keep going when many others would give up.

The Universe loves action, and rewards it, even when it seems like it's taking too long. So now... Thank God I'm an entrepreneur!

♥ ♥ ♥

Known as The Unwrapper™, Heather Vale Goss is an interviewer and writer who has worked in all media: TV, radio, print and online. She specializes in the entrepreneurship, personal growth, health, and parenting niches, and works both as a freelancer and with her husband, Barry Goss, at LWL Worldwide Inc. Together they create, publish and market personal and business development products that help people live a Life Without Limits at LWLWorldwide.com. Heather is the author or co-author of several books, and her blog, "Unwrapping the Mysteries of Life," can be found at HeatherVale.com. When not working, Heather and Barry focus on teaching the ways of the world to their young son Konan.

Thank God I Was Scammed

JACKIE HAUGHN

My story began in November, 2005. As I was getting into my car after work, I noticed a flyer on my windshield for 50% off a psychic reading. Since I have always wanted to have a reading done, I thought I would hold on to it for a while. So I kept it in my car for another time. A few weeks later, I decided to call and make an appointment.

I was surprised to see that the psychic did her readings in her home. Although I sensed this was a bit strange, I had nothing to compare it to since I'd never been to a psychic before.

When I arrived, we sat in her living room and began our session. I wanted to know when a man would come into my life and what my future held for me. She gave me very general answers and said if I wanted a more in-depth reading, I would need to pay for her to light twenty-nine candles at $25.00 each while she meditated and communicated with the spirits. As I was doing the math in my head, I decided it was too much money. She told me I could leave a small deposit for now. Since my curiosity got the best of me, I agreed, and we set up my appointment for the next day.

I arrived at her house the next afternoon. I was led inside by her daughter and was told she was meditating at church. When she arrived, she appeared concerned and said we needed to talk immediately. She then proceeded to tell me a curse had been put on me and my family. She said it was put on many generations ago, even before my parents came into existence. I believed her because I made the connection to my past, which had more hurtful than pleasant memories.

When I left her house, I felt frightened and worried. I couldn't believe a curse was the reason for all my suffering. I was ready to do whatever I needed to get rid of it. I really wanted a better life for myself and my family. She called me with very specific instructions for what to do next. She said I needed twenty-nine bills in the same denomination. However, they could not be a one or a five. I was able to gather twenty-nine, twenty dollar bills. I was told to place the $20's in the sign of the cross, alternating each bill, one at a time. The money was placed under my mattress while I slept, and I was to see her the very next day.

She also asked that I bring the money and pick up some other items. I purchased three grapefruits, a bottle of yellow disinfectant cleaner, sea salt, and a white candle.

When I arrived, she told me we were going to get rid of the evil spirits that had placed the curse on my family. She lit the white candle and had me rub grapefruits all over my body and repeat phrases she read from her prayer book. She then took the grapefruits and placed them in a black trash back and poured Mr. Clean and sprinkled salt on it. She closed the bag, started rubbing the grapefruits together, and saying, "Evil Spirit, go away, we do not want you anymore, you have caused enough suffering in her life." I stomped on the grapefruits until they broke open. When she opened the bag, inside the grapefruits was a tiny black skull. She immediately screamed, "Oh my God, Oh my God, I can't believe this. Do you see this?" I couldn't imagine how it got in there. I was terrified at what I saw and afraid to look at it. She took the money I brought and threw it on top of the skull, and we both spit on it.

She claimed this was just one of seven evil spirits. She needed more money to get rid of the rest. I went to the bank immediately and withdraw $5,000 because I was really afraid and didn't know what to expect.

Over the next few weeks, we were in constant communication. I would go to her house every day, on my lunch hour, as well as the weekends. She would call me several times a day and vice versa. I'd ask her if I would get my money back, and she assured me I would. She would tell me things such as: "God would never let me suffer financially." The money would be returned to me tenfold. She had an answer for everything!

I felt fearful and a sense of dependence on her. I kept our daily interactions a secret from my family and most of my friends. I certainly didn't tell them how much money I gave this woman. I felt alone and ashamed. However, I felt I was doing a service to everyone in my family by breaking the curse so they could have happiness and joy in their lives.

We performed several rituals to rid the evil spirits that cursed me and my family's life. There was always a bigger and more powerful spirit that required more and more money. Each time I handed her more money, she kept saying we were almost done. I felt since I came this far, there was no turning back. I felt as though all my sacrificing of money would have gone down the toilet, since the curse would not have been lifted and I would have continued to suffer. I felt trapped, helpless, and dependent upon her.

Within four weeks of our first visit, she received over $200,000 of my life savings. I took loans, sold stock, and ran up my credit cards. Even though I felt uneasy withdrawing this amount of money, I kept telling myself it was the right thing to do, so I ignored my feelings cautioning me.

Eventually, our daily visits and the phone calls became less frequent. What started out to be a "life changing" mission, turned into a "life changing" mess. I could not understand why the communication had slowed down so much, even though our "mission" was not complete. Was the curse that was placed on me and my family no longer important? Why was my situation no longer a priority? She assured me she would help no matter what. Where was she now?

During the time we didn't speak, I had my own internal dialogue going on. I kept going back and forth, trying to make sense of what was happening to me. If she really was scamming me, why did she even bother to call? She could have just disappeared since she had all my money anyway. Why would she risk bringing me into her home, when she knew I wouldn't be getting any of my money back? How could she know that I wouldn't seek revenge and burn her house down? Was she that confident with herself that she didn't worry about risking her family's welfare? Yes, she was.

In June of 2006, one of my friends whom I briefly told about my psychic visit, called me and told me about an article in the paper, that sounded very familiar. I quickly grabbed the paper to take a look. The headline read: "Psychic Accused of Bilking Two Women". The article mentioned a curse as well as a similar ritual of rubbing fruit over her body. After I read the article, I finally woke up from the nightmare I was living. I was so shocked that my body was physically shaking. I knew this was the same woman. I thought to myself, "Oh my God, I've been had." Strangely enough, I also felt a huge sense of relief! All the craziness in my emotional and mental world had come to an end. I immediately called the police, made a statement the following day, and cut off all communication with her.

I found out she had a long history of scamming people, and a long list of aliases she went by. I was informed by the prosecutor's office that if I wanted to press charges and proceed with a trial, in which she might serve prison time, there was no guarantee I'd get any of my money back. Since I was in a financial hole, I decided to take the money offered in the amount of $153,000. I was pleased to have received more than half, especially since my family told me I'd be lucky if I received a dime.

Today, I can honestly say that I'm grateful for this experience. This was the wake-up call that literally shook my inner world. This experience has put me on a path my soul has been crying out for all these years. Today, I listen to those cries and embrace them. I am kinder and gentler with myself. I've retired my role of being a victim and blaming everyone else for my problems. I claim 100% responsibility for my life and notice the blessings in all experiences.

It was no accident I saved her flyer that day in November. As a matter of fact, I don't recall seeing any other cars with her flyer on it. Was it a coincidence? I don't think so.

Everything happens for a reason. I see it as my ticket to experience the full-blown negativity that has been brewing within me throughout my life. I attracted this "horrible" experience because that is how I felt about myself. What I felt on the inside manifested on the outside. The psychic was only reflecting what I couldn't see within myself.

I no longer blame her for what I went through. It was all my choice and I thought I was doing what was right. I ignored many signals that could have made me aware that her activity was fraudulent. I did not notice those signals because I wasn't ready to notice them. In order for me to grow spiritually, I needed to go through this experience, and hit my rock bottom.

I learned listening to my intuition; I am guided in the best direction. It may feel different and scary, but that's a signal that change is necessary and to let go and trust in your higher power. I've learned to trust my feelings and not let my mind talk me out of the importance of feeling them.

I feel so much gratitude as a result of my experience with the psychic con artist. I continue to attract wonderful people and experiences into my life that help strengthen my spiritual gifts

I found my life purpose of helping people heal and transform their lives. My accomplishments would not have been possible had I not been scammed. It was more than just losing a large chunk of my life savings. My confidence, self-worth, and self-esteem hit an all-time low. I believe reaching those low points is what keeps me determined and focused on my personal quest for self-discovery and spiritual awakening.

♥ ♥ ♥

Jackie Haughn is a holistic life coach and healer, living in the northern New Jersey area with her family. She received her certification through the Empowered Spiritual Life Coaching Program. She received her Bachelors Degree from the University of Metaphysical Sciences. She is an angel therapy practitioner and studied with Doreen Virtue. She is also a Reiki master and intuitive energy healer.

She has taken courses in NLP, the Silva Method, advanced intuitive training by James Van Praagh, and Trust Your Vibes, led by author, spiritual teacher, and intuitive guide Sonia Choquette, PhD.

Her passions are spiritual development, teaching, meditation, walking, reading, dancing, bike riding, and martial arts. Website: www.jackiehaughn.com

Thank God
Cancer Is My Path to Gratitude

JUDYTH REICHENBERG-ULLMAN

It never occurred to me that I might be diagnosed with breast cancer. I had practiced yoga and meditation for decades, been blessed with a loving marriage, felt passionate about my life's work as a naturopathic and homeopathic doctor, and lived in the breath-of-fresh-air Pacific Northwest. I ate a healthy, organic diet and exercised. On the verge of turning fifty, I was svelte after having just shed twenty pounds.

During the previous five or so years, I had noticed a nagging, pulling sensation around my left armpit, but my yearly mammograms and ultrasounds were normal. One night around three A.M., I was awakened by searing, excruciating pain in my left breast. A magnification mammogram revealed micro-calcifications. Indelibly etched in my memory is that phone call, a week later, confirming the diagnosis of ductal carcinoma in situ (DCIS).

The two months following the diagnosis were extraordinarily intense, and the sequence of events seemed to take on a life of its own. The day I was diagnosed, and still stunned, my husband, Bob, headed off to the bookstore to buy Susan Love's Breast Book. Within two hours we were fully apprised of what we were facing and the most current conventional treatment options. At no time, from diagnosis to recovery, did I ever lose my desire to live a long, happy, and fulfilling life. There were so many things yet to experience, places to go, moments in nature to savor, spiritual depths to explore, people and animals to love.

Although there were obviously many decisions to make, the questions seemed to be answered as quickly as they emerged. The whole saga unfolded like a well-choreographed dance performance. The one word that best describes, for me, the entire experience is "surrender." Even for me, whom my husband calls "a force of nature," it was challenging to wrap my mind around the complexity of dealing with a potentially life-threatening illness. Had I brooded about why it happened to me, agonized over the prospect of a nine-hour surgery (mastectomy and free-flap reconstruction), or dwelled on our missing our long-awaited trip to New Zealand, I could have felt very sorry for myself. A mastectomy was not, by a long shot, my idea of how to celebrate turning fifty. But, true to form, I took charge and put one foot in front of the other.

Being a doctor myself, I was actually intrigued that a skilled plastic surgeon could create a natural-looking breast from the little belly fat I had left. I wasn't so wild about it being my body that was being refashioned, but so it goes. After that, I did not look back. The homeopath, the spiritual healers, my friends—they were all part of the team that quickly rallied to my support. In place of terror, I found myself becoming surprising peaceful, knowing on some level that I was in the best of hands and that it would all work out. Don't ask me why. After all, breast cancer can be a terminal illness for many women. But, somehow, any fear I had of the cancer was released. My closest friends say they were amazed at my courage. I just respond, "What else was there to do?"

The fascinating part about those six weeks between diagnosis and surgery was how clear and spiritually connected I became. As the surgery date approached, I felt more and more in tune with myself. I was not depressed, angry, or wishing that I could change places with anyone else. A friend joked that if I kept going in such a positive direction, maybe the cancer experience would result in my becoming enlightened.

That did not happen, but it did bring a renewed peace and love of life—almost a euphoria. I had a sense of being held in the arms of the universe.

There were many magical moments. Swimming in Kealakekua Bay on the Big Island of Hawaii, surrounded by twenty to thirty dolphins, who put on a delightful exhibition of leaps and spins. Bob remarked that they came to heal me. I remember, as if it were yesterday, my fiftieth birthday party, especially the healing circle, at the end, during which I, in the center, was showered with blessings, love, and song. The atmosphere was magical.

Several friends were convinced that the various powerful spiritual healings I received, had cured the cancer. At moments I, too, believed that, and certainly hoped for it. So much so that, upon my request, my surgeon agreed to remove a frozen sample of my breast tissue, in order to make sure the cancer remained, before proceeding with the mastectomy and reconstruction. She simply stated, "We all need to believe in miracles. If there's no cancer, there won't be any mastectomy." This meant that, once I went into surgery, I would be out either in two hours, cancer-free with both breasts, or nine hours later with a mastectomy and reconstruction. Amazingly, I was able to surrender, so that whichever ended up happening, I could accept. There were a few blips on the screen. Two weeks before the surgery, a close cousin of Bob's was diagnosed with an aggressive brain tumor. With just two days to go, my eighty-eight-year-old mother's nursing home called to tell us that she was at death's door. It appeared to all who saw her that she would die, either that same day or while I was in the hospital. I devoted myself, in between seeing my patients, to calling my aunt, and arranging with mortuaries and rabbis to transport her body to St. Louis. I couldn't quite believe all this was happening to me. It seemed too absurd to be real.

The day before entering the hospital, the surgeon outlined the area that was to become my new breast. Fortunately I had an artistic, as well as brilliant surgeon, who used a bright purple magic marker, instead of boring black. The fast the night before the surgery was reminiscent of the many healing fasts I had undertaken over the years. But this fast was for a different reason and would have a different outcome.

We arrived at the hospital for surgery at the crack of dawn. The anesthesiologist had a terrific sense of humor, which put me at ease. As I waited, in surgical gown, cap and socks, Bob read to me from one of our favorite spiritual books, Silence of the Heart, by Robert Adams, a realized being who was able to merge with divine consciousness from the age of fourteen. Robert's fundamental message is, "All is well." And that is what I took in as I was wheeled into the operating room. A friend had lent me a special Primordial Sound tape, which was supposed to elevate consciousness. I had asked that it be played during the surgery. The operating room was freezing cold. And the tape had been turned to fast-forward, and sounding like chipmunks in a Hindu temple! I found it quite amusing. The anesthesiologist cracked yet another joke, and I was out. No awareness of anything or anyone. Absolutely out.

The next thing I knew, a nurse was gently shaking me awake, informing me that I was in the recovery room. I awoke with the thought, "I am that I am," then asked what time it was so I could tell whether I'd had the mastectomy or not. "Five o'clock" was the response. Okay, I thought, no spontaneous healing after all. I was just happy to be alive.

Those four days in the hospital were somewhat of a blur. I do remember, groggily, receiving our close friends, who stayed with Bob during the nine hours of surgery. I can still hear the booming voice of Madonna in Evita, thanks to Bob's willingness to bring in a VCR to entertain me. I recall the morphine drip, the catheter, the drains, and the sauna-like hospital room, which was required for my particular post-surgery recovery. Hiker that I am, I was astonished that the first time I tried to stand up, on the second day after surgery, I lacked the energy to get out of bed. Then, on day four, my memory is clear that I woke up ready to go home! By that afternoon, I was happy to be in my bed at home. I certainly was glad to have Bob wash my hair for a few days and enjoyed the home-cooked meals delivered by our wonderful friends for the first couple of weeks.

I recuperated reasonably quickly. So did my mother—at least enough to be lucid and delightful for another year and a half. Only a year later, we took the trip to New Zealand that we had postponed when I discovered I had cancer. I easily finished fourth out of over forty hikers on the five-day Milford Track backpack, which was symbolic of my full recovery. The cancer experience brought me much closer to friends whom I had at times put second to my work, writing, and travels. It deepened my relationship with, and love for, Bob. I can much better appreciate what individuals with cancer go through; I can better help my patients with cancer who wish to combine the best of alternative and conventional medical care. I am grateful to every person who in any way helped me through my cancer journey.

Now, twelve years later, as this chapter goes to its final edit, ironically, I find myself again dealing with the possible diagnosis of breast cancer. I didn't give a second thought to my scheduled mammogram this year. So the call from the mammography clinic requesting that I return for additional views to me was completely unexpected. This morning, after magnification mammograms were done, as well as an ultrasound of the breast, the radiologist shared with me her concern about what appeared to be an abnormal appearance of the right breast tissue. A biopsy is scheduled for next week, and I find myself again riding the wave of having no idea what will unfold in my life over the next few weeks and months.

What is unquestionably clear to me is that I am remarkably blessed. Bob continues to assure me that we will deal together with whatever arises and that, one way or the other, it will be okay. I was clearly reminded today of what is most important in my life: my marriage, my connection to the One, my community of loving friends, being surrounded by the magic of nature, and our three playful and affectionate golden retrievers. Life is filled with beauty and wonder. Just yesterday I was moved to tears listening to The Total Experience Gospel Choir at the Seattle Folklife Festival. Today, as I drove home from the breast diagnostic clinic, I glimpsed, out of the corner of my eye, a guileless fawn, gracefully bounding across our neighbor's newly mown grass. Walking on the beach with our goldens, to get my mind off my breast, we met up with three bald eagles waiting patiently at the water's edge for prey, then soaring overhead upon being chased by the dogs. Then life went on as normal. I did my patient phone consultations, wholeheartedly enjoyed my Zumba aerobic dance class at the gym, and picked a delicious fresh spinach salad out of the garden for dinner. I have absolutely no idea what next week, or even tomorrow, will bring. All I can do is breathe in, breathe out. The longer I live, the less I can figure it all out, and the more I am filled with gratitude for the mystery of life. All is well.

♥ ♥ ♥

Judyth Reichenberg-Ullman, N.D., L.C.S.W. has been a licensed naturopathic and homeopathic physician since 1983, specializing in women's health, patients with mental and emotional issues, and children with behavioral and learning problems, and treats patients in person, by telephone, and by video consultation. In addition to writing Whole Woman Homeopathy: A Safe, Natural, Effective Alternative to Drugs, Hormones, and Surgery, she co-authored six other books on homeopathy with her husband, Robert Ullman, including Prozac Free, Ritalin-Free Kids, Rage-Free Kids, and A Drug-Free Approach to Asperger Syndrome and Autism. Judyth has been deeply involved in spiritual practice since 1970 and co-authored Mystics, Masters, Saints and Sages: Stories of Enlightenment, with a foreword by His Holiness, the Dalai Lama.

Judyth practices at The Northwest Center for Homeopathic Medicine in Edmonds, WA, lives on Whidbey Island, WA and in Pucon, Chile, and can be reached at (425) 774-5599 or www.healthyhomeopathy.com.

Thank God I Was Sexually Abused

KARMEN KIZZIE ROULAND

I remember coming home from church one Sunday during the fourth grade. I was in the car with my father and sister. My mom stayed after church to help count the money from offering. As we were driving home, I told myself, "It's okay. I want to tell. I can do this." I didn't know what the consequences would be or the aftermath. I suppose I didn't care. I knew that whatever the aftermath was, that it could not be worse than what already had happened. I really didn't understand why now I wanted to tell my parents. I had made up my mind and determined that I would say something. During the ride home, I told my dad I had something to tell him. He asked inquisitively, "What? What do you have to tell me?"

I said, "I don't want to tell you now; I'll wait until we get home."

When my dad pulled into the driveway we all got out of the car and went inside. I ran upstairs and wrote on a sheet of paper, I was sexually abused. The shame had kept me silent for so long. It was hard to "speak" the words of the abuse. After my parents read my note, they called a close family friend, who was a social worker, and asked her, "What should we do?"

That night, the abuser was arrested. We went to court. I didn't testify during the court hearing because my parents thought that I had been through enough. But as I got older, I realized that I was okay and that I could speak about this to other people.

You see, I made a decision early on not to say anything to anyone about what had happened. It was my secret, and I didn't want to share it with anyone. I have memories of the abuse—not just the acts, or several "instances"—but more so of the pain and parts of me that were being chipped away each time he touched me. I blamed myself for many years because of that first night; I should have come home and told my parents what had happened. I should have run out of his house screaming at the top of my lungs. I should have fought back. I wondered if he was abusing his daughter. I remember one day asking a friend, "___, does your father touch you?" She ignored me and didn't answer the question. I would say yes.

I was exposed to pain, abused, parts of me stolen, and I lost my innocence at an early age; and I am so grateful that I went through this ordeal. It took me all of my youth and most of my early adulthood to reach that point. Sometimes I feel alone and isolated; I feel so uncomfortable in social settings or so afraid of meeting new people. I wouldn't consider myself a shy person, but I try to hide this true part of me from people I interact with on a daily basis. When working closely with others, I feel that I cannot be myself because "the self" that I am, I believe, is not one that they care to know. I am a strong woman, who in her childhood was abused.

I started working with youth and, as a result, I understood my abuse to be the vehicle that would help me reach out to others and inspire others. Getting to this point wasn't easy for me. I found myself getting angrier and angrier. My perception of being abused changed when I started searching for ways to release my anger.

It was during the fall 2007 when a pastor said, "A lot of us have bitterness in our hearts, and we need to let it go. We need to acknowledge it, pray about it, and turn that burden over to God." He went on to say that many of us are broken and don't even know it. I was sitting in the congregation thinking, "He is talking to me. He is describing the exact way that I feel." I asked myself, "How can I grow closer to God with anger and bitterness at the very core of me?"

As I started on the journey of growth, I began praying more and speaking to God more. I wrote in journals and shared my story on the radio to show others that courage can, and will, inspire others. Experiencing this series of events has allowed me to have a deeper understanding and appreciation for God and deeper love of myself.

For people who have endured physical, sexual, or emotional abuse, know that by being silent actors you give the abuse and the abuser power. By acknowledging the abuse, you empower and uplift others and yourself in the process. Every day, I challenge myself to be more open.

If I could go back in time and erase being abused from my life, I would not. I used to think that I would have been a better person had the abuse not happened. But now, after some growth and prayer, I believe now that God chooses people to experience certain things so that they can be an advocate for someone else.

As a result of my experience, I am blessed with many things. I am blessed with a new eye on life, with good friends and family who love and care about me. I am blessed to be in a relationship where unconditional love exists. Out of this experience I realized that my gift is being able to inspire others so that they can begin the healing process.

God is moving in my life.

❤ ❤ ❤

Karmen is an educational psychologist and researcher living in the Washington, DC metro area. She has experience in working with youth development programs and public speaking engagements."

Thank God
My Girlfriend Left Me

LAWRENCE HARRIS

It was the day after Thanksgiving, a beautiful Friday in South Florida, and I had just finished a wonderful lunch of Thanksgiving leftovers with my girlfriend. I was informed upon my leaving that the relationship was over. This relationship, which had started over a year earlier, was a bumpy one. It was a relationship of manipulation and control, love and hate, learning, growing, and knowing who I am. Everything happens for a reason and although I am grateful that it ended, I am grateful that it started and existed for the time it did.

She was a beautiful woman, very majestic in appearance. I met her at a Barnes and Noble where I was giving a seminar. I met her briefly with her roommate. They started coming to my seminars monthly, until one day we started talking. She mentioned that she had been looking for me for a long time.

I was puzzled and wondered what she meant. Being an advanced energy worker, I had never met anyone as good with energy until I met her. She was good, and equal to if not better than me. She was tracking my energy for a purpose I did not realize until the relationship was long over.

Her energy felt very loving and pure. My problem was that I had love issues, and my heart was still partially blocked. I was in a relationship that was coming to a close.

This relationship was very complicated, and she was an expert in psychology and consciousness. She could read my mind and started working with me to open my heart. As it opened more and more, I fell more and more in love with her. She would constantly espouse the greatness of Creator and work to show unconditional love.

I'd had difficulties expressing myself most of my life. I further had difficulties expressing myself as she wanted. My expressions were constantly being criticized as she took a different meaning to them than was intended. We were in constant arguments over what was said and how it was said.

At the time, I had a large metaphysical organization from years of teaching energy work and healing people in South Florida. I had trained a number of individuals in the modality created through me called Transformational Energy Release™. This modality was constantly developing and evolving as it produced amazing results in a very short period of time. It was the time she had just "come out of the closet" to do something with her skills and was joining forces with me to teach and spread spirituality.

I was thrilled to introduce her to the group, from the organization, as her abilities and teachings were phenomenal. She presented herself as an avatar. I was in awe at what she knew. Her knowledge of many subjects was beyond most people, and she could carry on a conversation with anyone on any subject. She was a true genius.

During the process of my introducing the various members of my organization to her, one of my advanced trainees mentioned to me that she felt that she would destroy my organization. I scoffed at the idea as we were making plans for her to share leadership with me. She started teaching me how to open my heart and have more love and quality of love. She did a session on me to remove illusions in the subconscious mind; this was the first time I had ever heard or seen anything like this. The spiritual group had weekly sessions at her house, where we would all gather to discuss and study the process of ascension. We went through initiations and started expanding ourselves. She was the first one to recognize me as the soul extension of the Ascended Master Serapis Bey.

At the time I had no idea who Serapis Bey was. I did an Internet search and was amazed at what I found. I was constantly being compared to him as much of my personality matched what was printed on him. My worthiness issues prevented me from accepting that I was he, and it took me eighteen months to accept the fact, although I had constant verification from Creator and others. For all of this knowledge, I am extremely grateful, for this was the time when I was able to open myself to move far beyond the physical plane of consciousness and reality. This was the time I started to integrate into myself who I am and heal my Soul.

My challenge persisted with her; I felt that she was manipulative and controlling. There were constant situations where I was put off guard, and not being aware of her prowess at psychology, was manipulated. Being somewhat stubborn, I was constantly resisting some of her desires. I excelled at learning the information being taught at our weekly gathering, but I would not conform to the way she wanted me to act. She developed an organizational plan and drew circles for the group. Everyone was in the inner circle while I was in the outer one. I was a main part of the group, yet I felt less than the others. Something inside me knew that I was the glue that held the group together. Tensions continued to grow, and she even altered the relationship with me to allow one of my clients, now a group member, into her personal life.

They became close, and soon I was on the outs. She said she loved me, and we carried on a semi-relationship, with me hoping that she would be my significant other on a permanent basis.

I soon started noticing some very dark energy in her abdomen area. I did not know what it was, but I talked to her about it. She would not recognize it, and soon thereafter I noticed it in her roommate and my prior client, whom she had started having a relationship with. I soon noticed that the dark energy ran between the three of them and realized something was wrong.

I continued to tell her about the energy, and more tension was created. I felt that he, the prior client, was attacking her and her roommate, and that he was manipulating her. He soon moved into her house, and our relationship became more distant. I also become more despondent and angry at the situation. Soon Thanksgiving came, and I was not invited to the house for the main feast but for lunch the next day, when he was not there.

At lunch we talked. I explained to her what I saw was happening with the energy, and there was a disagreement on the subject. I was a little perturbed, and when I left the house, I said something to her. I do not remember exactly what was said, but it was nothing earth-shattering...at least, that's what I thought. A major argument ensued, and when I got home, I had a message on my answering machine where she threatened to destroy me. The energy from the tape was piercing, and I felt myself fill up with darkness and entities.

A number of months before this, I had met Alison. She lived in West Virginia and was sent for healing sessions with me when I was conducting a seminar in her area. Alison was a very advanced being and was suffering from Lyme disease. As I helped her heal, we became best friends.

During my breakup with my girlfriend, Alison could feel the pain that I was in. I was in love with her, or I thought I was, and in excruciating pain like I had never felt before. Alison would help me with the pain in my heart. It was during this time that we both started being attacked in ways that we had never encountered. These attacks forced me to develop my energetic skills further than I had ever expected, and in ways that at that time were completely unknown to me.

I discovered the attacks came on different dimensional levels. I figured this out as my Soul, Spirit and different dimensional levels came under attack.

Through the process of determining which part of me was being attacked, I discovered that our energy systems are set up dimensionally. This process showed me that our Soul was fourth dimensional and our Spirit was our fifth dimensional. This information assisted my healing work move light years ahead, for which I am extremely grateful.

Each dimensional level we interacted with taught us more and more about how the human race required healing multidimensionally. This information accelerated healing in others and me by developing my ability to work multidimensionally and finding where blocks and limitations were in people. I was extremely grateful.

During this time another Soul contract became apparent to me. That was to bring forth a healing system to assist humans to release large amounts of density in a short period of time and to remove the blocks that I believe the dark entities placed in our race. Once again, if it were not for the relationship ending, I would not have been graced with this blessing.

Once the relationship was over and my pain subsided, I had a chance to reflect upon what had happened. Even though much of my business was destroyed, the knowledge and growth I received was phenomenal. It became apparent to me how the ascension process works to get to enlightenment. I was shown how the human race has been segmented and limited, and how to remove the limitations and integrate the whole system into alignment energetically with that of Creator and the universe. This also included the etheric blueprint changes that were placed in us by darkness. Yes, I am grateful, for I am blessed with this knowledge, how to help others and how to help myself, and for having been able to open my heart. The breakup with my girlfriend brought me into my power. It showed me about transformation from dark to light.

I also realized the need to heal after the ending of a relationship. Previously, I would jump from one to another and realized that healing was required after each one. Time to reflect on events and feelings also led to my healing of issues that caused disharmony.

I think back and realize the wonder of Creator and how he got me to this place. The relationship with my past girlfriend was the main catalyst. Thank God it happened. It was the ending of the relationship that propelled me into my greatest challenge. It was the blessing of learning to live on my soul's path.

♥ ♥ ♥

Rev. Lawrence J. Harris was chosen to be a healer. He was a successful businessman and accountant, when most of his life fell apart. Partly for something to do, he started teaching people about energy awareness, which he studied many years before. About that same time, he started receiving dreams and visions about how to heal himself and his life. After some time of resistance, he started to use them. The techniques were effective, so he began to facilitate others in their own healing as well.

He calls this program Transformational Energy Release™. He is a talented energy healing facilitator, a recognized speaker, an ordained minister, and the founder of the Transformational Energy Institute™.

Thank God I Was Adopted

MARIE BECKER

Have you ever seen those reunion shows on television? You know the ones where a person, typically female, is in tears about how she had been adopted and has felt this void in her life for this family that she never knew...then, surprise... her long-lost family members miraculously appear from backstage, and everyone is happy and crying. When I was younger, I used to wonder if that would be me someday.

I was told that I was adopted when I was six years old. I didn't really know what that meant until I made the mistake of mentioning it to a few kids at school, and it became a reason for them to torment me. The "your mamma didn't want you" comments, although hurtful, promoted a creative side. I would make up all sorts of stories about how my mother couldn't possibly keep me because of some strange yet noble reason, which of course would have been completely out of her control.

Growing up I was relatively happy with my life. I was well taken care of and, although we were by no means wealthy, and slightly dysfunctional, I didn't want for any material things. But even still there was that little voice in the back of my mind that wondered... what if? Every time someone mentioned that I looked just like someone that they knew, a part of me would wonder if there was a reason for that. I would also make up the occasional story about various celebrities being one of my parents, and it was a great conspiracy that had to be kept secret or ruin their career. Then there were those reunion shows. No matter how I looked at it, finally finding my birth mother would be this grand and wonderful thing, if I ever got up the nerve to do it.

I was twenty-three years old when I finally got the nerve. I was getting ready for my upcoming wedding to my second husband and had only very recently dug myself out of a very chaotic, abusive ex-husband, financially ruined, single parent situation. For the first time in a long time I was feeling that I finally had things under control and going in a much better direction. I had found a great guy whom my young daughter adored and was feeling pretty good about life in general.

I was nervous about meeting my biological mother, so when I contacted the agency that I had been adopted through, I did it under the pretense of wanting my medical history. They looked up my file and said that they could try to find her from their outdated information but that they charged an hourly fee. I didn't have a ton of money but thought, "What the heck?" The woman at the agency started her search and called me back half an hour later. She had tracked her down and was going to send the necessary paperwork. When the documents came back, the agency would forward them on to me.

I remember thinking that this must really be meant to be because it happened so quickly. How wonderful! I could hardly wait. It wasn't like being on a talk show, but I just knew it was going to be fantastic.

It only took a couple of weeks to get the information back, and the agency said that my birth mother was as just as excited about my attempting to contact her as I was about finding her. Could it get any better?

The day I read that paperwork was a day that changed my life forever. Despite all of the stories that I had made up to try to be ready for whatever the truth might be, nothing could have prepared me for the reality.

My birth mother had been raped.

Nowhere, in any of the stories that I played through my mind, was rape a possibility. Life stopped for me that day. I had opened the envelope in my car because I wanted a few moments with it by myself before I told my roommate my "great news." I am glad I did because the tears were violent, the pain was raw, and I was thankful to not have an audience.

I'm really not sure how long I was sitting there, but I knew I had to go in the apartment sooner or later. I pulled myself together and planned to not mention the envelope to my roommate until I had more time to deal with it.

I went inside and she told me that some strange woman had called for me and wanted to know when I would be back. When she told me the name, my brain flipped, my heart dropped, and my stomach was threatening to betray me. My birth mother had called. I was not ready to deal with that. I said, "Oh?" as I walked by her to my room. I really don't remember much about that day or the next month.

The next day I went to see my fiancé. I was proud of how well I had kept myself together at work. The moment I saw him, my emotions erupted. He held me while I blubbered on, and when I was finished, he said something exceptionally profound. It wouldn't mean anything to me for a few weeks, but it was huge. He told me that it didn't matter, and regardless of what had happened to her, it didn't change who I was.

I called this statement profound, and it was, but not because it was correct. In reality it couldn't have been more wrong. It was profound because that statement was a key factor in helping me deal with the situation and be able to move on.

It took about a month before this haze I was in went away. Call it depression, call it sadness, but whatever it was, I hated it. I was numb. Nothing mattered. It was as if this one event had completely stripped all possibility for emotion from my body, and there was nothing left. I kept rereading the paperwork. I'm not sure if I was trying to memorize it or discover that I had read it wrong the first time. Two notable discoveries were that she had been divorced because her husband was abusive and she never had any other children. I was her, save the rape part.

The third notable point was that the documentation from the case worker told a story about a young lady who had made sure her child had been named and baptized in hope that she could convince her parents to allow her to keep the baby. It was a little reassuring to know that all those kids in school had been wrong after all.

I still had that phone message looming over my head, and I couldn't make myself call her. Not wanting to ignore her, I wrote her a letter. I did not tell her what I was feeling, but that I didn't feel ready to talk to her just yet. We wrote back and forth a few times before I realized that I would not have the type of relationship with her that I wanted. She started to promise things and not follow through with them. She wrote about strange situations she continually found herself in, and they were getting more and more bizarre with each letter. She invited me to the family reunion but, for me, that was not an option. This correspondence proved to me that everything happens for a reason.

I don't think my birth mother is a bad person; on the contrary, she was very kind. But every time I read one of her letters, I felt like I was being pulled back into that chaotic and drama-filled lifestyle that I had only recently left. Hadn't I just dug myself out of that hole? Hadn't I worked hard to make a better life for myself and my child? I sure as hell wasn't going to go backwards now.

That profound statement my fiancé made helped me to put things in perspective. He said that this information didn't change who I was, but it did. It allowed me the opportunity to reevaluate my life: my temper, how I deal with my children, the choices and decisions that I make every day, the way I look at and deal with people.

Perhaps I dealt with the pain by pushing it away and not really dealing with it at all. Perhaps I was being selfish and got what I deserved for putting such high expectations on it. But either way, it made me realize that I hadn't looked her up in order to find a new life or even to find a new mother. I had wanted the happy ending that I had seen on TV. I wanted something that didn't exist for me, not in that way.

I made my own happy ending, and if I hadn't looked her up and found out the truth, I would have lived my life with part of me still searching for some mysterious happily ever after. It helped me to appreciate the life I already have.

This poem stayed up on the wall in my bedroom as a child. I don't know who the author is, but it is the only poem I know by heart because I read it and felt it every day.

"Not flesh of my flesh
Not bone of my bone
But still miraculously my own.
Never forget for a single minute
You didn't grow under my heart, but in it."

♥ ♥ ♥

Marie Becker is a ghostwriter, screenwriter, playwright, novelist, and very busy mother of four beautiful daughters. She fell in love with writing in high school and is still infatuated to this day. She and her husband, Lucas, have been married for eleven years and reside in Richfield, MN.

Thank God I Was Broke

MARIE BECKER

I have learned that the word "broke" has a lot of different meanings to a lot of different people. For me, "broke" refers to a time in my life that I try not think about much. I can't ignore it—it's a big reason I am who I am today.

Sixteen years ago, there were many parts of my life that were "broken." Financially, spiritually, and emotionally, I was broke and broken, and it sucked. That was the lowest I had ever been in my life, and it's still a little scary to think about. I learned a lot, and gained a lot of knowledge.

I was living in a studio apartment in a rough neighborhood of Minneapolis. I was a single mother living on not much, and I hated men. The apartment was okay, plenty big enough for my infant and me. There were no bedrooms, so I slept on the floor in the living room, and she slept in the closet. There was room for her port-a-crib, her dresser, and all of her toys, and she didn't seem to mind.

I had a job as a desk clerk at a hotel, which paid barely enough. I had a few angels who helped me out along the way. I don't know how I would have survived without them. One was a good friend from college, and the other was her mother. The friend helped me find an apartment that I could afford, which wasn't easy. Her mother did daycare for me for only $30 a week. I couldn't always pay her, but she never complained. I swear this friend was psychic, as she always seemed to know just when I would run out of diapers. I would be down to my last one with nothing in my checking account, and she would magically appear with a whole case.

When you have no money, you learn to be very clever with it when you get some. I had writing a check down to a science. I could tell you to the hour when a check would clear from various businesses. For example, I knew I could float a check to the local gas station, if I needed to, because they wouldn't cash it for at least a week to ten days. However, if I needed to go to the grocery store, the money had to already be in my checking account because that sucker would clear at midnight.

Trips to the grocery store were not much fun. I had only fifteen bucks to spend a week, and after baby food and a gallon of milk, I had just enough left for packaged noodles and Kool-Aid. When my daughter turned nine months, I switched her to real food so that I could buy a second gallon of milk, peanut butter, bread, and the occasional box of macaroni and cheese for a special treat.

People kept telling me to go on Welfare, but I couldn't make myself do it. I was only twenty, stubborn and determined. The way I looked at it, my stupid mistakes had gotten me into this mess. I was going to get myself out of it no matter what. I felt like if I took the money, I was giving in somehow. I was admitting that my situation was so bad that I could not fix it. I just kept telling myself that it really couldn't get any worse, so the only place to go was up.

Of course it did get worse before it got better, but my daughter and I did not go hungry, and we were never homeless, although we came close a couple of times. I consider that a success!

I was broke spiritually for a long time. I had not been to church in years, and I wasn't sure what I believed in anymore. I experienced first-hand "ask and ye shall receive." I couldn't remember the last time I had prayed, but when I did, God answered. If I couldn't make the rent or my daughter needed to go to the doctor for yet another ear infection, I would find myself praying and somehow I would get money in the mail. My mom would have sent me a surprise check, or a rebate I had forgotten about would suddenly appear. These were not large dollar amounts, but they were enough to scrape by.

It was then that I realized that I wasn't going to have to live like this forever. God was taking care of me, and if I trusted in Him, I would never go hungry. I started going to church again, and I met a great guy. He was the pastor's son. I took that as a sign. I didn't trust very many people then, but my daughter adored him instantly. So I figured he must be okay. He turned out to be another angel. He didn't like the neighborhood I lived in much, so we spent a lot of time at his place. He started doing daycare for me because I worked evenings. He started bringing me food and stocking my fridge. He thought I was broke because I was bad with money; he wouldn't realize for years that I was good with money, I just didn't have any.

To this day I don't know what kept him around. I started to get expensive, and I kept waiting for him to leave. My car got towed, and I called him in tears. He didn't even think twice. He just came down and paid the fee. I got a flat tire on the side of the road, and he paid for four new tires without being asked. I got into an accident with a squad car, and it won. My car was totaled, and he co-signed for a new one. We were still dating at that point. I just kept thanking God but waiting for him to leave. He never did.

I will remember deeply that time in my life and all that I gained from it. I am a much stronger person for it, and it taught me to appreciate so much. I know it may sound cliché but it's true: You don't know what you've got until it's gone. Even better: When you get it back, it means so much more.

I thank God that I'm not 'broke' anymore.

♥ ♥ ♥

Marie Becker is a ghostwriter, screenwriter, playwright, novelist, and very busy mother of four beautiful daughters. She fell in love with writing in high school and is still infatuated to this day. She and her husband, Lucas, have been married for eleven years and reside in Richfield, MN.

Thank God for Arthritis—It Enriched My Life!

MARK WILLIAM COCHRAN, PHD

The very thought of getting out of bed that morning was more than I could bear. My pain was so intense and agonizing—again—that I looked up and said to God, "Enough is enough. Either cure me or take me." His answer was immediate and clear: "Cure yourself or take yourself." This blunt response did not come to me as a booming voice from the heavens; rather, God spoke to me from somewhere deep inside...

Arthritis? I've been there. Boy, have I ever been there! I know the pain, the anger, and the fear. I've been on the fruitless search for that ever elusive silver bullet that would kill the pain once and for all. I've had new hopes dashed again and again, unable to shake the dark fear that maybe my disease would never go away. The heartache of not being able to run and play with my little boy...the despair of being stuck on the sidelines as my friends enjoyed a raucous game of softball...the crushing loss of self-worth when the U.S. Marine Corps told me I no longer measured up and had to go...I've been through it all.

In high school, I competed as a varsity track and field athlete. I went through college in the Naval ROTC program, and upon graduation was commissioned as a second lieutenant in the U.S. Marine Corps. At age twenty-three, when I was stationed at Camp Pendleton, California, I began to feel pain in one of my hips during physical fitness training. The pain not only interfered with my training, but also it began to affect my lifestyle. My first course of action was perhaps the most commonly attempted cure in the world. I didn't do anything, hoping the problem would just go away on its own. Looking back, I'm reminded of an episode of the '70s era TV show Sanford and Son. Fred Sanford, a cantankerous old junkyard owner, was getting late notices on his bills. He just kept putting them back in the mailbox hoping they would go away. I was doing the same thing with my pain, and my "late fees" kept growing and growing. Before too long, my mailbox was full, and the pain was interfering with my life so much that it finally drove me to go in and see my battalion physician.

After endless questions and all sorts of tests, I was diagnosed with a potentially crippling form of arthritis called ankylosing spondylitis. This was devastating news because, as a Marine, I had to keep myself in top physical condition. I was also an avid scuba diver and outdoor enthusiast. Needless to say, arthritis pain was not compatible with my active lifestyle, and it wore out its welcome in a hurry.

The days of pain turned into weeks, which dragged into months. Over the next few months, different doctors prescribed various drugs. Some relieved the pain to a degree, but none rid me of it. I was aware that alternatives existed, but at first I scoffed at them. Conventional medicine was the only form of healthcare I had ever used. All along, my wife had been prodding me to see a chiropractor. But when I was young, my mother once told me that chiropractors were "witch doctors," so I wanted nothing to do with them. After my being unable to participate in physical training (PT) for a couple of months, my commanding officer (CO) called me into his office. He told me that if I wasn't back on the PT field soon, he would have no choice but to start processing me for a medical discharge from the Marines. He might as well have punched me square in the stomach. The Marine Corps was my life; it was my identity! But my CO was right; I just wasn't cutting it. I was a liability to my unit. No one had to tell me that if we were to go to war, I would be a danger to my fellow Leathernecks. My commanding officer was a good guy and wanted to keep me around, so he gave me the phone number of his chiropractor. At this point I was ready to try anything—even a witch doctor—so I called and booked the earliest appointment I could get. And whaddya know? Chiropractic care did the job. Not only did it help with my pain; it also opened my mind. As my healing unfolded, I started learning more and more about alternative healing, and trying new approaches.

A long, difficult and tortuous journey still lay ahead. For years I experienced ups and downs at the hands of my tormentor. As a Marine, I was a fighter, and the only acceptable outcome for me was victory. Initially, I committed myself to an endless quest for the secret weapon that would vanquish my attacker once and for all. For years I remained mired in a self-defeating focus on the problem. Arthritis became my new identity. In retrospect it's no surprise that the pain finally won the battle and forced me into an early retirement from the U.S. Marine Corps.

Chiropractic had done wonders for me. Although I had a crippling disease, regular chiropractic care had allowed me to serve productively in the Marine Corps for seventeen years. It had such a profound effect on me that I decided to make it my life's calling. When I left the Marines, I enrolled at Palmer College of Chiropractic in Davenport, Iowa.

During my first year at Palmer, I had a vision of myself as a doctor going out into the world to cure pain and disease. But something didn't quite feel right. I sensed that I needed to follow a new path; however, I wasn't sure how to find it. Well, as the old adage goes, "when the student is ready, the teacher will appear." One afternoon I went to listen to a visiting speaker, Dr. Arno Burnier, one of the chiropractic profession's most inspiring and passionate voices. That afternoon I was but one anonymous face in a packed auditorium, but I felt like Arno was speaking straight to me when he said: "You cannot fight darkness; you must turn on light. You cannot fight disease; you must turn on life."

It was a seismic, life-changing moment for me. Arno's simple words shifted the tectonic plates of my old paradigm and allowed a new consciousness to break through. From that day forward, turning on life became my new quest.

But it wasn't magic. Soon, I had another flare-up and my dark dance with arthritis resumed once again. I couldn't believe it. I was doing all of the right things to stay healthy, but the pain came back anyway. I was furious! And this time, it hung around for well over a year. I shuffled along like a tired old man and was late to every class. One of my professors told me that a lot of students who didn't know my name just referred to me as, "the guy that limps." I even began to doubt whether I could ever be a chiropractor. I could hardly get around; how would I ever be able to work all day in a busy chiropractic practice? And if I couldn't keep myself healthy, what credibility would I have with those I served? It was one of the lowest points of my life. I felt utterly powerless.

It was during this low point that I had my "cure me or take me" conversation with God. Getting through another day was such a painful chore that I just did not want to do it anymore. Every morning when I woke up, I would think to myself, "Oh man, not again." Though I hadn't considered taking my own life, if I had gone to sleep one night and simply didn't wake up to the light of day, that would have been just fine with me.

It was at this low point, with all of my illusions, delusions, and ego stripped away that my new enlightened perspective really began to sink in. One afternoon, when I went to the Campus Health Center for my weekly adjustment, my student doctor, following standard clinic protocol, asked me for the umpteenth time to rate my pain on a scale of 1 to 10. I was tired of focusing on pain and told him that I was not going to answer that question again. I said, "Look, I'm not here for my pain; I'm here for my health. Just adjust my spine so we can turn on some life!"

Rather than see myself as a guy with a disease, I began to realize that I was a beautiful and perfect being.

My self-identity began to shift from that of someone in constant pain to that of a person with vast and breathtaking human potential. For years, I had hated my body. I felt like I had been dealt a bad hand, and I resented it. Now I started to love myself: my body, my being, my mind, my spirit, my circumstances—even my pain. I came to realize that good health doesn't come from "doing all the right things." More important than the do-ing is the be-ing. Everything in our lives comes about as a result of our consciousness. You must be healthy in mind, heart and soul if you want to be fully healthy in your body. If your consciousness is one of fear and anger, you manifest disease. On the other hand, if you embrace each new day with a sense of love and gratitude, you manifest a life of joy, vibrancy, love, and abundance. There may be pain in your body, but life can still be wondrous.

By shifting your focus from your woes to the fullness of life, you raise your level of vibration. Over time, an increased level of vibration can lead to miracles. In my case, this fulfilled way of being has allowed the athlete within me to step forth once again. At age forty-seven, I was able to start running again after not being able to run for over eleven years. At age forty-nine, I competed in my first two triathlons and my first marathon. As I write this, at age fifty, I enjoy greater health and vitality than when I was on my high school track team.

For many years I saw my disease as a limitation imposed on me from the outside. I now embrace it as one of my life's most beautiful gifts, and one that came from within, just as God's words did on that morning of despair. I enjoy my newfound state of vibrant health in great part because of the new window on life that debilitating arthritis pain opened for me. Most importantly, living so many years with chronic disease has given me an abiding sense of empathy and love that allows me to touch other people's lives as a healing facilitator.

Now, whenever I step off on an invigorating trail run, I open my arms to the heavens above and feel an all-consuming sense of love and gratitude for the robust health and abundance in my life, and for everything—everything—on my path.

♥ ♥ ♥

A lover of Nature and the great outdoors, Dr. Mark William Cochran is blessed to live, love, work, and play amid the towering pines, majestic mountains, and sparkling lakes of the Idaho panhandle. Mark's unique and gentle approach to healing calls upon ancient spiritual healing concepts to help awaken each person's own natural potential for vibrant health. He is also a writer and speaker, passionate about helping his audience embrace the elegant simplicity of Nature in the pursuit of health. Mark is the author of the award-winning book, Oby's Wisdom! A Caveman's Simple Guide to Health and Well-Being. Learn more about the book at www.ObysWisdom.com. Mark would love to hear from you at TurnOnLife@juno.com. Please visit his blog at http://DoctorMarksHealthyThoughts.blogspot.com

Thank God
I Had Colon Cancer: Flush, Flow, 'n' Glow

MARY ANDREWS

I was diagnosed with colon cancer on Halloween 2002. Cancer showed me that I had been wearing a mask. My authentic self was buried under layers of conditioning, and repressing it was literally killing me. I believe that for me, cancer was a messenger. It was a rude, ugly, painful, and stinky messenger, but it delivered gifts to me that prior, more subtle messengers could not do. For that I am truly grateful.

Cancer brought my "stuff" up, and I was faced with a choice: Do I focus solely on a superficial cure for the cancer, continue to ignore the shadow side of me and go back to living the way I had been? Or do I dare dive into this unexplored side of myself, and perhaps meet with true healing along the way?

I had been an avid student of general "self-improvement" for years but was still searching for some missing pieces of the puzzle.. Although I had invested a lot of time, money and energy in many different products and programs over the years, my spirit was restless and still searching.

I was great at following the instructions, strategies, habits, techniques, formulas, rules, steps, keys, and tips from the "experts." I was even better at ignoring the wise little voice inside me that was lovingly guiding me to personalize things based on my own style, spiritual path, and purpose. I had been using a lot of energy to suppress my intuition and to suppress "me." When I read one definition of cancer as the body fighting itself, I froze for a moment because I knew, that at least in my case, it was true. I had been fighting and repressing my authentic self.

I don't believe it was any coincidence that I had cancer of the "gut." I hadn't really ever trusted my gut—my intuition. Sure, cancer is physical, but I knew that for me, there was a mind-body-spirit thing going on. I remember vividly the face of the gastroenterologist as he told me that a part of my colon was "almost completely obstructed." I didn't consciously see it then or during the ensuing whirlwind of diagnosis, surgery, chemotherapy, appointments, tests, procedures, panic, fear, anger, regret, guilt, blame, sadness, and confusion, but on a deep soul level, I knew that I had a physical manifestation of my blocked intuition and connection to God.

Cancer was the beginning of a new part of my spiritual journey as my sense of God naturally began to extend beyond the limiting walls of religious rules and social beliefs. For the first time in my life, I allowed no rules except one: to follow my gut.

I immersed myself in any kind of teaching that called to my heart. If it felt good or caught my interest even a little, I moved toward it. If it didn't feel good, I passed. This was a new strategy for my conditioned, repressed self but was surprisingly fun and interesting. It felt as if along with cancer, the Universe handed me a "Get Out of Self-Imposed Prison Free" card.

I also saw a strange humor in how the chemotherapy side effects afforded me an unusually large amount of quiet, solitary time via the bathroom to process these new concepts. Although I wasn't laughing at first, it felt like God's interesting way of telling me to slow down, evaluate my life, and see things from a different perspective.

I wasn't particularly afraid of death, but as cancer taunted me with the possibility of not being around much longer in a physical, human way for my children, (ages eleven and thirteen), the emotional pain was excruciating. I wanted to live.

At the beginning of the "cancer time," my beautiful, peaceful prayers quickly turned into fearful, anxious, desperate pleadings. I tried to shift my thoughts and prayers to a more positive focus but couldn't seem to do it using any of the prayers and meditations I'd practiced before.

I had been keeping a very informal journal about my cancer experiences and process. I wrote about frustrations, fears, epiphanies, observations, and theories. I freely expressed my perspective and feelings about what was going on in both my outer and inner worlds. Sometimes I was in an optimistic, loving, hopeful mood, and sometimes I wrote with a scared, angry, sad, or sarcastic tone. Whatever it was, I let it flow without judgment. I was learning to relax and to unapologetically be and love all the parts of myself.

I knew about the power of gratitude and had also been keeping a gratitude journal. During the cancer time I went through a period where I didn't feel thankful, grateful or appreciative for anything. I was physically uncomfortable and emotionally exhausted from "trying" to be positive, from blaming myself for the cancer, from worrying about my family, and from a deep, sad knowing that I hadn't accomplished whatever it was my soul came here to do.

Too tired to resist, I allowed myself to feel what I felt, when I felt it, how I felt it, for as long as I felt it. I cried, yelled, whined, and complained. It was clear that I needed to express and release that emotional pent-up energy. The metaphors kept on coming as it occurred to me that before I could go forward, I needed to "flush all the crap" up and out.

Soon after this "energetic flushing," I had a pivotal experience that gave me a new understanding and appreciation for the power of gratitude. Since it was extremely difficult for me during the cancer time to quiet my racing mind, I found a powerful ally in simplicity. I decided to try one of the most basic and simple meditation techniques: to simply close my eyes and focus only on my breathing. I wasn't sure how long I could relax for, but it turned out that all it took was one breath to change my perspective.

I closed my eyes and breathed in. On the exhale the thought popped into my head, "It doesn't hurt when I breathe." It was the first time in a long while that I felt grateful for something. I used to journal only about big things I was grateful for, and I realized that there was an abundance of things I had been taking for granted.

I went to my gratitude journal and thought it might be helpful to rephrase this newest gratitude in a positive, creative way. I tried to rephrase it to, "Breathing is easy for me," or "It feels good to breathe easy," or "I am grateful for my healthy lungs." But my hand physically wouldn't let me change the words. The most positive I could be that day came in the form of a negative: "It doesn't hurt when I breathe." I felt through my whole being the enormous power in the simplicity of gratitude and appreciation.

As I continued the process of honest expression through journaling, I continued to feel consistent inner shifting. Acknowledging all of the parts of me that showed up, even the parts I didn't like, somehow lifted the resistance around them. As that happened, another gift came out of the blue: I started laughing. There was a strange thread of humor running through my cancer experience. I didn't understand it at first, but it felt so good to laugh that I just flowed with it.

A crazy idea came to me to write and perform a colon cancer comedy. I dismissed it immediately as a cute but ridiculous concept. I had no comedy, writing, acting, or performing experience or training of any kind. There was no way I was going on stage in the first place, never mind to talk and laugh about the most uncomfortable and embarrassing time of my life!

But not only did this idea continue to follow me, it kept expanding. I got the title: "The Poopinator!" and in my mind I saw segments of the show. I tried to bargain with God, "Oh come on, God! I know I said I was ready to be authentic, to start living out my creative purpose, whatever that turns out to be, to release fears and start living and flowing with joy, but come on! This is a little ridiculous, don't you think? I had a gentler, more gradual, private, semi-normal process in mind, you know?"

Instead, the Universe was offering me the opportunity to take my masks off at once. I was being invited to expand my awareness in the areas of self-love, intuition, perfection and imperfection, joy, laughter, humor, fear of what other people think, appreciation, gratitude, authenticity, courage, and fun.

I accepted this bizarre, but surprisingly exhilarating invitation. I started writing, and soon had the honor of being on stage in front of a small group of loving, supportive people as I nervously performed "The Poopinator: I've Got Good News and Bad News." It was far from perfect, and I learned that somehow there's perfection in our imperfections. I wore no masks this time, except for the ones I chose to wear for the sake of entertainment. I felt the tremendous healing power not only in gratitude, but also in honesty, humor, laughter, creative expression, appreciation, and love.

"The Poopinator" showed me that the best way each of us can serve the world is simply to be who you are and to joyfully follow your own spirit. My experience with colon cancer taught me to "flush, flow, and glow." When we flush regret, resentment, judgment, and fear of what other people think, and flow with appreciation and authenticity, we can't help but glow brightly from the inside out with joy, inner peace and love.

♥ ♥ ♥

Mary Andrews is the writer and performer of the colon cancer comedy, "The Poopinator: Patient 295." She is also a life coach and uses tools such as Human Design to help others understand and love themselves more. For more information visit www.Poopinator.com

Thank God My Mother Did Not Abort Me!: "Shattered Glass to Stained Glass"

MEREDITH BROMFIELD

Whenever you drop a glass, it shatters. You try to pick up the large pieces, but the tiny shards go everywhere, piercing anyone who is near. As desperately as you attempt to pick them all up, many pieces still elude you, some never to be found as they are swept away... hiding... looking for an opportunity to pierce yet another. No matter how hard you try, you will never be able to put that glass back together the way it was originally created.

The exciting thing is that a master artist can take that shattered glass and transform it into stained glass that has new shape and beauty much greater than its original intent. That was my life. I was that "shattered glass" and now I am that "stained glass."

Let me tell you my story and the keys I discovered along the way!

For you to understand why I am grateful that my mom chose not to abort me, I need to tell you about my mom's story. My mom's history is very sketchy, so I will give you the pieces that I have been able to put together living with her for part of my life.

My mother came from a wealthy family in Poland. She was the oldest of five children, and somehow she ended up living with a wealthy aunt, who cared for her. It was 1939 when the Nazis came to her village and took her to a "work camp" in Germany. My mom was fourteen. She was the only member of her family taken, although many others from her village were also taken, mainly children.

In this camp she was raped, and there was experimentation done on the children. (To this day my mother cannot take it when a child cries.) Mom recalls, one time, being in a line for the showers, and in the next moment she fainted. When she finally woke up, she was placed in another set of barracks and never saw the original people she had come with to the camp.

Soon after, the Air Force rescued her from the camp. She ended up working for the Air Force, in the officers club, and living with a family that happened to have a butcher shop in Germany. She learned to butcher animals and sold the meat on the black market. I remember her telling me that the only animal that she hated to butcher was the lambs; they would cry like a baby just before they were butchered.

My mom was very secretive about who my biological father was other than that he was an officer in the Air Force. When my mother found out she was pregnant, and also had syphilis, everyone encouraged her to have an abortion: she was alone, no family, and she never told my father that I was his. The prognosis for a syphilis baby was not good; besides being born blind, I could be born with multiple medical challenges and probably would have severe mental challenges as well. At the same time, the medical professionals informed my mom that having this baby could take her life.

I don't know where my mom got the strength, or the fortitude, to not go along with all the advice and encouragement she was getting to abort me. In spite of all the challenges that my mom was facing, she decided to have me, and on May 23, 1949, I was born a syphilis baby. I had sores all over my body, and I was blind. I was born in a Catholic hospital that catered to women who had syphilis. Obviously that was a major problem after the war. My mom wanted to name me Sonya, but she was very ill, and the nuns thought she was going to die so they named me Maria. One of the nuns prayed for me and had me stare through a key; this supposedly gave me back my eyesight. My mother and I were in the hospital for a very long time.

My mom never told my dad that I was his. I don't know why—she never told me. After the war my mom's father found her and asked her to come back to live in Poland. She had vowed that she would never return to her "homeland" and wanted to raise me somewhere safe. That was the last time my mom spoke to her father. She never reconnected with her mother or her five siblings.

So why am I glad my mother did not abort me?

I could give you many reasons why I thought she should have aborted me. Here is the list of my life:

Living in an alcoholic foster home
Having my mom leave after every visit
Being sexually abused
Being beaten for asking questions
Being emotionally devalued for being illegitimate
Bearing the shame in school of being "different"
Needing to be responsible for my foster parents in the midst of chaos as a child
Coming to Chicago at age twelve—I was made responsible for myself
Hating men
Hating myself
Having difficulty in trusting anyone, especially men
Feeling fear of having to care for my mom with her schizophrenia
Getting pregnant and not being married
Attempting suicide twice
Getting fired for stealing
Doing drugs
Running away
Having three children under the age of four, and my husband losing his job
Fighting with my husband
Leaving my husband
Finding out my brother had committed suicide
Becoming my mother's caregiver after she had her stroke.

But somewhere along the way, I met my Maker. He assured me that I was loved, that I had value, and that if I could take all of these broken pieces of my life, He would make something beautiful out of my life.

So here are my reasons that I am so grateful that my mom chose not to abort me:

I became a teacher for challenged kids
I became a counselor to troubled teens
I share my journey and help other people struggling with their issues
I have four beautiful children
I have three beautiful grandchildren
I had forty years with my brother before his life ended
I healed the relationship with my mom, over all the anger and hatred I felt towards her while growing up
I forgave my abusers before they both died
I healed all my past traumas through Theophostic ministry
I obtained a master's degree in counseling
I have traveled with my children to many wonderful places
I created my own company, called "Crossing Your Bridge"
I created workshops that I give on helping people find their passion
I help people become financially free
I counsel people who experienced trauma in their lives
I made a difference when I traveled to Kenya to work in the slums of Mukuru
I influenced my children to believe that they were created for greatness and that they are limited only by the dreams that they have
I stayed married for thirty years to a man who refused to give up on our marriage or me
I became my mother's caregiver when she had her stroke.
I led many to a relationship with the God of the Universe through His son Jesus.
I impacted my community by becoming an elected official
I was given the opportunity to travel the world and see such fabulous and wonderful sights
I traveled with my daughter to Europe, New Zealand and Australia
I have many meaningful relationships
I have helped many with my weekly words of wisdom that I offer through my website www.crossingyourbridge.net
I wrote a book called "Choices" about the lessons that I learned along my life's journey

I learned many lessons that made me the person I am today, and because my mom chose not to abort me, I am privileged in helping others.
I give thanks and realize that I can't control my circumstances, but I can control my attitude.
And if that wasn't enough:
Believing that I was destined to be free and programmed for greatness and abundance.
Communicating what I wanted in a clear concise mental picture.
Determining that words of my mouth will decided my future.
Expecting good things to happen to me.
Fearing not the future.
Giving of my time, talents and assets.
Trusting my gut!
Living in joy!
Never quitting on my dreams!

So as you can see, even though there were many challenges, each of them became a stepping-stone that has made me the strong, caring, compassionate person I am today, and for that I am grateful. For every challenge, there is an opportunity for even greater good.

So after looking over my life, I am, today and forever, grateful that my mom chose not to abort me!

❤ ❤ ❤

Meredith "Kit" Bromfield is an author, an inspirational speaker, and founder of Crossing Your Bridge©. Her years of counseling on life issues (finances, relationships, emotions) have given her the expertise needed to help men and women navigate through this complex world. Meredith's passion is twofold: first, to make a difference in the lives of the people she comes in contact with and second, to travel the world making that difference. Her focus is on helping individuals face the challenges of change. www.MeredithBromfield.com

Thank God
My Dad Died:
How Connecting With My Father's Spirit Helped Me Regain My Own

PAUL E. LANTHOIS, PHD

I had a thriving business; a loving family, and was financially secure, yet I felt a sense of emptiness... a sense that I was meant to do more with my life. My life was nice and comfortable but I realized that it had lost its spark, its passion, and its vitality. My life had lost its spirit.

On February 4, 2006, as I was driving to visit my ill father, I made the conscious decision to reclaim my spirit and live the type of life I had dreamt of. In the car I decided that after Dad passed on (which I thought would be sometime within the next two years), my family and I would sell and move to the other side of the country. What I was going to do and how I was going to do it, I didn't know. All I knew is that we had to move...
...That visit to my father was the last time I saw him alive. Dad died two days later.

On February 6, 2006, while I was doing a consultation, I was interrupted by an urgent phone call: "Dad's dead! He's here and he's dead. Dad's dead!" The sheer intensity and raw emotion in my brother's voice on that day over the phone will be forever etched in my memory. My heart went out to my brother. I wished that he weren't the one who had to experience the shock of finding Dad's lifeless body. I wished it had been me because I had been working in the health profession for fifteen years; at least I had some experience in dealing with the topic of death.

I quickly got into my car to meet my brother at the apartment where Dad was staying. Although Dad's death was hardly a surprise, it was still a huge shock. I thought it was going to happen someday soon, but now? As I was driving to Dad's apartment, an eerie calmness came over me. I recalled the thoughts I had two days earlier as I was driving along the same route. Taking a few deep breaths, I contemplated the impact of Dad's death. I realized that the time for a major change in my life was now.

When I arrived at Dad's apartment, my brother and I sobbed and hugged each other so tightly, in the hope that it would somehow ease the pain... It didn't.
I went into the small, dark apartment, where on the bed lay a lonely figure draped with a white sheet. It was surreal. I gathered myself by the side of the bed and finally mustered enough courage to lift the sheet. I hugged my dad's lifeless body, struggling to comprehend how my big, strong, wisecracking father could be reduced to this. He was so different without life coursing through his body... just an empty shell.

Refusing to give in to reality, I even checked Dad's vital signs, hoping for a flicker of life, but there was none. For the next thirty minutes, I hugged and looked at Dad, trying to take in as much information about him as possible to ensure that I would not forget him.

After my father's funeral and after finalizing his affairs, I visited one of my mentors, Mardi, who does spiritual energy balancing. I told her that I had no idea of any direction in my life and that all I knew was that I had to move to the other side of the country. Mardi said that I would start to attract the people, places, events, and circumstances that would assist me in my journey. How right she was!

That night I went to a health talk and began sharing my intention to move to the other side of

Australia. There I met an amazing nutritionist and author named Erica, who, by chance, used to live in the area I was moving to. I was intrigued by this person, as she seemed completely different from anyone I had met before, yet strangely familiar. I was certain that I was meeting this person for an important reason, especially when she revealed that the translation of her surname meant "angel."

We shared stories of remarkably similar journeys in our lives. I was inspired by her stories of what it meant to be able to make a difference in other people's health on an international scale.

I returned to work with a renewed sense of vigor, buoyed by the knowledge that I was somehow being guided in my journey.

Within two months I had sold my practice to an exemplary young man and agreed to stay on for the following six months in a part-time capacity, to assist with the transition, as I waited for my children to finish their school year.

Around this time, I had become so focused on the changes in my life that I forgot about my wife, Angela. She was understandably hesitant about our comfortable lifestyle being turned upside down in the selfish pursuit of my dream. Our marriage had been so strong, and for the first time it, too, was uncertain. Just the thought of this sent my world into a spin.

I didn't know what to do, so I went for a walk in nature to clear my head and get some sort of perspective on my life. I rested on a rock, where I realized that the only person in the world who I really wanted to talk to about this was Dad. This triggered an expression of grief so raw that it felt exactly like when I was crying by my father's gravesite. My crying continued unabated for the next fifteen minutes. I was at my lowest ebb. I looked to the heavens and surrendered. "I give up. What in the .... should I do now?" I screamed at the top of my lungs until there was no more grief, anger and desperation inside of me.

I gathered myself and began the hike back out of the forest, thinking about how I longed to speak to Dad.

I had walked approximately fifteen steps when I heard my father's voice over my right shoulder. "You know I am here if you need to talk." My body tingled with goose bumps of exhilaration as tears of joy washed down my cheeks. "You can write books and teach people how to regain their spirit. You can call it 'Teen Spirit'."

Instantly a vision flashed into my mind of going on a book tour and giving presentations on health, energy, and life fulfillment to groups all over the world. This was accompanied by an amazing sense of euphoria for rediscovering some purpose in my life. I then thought to myself, "How do I go about writing a book?" A picture of Erica (an author, who I had met a few months earlier) flashed into my mind.

My feelings intensified as I appreciated the synchronicity of the recent events. The pieces of the puzzle were starting to fit together. It was amazing... within five minutes of experiencing some the most intense feelings of grief I can ever recall, I was now feeling one of my life's most amazing highs. I laughed at the inevitable ups and downs of life that I had long striven to avoid for the sake of stability. The intensity of this experience really jolted my senses, and I was now feeling alive like never before.

Later that afternoon, I tracked down Erica's number and plucked up the courage to call her. She not only supported my book idea but also actively encouraged me to make a difference to others with this book. She passed on a lot of what she had learned throughout her writing journey and recommended that I go to a writing conference in Hawaii to fast-track my learning.

I began doing a lot of research and writing in my spare time as I completed my work commitments amidst organizing our belongings. After Christmas 2006, my family and I travelled to our new home, 5000 kilometres away in Queensland. Motivated by my life's purpose, I continued writing and decided to go to the writer's seminar in Hawaii.

During this conference I lost my way around the hotel and unintentionally ended up at a presentation by one of the people featured on *The Secret*, Lisa Nichols.

Towards the end of her presentation, Lisa mentioned one of her teen support programs called "Teen Spirit." Recognizing my father's very own words, my ears pricked up as I realized that I was again being guided. As Lisa walked off the stage she pointed to me and mouthed, "I'll speak to you soon."

People sitting adjacent to me turned to me saying, "Did you see that? Was she talking to you? What do you have to talk about?" The hairs on the back of my neck were again on end as I knew that I had to go and speak to her to find out about this program.

After speaking with Lisa about "Teen Spirit," I became quite emotional, so I walked out to the hotel foyer, where I took in the incredible view of the ocean. There I heard that same voice in my head...it was Dad again. "Thanks for remembering, mate." he said. "I'm proud of you."

For the next forty-five minutes, an enormous feeling of love overwhelmed me. I cried with joy as it felt like everyone in the world was hugging me, saying, "I love you." Staying connected to this feeling, I became aware that part of Dad's purpose in his life was to help me become inspired about health. "You went through all of that to help me?" I exclaimed while recalling the suffering he went through in the second half of his life. I felt so humble.

I resolved that if Dad went through this to help me find my inspiration, nothing was going to stop me from helping others to regain their energy and spirit. I strode with an air of confidence into my meetings with the interested publishers and agents

For the first time in my life, I was completely clear and assured about who I really was as a person and what my purpose in life was.

My father, in his passing, became my ultimate spiritual guide, leading me through the most incredible range of people, places, coincidences, and experiences, which resulted in my rediscovering my life's purpose. It's taught me to appreciate the part of people that we don't typically see...their spirit, because that is the real part of them. I now see my spirit as a real part of me.

I am sharing this story to help other people who may be facing a similar situation in their lives. Yes, you will probably be experiencing some pain, sadness and desperation as you face the mortality of a loved one. But I say this to you with the utmost conviction and clarity because I know deep inside that this is the truth: Amidst this suffering there is joy, happiness, peace, and contentment.

How do you find these gifts amidst your despair? Start to look for them. Start by interpreting your current events in a different way. Look at it with a different perspective, and pay attention to your emotions. Use your emotions as a guide. As you explore different interpretations of your circumstances, pay attention to interpretations that make you feel better.

If you're feeling bad, that is your heart and soul saying that there is another way of looking at things. It's your body telling you to look deeper. The stronger the pain, the more important it is to delve deeper.

Your body will let you know with bursts of positive emotions when you have found these gifts amidst your sorrow. As a result of the beautiful gifts that have arisen from my wonderful father's death, I can say from deep in my heart, "Thank God my dad died."

❤ ❤ ❤

Dr. Paul Lanthois is a chiropractor, speaker, author, and corporate wellness consultant. He is the director of The Work Life Balance Foundation (www.WorkLifeBalanceFoundation.com), where he helps improve business revenue and productivity gains through improving personal productivity via his popular From Burnout to Balance Workforce Sustainability and Productivity Development Programs for business. His latest book is the business health book From Burnout to Balance in Four Weeks.

Thank God
I Have Asthma

REN'E COSBY

The greatest gift I can offer to you is to pass on the knowledge that only experience has taught me. I want to share my story for those who may have endured the same challenges as I did, and the opportunity to learn through my story.

In 1958, I was born to two young parents: a seventeen-year old mother and twenty-year-old father in L.A. County. Shortly after my birth, I was diagnosed with chronic asthma, the same condition that my father was also burdened with. His day-to-day life was a struggle to live with his own condition, and it became equally difficult for my parents to try and attend to the asthmatic condition of an infant.

I know this was difficult. I was their firstborn child. I constantly fought just to breathe, as only minimal amounts of air managed to reach my tiny lungs. Besides the severe allergies I had, my body was entirely covered in bleeding scabs caused by eczema. Doctors tried to help, but little was known about the cause of these allergies and breathing problems. My parents were warned not to give me milk, even though food wasn't considered a major factor in symptoms such as mine at the time. My parents failed to realize that other dairy products such as cheese, ice cream, and butter also fell into that category of "milk."

In an effort to keep me alive every day, my parents would occasionally drive me over an hour and a half away to the beach in the middle of the night, when I could not breathe, just to try to get me some fresh air. My dad gave me large amounts of carrot and other vegetable juices to try to lessen the severity and increase the strength in my undersized body. I used a nebulizer constantly, which was a hand held pump-inhaler used for asthmatics during that time. An air purifier was also placed near my bed.

My sister Denise was born sixteen months later. This was hard for her as well because our parents spent a lot of time trying to help me breathe. In a way, she was neglected a lot because more time was focused on caring for her sick older sister. My condition did not improve, so things were not easy for anyone in my family. In fact, things became worse, as my asthma attacks became steadily more severe each day.

My sister and I were very close growing up; however, she became understandably resentful as the years passed. My parents then turned to God and took on a very religious lifestyle when I was about three years old. This restrictive lifestyle limited me even further concerning normal childhood activities and associations.

We were extremely poor when I was growing up, so much so that I remember wearing rubber bands on my socks to hold them up. This made paying for expensive medical bills and specialists impossible. Proper care was unavailable to me. We made frequent trips to the hospital; however, there were many instances when I needed to go but preferred to suffer as I became afraid of hospitalization.

Because it was hard just to live a single day, I ended up being absent from school quite a bit. I wasn't allowed to play or run around like most children, thus I did not make friends, and this left me feeling very isolated and alone. This loneliness made me feel like something was wrong with me, and I began secretly cutting myself at the age of ten. I became afraid of everything and would not try to make new acquaintances or talk to people. Fortunately, my parents showed me a lot of love by taking turns getting up almost every night to watch over me. The entire household would wake up to me screaming, trying to catch my breath. Even after allergy shots and tests, I never seemed to find any relief from this terrible affliction. Six years later, my second sister was born; then my baby brother PJ came fifteen years later. So our family had grown significantly, and all of us had at least a touch of asthma, but none so severe as that of my father's and my own.

My dad was a functioning alcoholic for as long as I can remember, as was my mom. All my energy was put towards staying alive, which made me feel worn out, and I felt like giving up completely. I began to wish for death to take me, since it had been after me for so long. Although I had always despised my father's drinking habits, as a symbol that I had officially given in and given up, I decided that I too wanted to take up drinking when I was fifteen. As the old cliché goes, "if you can't beat 'em, join 'em." It didn't take long until I became a full-blown alcoholic myself, drinking nearly every night with my parents, despite our religious affiliations.

I finally moved out at twenty-one years old and realized I was a lesbian, despite my rigid religious upbringing, and to my parents' disappointment. Even though my parents still spoke to me, it was clearly understood that I was living a lifestyle that was not approved of and would keep me at a distance from my parents so that we would not have the closeness we had in my youth.

I ended up feeling rejected and more lost than ever. My drinking habit became worse and, wanting to escape this harsh reality, I delved into a hallucinogenic world of drugs.

During this young adulthood, I maintained a rigorous job where I made quite a lot of money. I also became involved in a tumultuous, physically violent two-and-a-half-year relationship that left me with some large concussions to my head from being shoved through walls. I became a victim of domestic abuse, and of course, this just agitated my asthma attacks and caused me to retreat further into drugs and alcohol. I found myself going in and out of the hospital for one to two weeks at a time and simultaneously, I ended up going in and out of jail for drunk driving, which led to several car accidents. Although I came away with no broken bones, I suffered chronic body pain in my back, neck, and shoulders.

I really felt that every day was going to be my day to die. My relationships started repeating that abusive pattern; however, this time, I became the violent one. Never wanting to be treated so badly again, I took on that role before anyone I was with could hurt me. I didn't even realize this was the reason I became both physically and verbally abusive to my girlfriends. I had one unhappy relationship followed by another.

After a lot of coaxing from my baby sister, Deneen, I finally moved away from the unhealthy, bad environment I had found myself surrounded by in LA to San Diego. For a long time, I knew that I was on a self-destructive path, and as stubborn as I can be, I knew this move was the first step towards caring about my life and the possibility that I might have a future. My job allowed me to live anywhere I wanted to, so that wasn't an issue. Initially, I thought San Diego would be a much better environment for me – it was away from my old friends and drug lifestyle. I wanted a new life. It didn't turn out that way when I ended up moving next to a meth dealer and had all the free methamphetamines I could want. I was hospitalized yet again for two more weeks. This was my last stint with drugs, and it was also the last time I have been admitted to a hospital to date. Getting clean was indeed one of the hardest things I have ever accomplished to this day. I owe it to my support system and the love of my family, but most of all I congratulate myself. This was one of the first times I realized that I possess within myself a strong desire to live.

With fond memories of going to the beach in the middle of the night so that I could breathe, I longed to live at the beach, and that is where I settled... in Oceanside. I got a small studio right on the sand. I was still wrestling with my alcoholism on a daily basis and then, one day, I was arrested for being heavily intoxicated on the beach. Now that I was in my thirties, I realized how irritated this lifestyle of being arrested was to me and wanted to settle down. I didn't want to go to jail again, and the only way to do that was to stop drinking altogether. Somehow, something finally seemed to click, and I began my journey towards sobriety and developed a relationship with a woman named Mary Ann, who helped me on that path.

I literally thank God every day that I made it through this time of my life and can look back on eighteen years of sobriety today. Yet, I still had the same problems I'd been at war with since childhood: my asthma with a constant bombardment of one attack after another. Quite wisely, I decided to finally quit smoking after the doctors decided to give me an oxygen tank and said I had the beginning stages of emphysema.

The uphill battle to breathe got worse, but I refused to ever go back to the hospital. I vowed that I would not allow myself to go back to that loathsome place where I'd spent the majority of my childhood. I admit, things did get pretty bad, and death breathed its name across me several more times, but I still came out victorious. My general quality of life was extremely low. For about a month, it could take me as long as an hour to get across my 1000-square foot apartment to my front door.

I tend to tackle one issue at a time. Breathing effortlessly was obviously the last issue I was going to tackle, since it was the first and hardest battle to fight. I was clean and sober, I'd quit smoking, but I still had to deal with my acquired violent tendencies. I became grateful for life and everything in it, and after overcoming my depression, isolation, and feelings of rejection, I was pulling myself together and actually enjoying the person I was becoming. I went to two years of intensive therapy and anger management to put my life into perspective; I eventually put an end to my violent tendencies.

I kept thinking that it was too late to try to fix myself. I started giving up on the fight with my asthma as I became more and more exhausted each night trying to sleep and breathe. One night, I told Mary Ann that I just couldn't make it through another night. I apologized, and said good night and goodbye. I turned off the light, put my head back, and waited to die ...with my mouth wide open, gasping desperately for air to reach my lungs.

I abruptly sat up and came to a second realization. I did not want to die after I had worked so hard and so long to live and improve my life. There had to be a way to survive this. There had to be answers. I had resolved to live and to do whatever it takes to do so. I remembered someone had recently told me about a doctor in Mexico who might be able to save me. It was worth a try. So the next day, Mary Ann and I drove there in about three and half hours. This doctor was widely acclaimed and had people come visit him from around the world. He gave me a three-month supply of natural pills that were highly sought after. I wanted this to be my chance to pull through my torment. I started taking the medication, and it worked so that I could actually speak; my condition improved drastically within one week's time.

For some unknown reason, right after I started taking that medication, I picked up a book that I had received from a friend a few weeks earlier. I wanted to read it while I was in recovery at home. The book was about going on a special fast to clear my lungs. As intense as it sounded, it seemed worth a try, since I was desperate to improve my quality of life at that point. I did an intense water-only diet for two straight weeks and, as agonizing as it was, I felt better than I had in my entire life. My desire and determination to live became stronger than ever. I would not allow my breathing ailment to control me any longer. I was to be in control of my own life.

I took up juicing again, which my father had taught me to do as a child. After numerous trial and error attempts to improve my diet, and taking the miracle drug from Mexico, I gained over 100 pounds, a side effect of this remedy. This weight gain took place over a short period of just two years. When I stopped taking the drug, my chronic asthma symptoms worsened, but my determination to live was unhindered. Being sick and having someone worry about you constantly can wear down a relationship, and mine got to the point where we could no longer make it work. It ended, but we parted ways as friends.

Soon after, I met someone who would become my best friend and who helped me find my way to freedom from the extremity of my affliction. Sandra helped me to shed the 100 pounds I had gained. I accomplished this through rigorous exercise and cutting carbohydrates out of my diet. This was a slow process, as exercise was not something I was physically capable of due to my asthma. Together, we discovered that most of my symptoms could easily be avoided by a strict change of diet. I owe a majority of my survival to her, and she continues to support me even after ten years. She watched my daily food intake very closely, discovering various reactions to food products such as cheese, soy, seeds, olive oil, nuts, seasonings, corn, and more. After forty years of coming so near to death, I finally found out it was my daily intake of sustenance that was killing me! So, as often as people exclaim how difficult it must be to not be able to eat my "favorite foods" anymore, I am far more grateful that I am alive and no longer have to wonder why I can't breathe throughout the night and if I will live to see another day.

So there I was: I'd taken on many battles, I got the upper hand in all of them, however the game hasn't ended. I've taken on alcoholism, drug addiction, overeating, violent tendencies, smoking, and asthma, but these issues I still fight to quell within myself at times. They are all essential aspects of who I am and define my strength and desire to be here now. I decided I owed something to myself and to people who were also fighting various illnesses, disorders, allergies, asthma, pain, and discomforts that gave them a poor quality of life. I dedicated myself to the study of holistic health with my friend Sandra. If I can help even one person avoid all the pain and trauma I've endured in my life, I feel a sense of accomplishment and purpose.

I am, now, in love with life and my ability to take in each day. I am grateful for my asthma because it helped me to be strong enough to take anything head-on and come out undefeated. I was so afraid of everything as a child, but fear does not control me when I am determined. I am grateful because now I have the opportunity to help others with what I learned in my own personal hell, plunging back into each asthma episode and coming out of it with a new sense of how to survive the next attack. I have a strong desire to help other people feel like they can also live and have a wonderful, active life to look forward to.

I celebrate my life as I now reside at the beach with my wife, Celeste, the love of my life, and continue my voyage with her and my health to accomplish everything and anything we want. I had done all the work on myself to be clean, sober, and at peace within myself so that I could allow such a wonderful and loving person to come into my life. Aside from my love of life itself, my perseverance has stemmed from a desire to find that one true love that makes life worth living, and I have found exactly this in my relationship with Celeste. I make a commitment to offer advice and help to anyone who comes to me in need. I know Celeste understands and supports my decision to live by watching my food allergies and developing new concepts to help me achieve my personal goals.

Life is beautiful. Air is beautiful. Just breathe.

♥ ♥ ♥

Ren'e Cosby was born and raised in Southern California. As mentioned in her story, she has pursued her interest in holistic health in hopes that one day she will be a part of the development of a natural cure or treatment for asthma. Every day continues to be a struggle and a learning process as part of her journey towards health and a balanced life. Ren'e lives with her partner, Celeste, whom she married in November of 2008. As a couple they both have a passion for living on or near the ocean. Together, they have a company that does property preservation work for banks, but she wants to branch out and also does network marketing. Ultimately Ren'e just wants to relax and have fun and be able to enjoy the life she has struggled so hard to just be able to live.

Thank God I Had a Heart Attack

RICK EMMERICH

"Go...go...go!" The words rang out as the gurney was wheeled into the ambulance. It had been a smooth elevator ride down, and we were off to 60th Street and north to our destination. They asked me one main question: "Which hospital do you want to be taken to?"

I remember thinking it an amusing question. My first answer was, "the hospital closest to us." This resulted in all of the EMTs shaking their heads No. Since that narrowed down the options, I had a real good chance of making their heads nod up and down. "Wisconsin Heart Hospital?" Bingo, we were off.

That was one of about four smart decisions I made that day. This after years of particularly bad choices as far as nutrition, exercise, my expectations, and the ways I handled stress. When I thought I might be experiencing symptoms of a heart attack, another good decision I made was taking two regular aspirin when I sensed trouble.

Minutes later we hurried into the Emergency area. I lapsed in and out of consciousness, but before I knew it I was in place and an angel appeared. Dr. Frank Cummins was on that shift and is known as an aggressive cardiologist. With cardiologists, like attorneys and hockey players, aggressive is good.

After I was given a cocktail of happy juice into my I.V., which put me out, they put a hole in my thigh and went to work. Dr. Cummins expertly removed plaque that blocked three out of my four coronary arteries. The fourth wasn't a picnic, but he did his best under the circumstances. I was maybe one Italian sausage away from complete disaster.

The next day I woke up in my room. This hospital was brand-spankin' new! I had a brand new flat screen TV, a room of my own, and some cards and flowers. People appeared and "loved up" on me. I told my minister and friends that I really hadn't done this to get attention. I thanked Dr. Cummins in person.

One of the other smart decisions I had made the day before was when I had the "This could be it" thought. I hadn't talked to a lot of heart attack survivors, but I know you have that thought. I did, and instantly thought, "No, I am not going to die—God is with me."

A couple of days more at this "Taj Mahal," and I was released and back home, a changed and fragile person. It seemed like I was coming out of a cocoon. The original "old me" had been a teenage partier who cared about no one, not even himself.

Twenty years of that behavior and I had finally shaped up and quit swearing and drinking. There are plenty of people I hurt during that period, and I did my best to make amends. At thirty-eight years old, I made the decision to become a baptized disciple of Christ. I made many life changes.

At forty-eight, this "old me" had almost killed my God-given body. I lived in Milwaukee and enjoyed every food representing the Beer City and America's dairyland. (Quiet, California...Wisconsin's cows are still better.) I ate red meat, bratwurst, all dairy, white bread, and on and on. Of course I skipped healthy salads, vegetables, and fruit.

Additionally, I mismanaged my money and let the stress really get to me. I internalized it. I feared the worst. I stayed two to three years too long in my job, because I was too afraid to venture off to another career. It was safe to stay and keep that steady paycheck.

My home environment (if not toxic enough already) included a lot of electronic stuff—the computers, cell phones, routers, and televisions, with the EMFs (electro-magnetic frequencies) that they were emitting. To me sleep had been a necessary evil. Caffeine and sugar fueled my days at work. At the time of the heart attack, I had one crazy roommate and had just succeeded in evicting another.

Soon after, a Harry and David Fruit Basket arrived at my condo. Malia, an angel in Hawaii, really knew how to respond in a crisis. More changes in my life followed. Friends helped me to start working out again. Fruits, vegetables, juices all found their way into my home and refrigerator and body. I tossed the carbonated soft drinks, gave up the milk and ice cream. I went from having red meat fifteen times a week to maybe once a week.

My new outlook was more relaxed. I let stress float off my body. Eventually, with a lot of love from my brothers and sisters in Christ and family, the color returned to my face and I was "back." God continued to smile on me.

Malia became an even better friend to me, and we talked on the phone often. We met halfway, in Southern California, that October. She was wonderful, and we married the next summer. A holistic chiropractor, she opened up a whole new window in my life.

She assisted in teaching me how to eliminate the stress that has been trapped in my body for years. We realized that we were perfect for each other. What a wonderful week-long celebration with family, friends, my church-brothers and sisters, and my new bride in July of 2005!

I went from being an unhealthy, emotionally toxic, single Wisconsin resident, to a healthier-than-ever, newlywed in the paradise known as Hawaii. These islands really are a hotbed of raw and natural foods, with alternative/complementary healers as Eastern meets Western Medicine.

Through businesses I have built and contacts I've made, I have also been fortunate and grateful to have met some dynamic health care professionals and networkers. I am blessed in so many ways to have mentors and selfless leaders.

My outlook on life, the words I speak, and those that roll around in my mind are inspired. I expect great things to happen. One of my teachers, Dr. John Demartini, taught me a lot. Most importantly the belief that I am perfect the way I am. I am worthy of love. When I speak from my heart, people hear it in theirs. Sleep, previously an inconvenient pause between emails and projects, has now become a highlight of my life. I refresh and heal this God-given body and brain.

At my doctor's office, in August of 2009, she told me I had to go on statin drugs to make sure I got my cholesterol and other levels down. I told her confidently, "No, I'll get them down myself." I had no idea how, but I knew I didn't want pharmaceutical drugs.

A month later, another angel (Anela) shared a raw whole food product (Mila) with my wife, Dr. Malia. Soon I was taking it, and within four months all those levels were where they should be. After another review of my health, my doctor proclaimed, "Whatever you are doing, keep it up." Here are the results from before and after I started taking the product.

	August	December
Weight	207	194
Total Cholesterol	264	197
Triglycerides	332	115
HDL(Good Cholesterol)	36	43
LDL (Bad Cholesterol)	162	131
Fasting Glucose Level	113	100

Heart Pump. Eject. Fraction 54% (50% is normal)

Thank God I had a heart attack and discovered my heart!

♥ ♥ ♥

Rick Emmerich, now fifty-four going on thirty, is enjoying every day of life in Hawaii. He helps promote the EZ to Use Island Pages Yellow Pages and search engine from his home in Honolulu. He discusses heart health, lowering Cholesterol, God, and other stuff at http://www.rickemmerich.com also on FaceBook: Rick Emmerich and twitter @hearthealthguy And bringing Mila by Lifemax to a town near you. More about Mila http://www.lifemax.net/drmalia God bless.

Special Thanks

Mila, by Lifemax, changed my health and gave me yet another great story to share with others.

Dr. Malia Emmerich (DC) helps patients at Holistic Chiropractic, 1010 S. King St. in Honolulu. Her specialty is Neural Emotional Technique (NET) which allows emotions trapped inside of us to be released. She has many other skills as well. I am grateful every day for the progress I have made thanks to her.

Dr. Cummins and his assistant, Mike Sween, took a very personal interest in this patient. Also, Mark Decker, brother in Christ and health care professional, monitored my progress, accessed hospital records, checked stress tests, and gave me advice. He was my best man.

Also, James Hamann, my evangelist at the time, was an incredible support. Others include Damon Brog, Tim Brudnicki, Ron Norwood, and that great servant, Tony Vraniak. Of course my mom and three sisters were a great support.

Thank God I Met Lange

ROBERT JOSEPH IWANIEC

Lange was such an odd bird, such an odd bird indeed. He thought he could fly. People made fun of him. Not to his face much because he had a disability. In school, teachers told us that his brain worked different than ours; other than that, he was normal. They said that kids with autism live in their own little world. I can tell you he certainly did that.

I think he truly believed that he could fly. He would stand up in the middle of class and climb on the chair and flap his arms and yell, "I'm flying, I'm flying," at least a couple of times a day. Mrs. James, our second grade teacher, would smile at him. "Get down off the chair, Lange. You cannot fly." He always insisted that he could.

I remember one summer I was invited to his seventh birthday party. I didn't want to go, but my mom thought it would be nice if I did. So I went. She asked me what I thought I should get him for a present. I had no idea. I told her, "He doesn't talk to me much—all he talks about is flying. That is his favorite thing." We talked for a few more minutes; then I came up with what I thought was a great idea. I was going to buy him a Superman cape.

His party was interesting to say the least. He didn't play with anyone. I ended up playing kickball with the other kids. We sang "Happy Birthday" and ate cake and ice cream. Lange then opened his presents. The superman cape that I got him was his favorite. He put it on and ran around the room and yelled, "I'm flying, I'm flying," for at least ten minutes.

His mother came over and told me how Lange pretends to fly all the time. "He climbs on the sofa and on the swing set and yells, 'I'm flying I'm flying.'"

I told her, "That's what he does in school too." I asked her, "Does he really think he can fly?"

"I don't think he really thinks so," she said.

My mom picked me up at two o'clock, when the party was over. On the way home, I thought about Lange for a while. I felt really good that he liked my present, and I felt lucky that I wasn't different, like he was.

When I returned to school in September, Lange was nowhere to be seen or heard. I checked to see if he was in another classroom, but he was not. I asked my new teacher, Mr. Smith, where Lange was, and he said that they would be addressing that in morning orientation. I got a bad feeling in my stomach. I could sense Mr. Smith was not telling me something.

When we got to the orientation, Mrs. James stood up and said, with tears in her eyes, "Lange, the little boy in our class last year, died in an accident. I just thought you should know." Then she asked us to bow our heads in a moment of silence in memory of him.

All I could think of was him standing on his chair, yelling, "I'm flying I'm flying." Then I started to cry. Later that day I walked up to Mrs. James and asked her what had happened. She told me that he was playing at home in his tree fort and fell off and hit his head.

I couldn't speak. I thought to myself, What if he was wearing the cape that I gave him and he really thought he could fly? What if it was my fault? That day I could think of nothing else. I went home and told my mother what happened, and I cried and cried. She assured me that it was not my fault, and that God has a special time for each of us. It took quite a while for me to get over that. In time things returned to normal.

Then, five years later, when I was in the seventh grade, I became very sick. I was diagnosed with a rare form of leukemia. I was in and out of doctors' offices for over a year. I had chemotherapy and radiation. I even went to a special doctor who used herbs and other alternative therapies, but I was not getting better. I was getting scared. At night, I would pretend to sleep so I could listen to what the doctors and my parents were saying about me.

One night I got really scared. My mom was crying uncontrollably, and my dad burst out of the room. I heard the doctors tell my parents that I had less than a month to live. I tried to hide my tears, but I couldn't. The next few weeks were tough. All of my friends and relatives were stopping by, to say hello and I guess, to say goodbye.

I was tired. I just wanted to sleep.

I remember, one morning, I could barely open my eyes. I thought, I must be dreaming. There he was, Lange, my friend from the second grade. He was dressed in white, wearing a white cape. He was flying. He came over to me and smiled. "I told you I could fly. You can too." He took me by the hand, and we went flying.

Quick
Don't be quick to judge
Be quick to love

♥ ♥ ♥

Dr. Robert J. Iwaniec, a professional speaker, chiropractor, author, poet, and success coach, has dedicated his life to the study of health and human performance. He is the author of several books including, Breakthrough Secrets to Live Your Dreams, Inside Out, Pieces of Eight, Charm, Four, Nonsense, Retrogenesis, and Almost Home. He has also authored two children's books, Flowers and Billy Burka and the Burka Trees. Dr. Iwaniec resides in Clifton Park, New York, with his wife, Diane, and their three children, Jenna, Robert, and Nicholas.

Thank G-d I'm Neurotic

ROBERT LANSBURG

I always knew when it was springtime. That's when they announced the annual celebration to honor the Spanish Inquisition. Actually, by "they" I'm talking about the annual spring fair that was held at the local Jewish community center. There were various booths showing different aspects of Jewish life from Biblical times and the Middle Ages.

Now, while the Middle Ages was never known as a particularly touchy-feely time for the Jewish people, The Inquisition was certainly a remarkable achievement for its excess. The Spanish Inquisition booth was my favorite, if only because at seven years old, I did not really understand what was going on. The basic premise of the booth was that during the Inquisition, Spanish Jews were forced to convert to Christianity or die a horrible death. Actually that's not completely true, as in most cases they really weren't even given the chance to convert, as it was much more fun to just inflict death and mayhem.

In any event, at the booth we were forced to kneel and someone would play the Grand Inquisitor. (This role was usually given to my neighbor, who had a horrific case of halitosis that was enough to knock over a water buffalo. On top of which, his two front teeth were severely gap-toothed. When he talked, you were showered with an avalanche of spit.) So after being subjected to the rancid smell of fried onion breath and covered with spittle, you were definitely ready to renounce anything.

My other favorite booth was "The Eating Of The Pork." There was a booth where we were forced to renounce Judaism, and to show our willingness to do so, we were made to eat pork. Actually, most Jews I knew ate bacon, so it really wasn't much of a test. We were supposed to say, "No, rather you strike me dead than I eat pork."

What makes this whole festival so absurd was this was punishment of Jews upon Jews. We didn't even need the goyim to make it worse. Growing up in the Midwest, actually Iowa, to be precise, made me feel at times like I was enjoying that rich shtetl ghetto experience that was denied to me by my grandparents escaping Russia.

At one time or another we all experience a sense of alienation. In school, I remember fondly going to pep rallies, where we were forced to root for the local football or basketball team. We were all herded into the auditorium, and everybody would join in some demonstration of solidarity reminiscent of a Leni Reifenstahl movie. Hundreds of hormone-crazed teenagers shouting for their home team, and all I could think was, "When can I get out of this place before I lose my mind?"

To add insult to injury, the pep rally usually came right after shop class. Now, at fourteen years old, I didn't know much about anything, but one thing I knew for certain is that there were fewer Jewish handymen in the world than Jewish athletes. I mean, let's face it, the last time any of my people built anything was the pyramids, and after that, everybody said, "Thanks, but I think we'd rather spend the rest of our days hiding under the bed from Cossacks."

So while there is an obvious sense of irony in being Jewish in a place like Iowa, the fact is that nobody really fits in anywhere. Everybody wants to fit in to some degree, to have a sense of belonging.

Sure, being born Jewish in Iowa isn't exactly like having to survive cancer, or some other extreme calamity. The very real lesson in life is to make a determination in our realization of our uniqueness, and truly explore and embrace that side of ourselves, rather than run away in fear/shame/disgust/self-loathing/self-pity/pill addiction/alcoholism/mindless sex/endless television/worthless hobbies.

So in my humble search for meaning, I left the cornfields and went to India. India can only be described as a Fellini movie come to life. It is a bizarre juxtaposition of the magical and profane, where joy and pathos constantly vie for your attention.

Just the sheer volume of people is enough to be daunting. You have a country of a billion people compressed into a land mass roughly a third the size of the United States. Imagine three billion people living in the United States, and picture how things would work here. It's the living embodiment of the chaos theory in action.

A lot of people I knew had just come back from India and complained about the beggars, or myopically raved about some of the fabled temples, but one of my most indelible impressions was just walking on the streets of Calcutta....

Calcutta has the infamous sobriquet of The Black Hole of Calcutta, a reference to 1756, when the Indians and the English were fighting. An Indian king captured one hundred forty-six English prisoners and put them in a cell so crowded, that only twenty-one survived the next day.

Calcutta has its reigning deity, which looks over the city, and that is Kali. Kali is the ultimate boogey-woman. She is usually pictured with an extremely angry expression on her face and a lot of blood on her from ripping people up. Songs celebrate how she causes people to suffer and the ruin that follows in her wake. (Think of her as Ann Coulter on a particularly bad day, but with a spiritual side.)

One poet has celebrated her by saying, "You have cut off the heads of the children of others, and these you wear as a garland around your neck." The poet goes on to say that Kali does not give what is expected, and the goal of the devotee is to become reconciled with death and to learn acceptance of the way things are.

As with many things in Eastern thought, there is that intertwining of opposites. On the surface, everything connected to Kali appears terrifying and negative; however, it is the very fact that Kali doesn't give you what you want that actually liberates her followers. She encourages them to see greater truths that go beyond simply asking and expecting you'll be rewarded just because you want or expect to be.

Back to the streets of Calcutta. I'm walking along the streets and I see literally thousands of families living in cardboard boxes, row after row of them. Children are running around, women are cooking, people are sleeping, and they're all doing so in make-shift houses of cardboard. The realization was so immediate and obvious. The same quirk of fate that gave me birth in a middle-class home in the Midwest could just have easily placed me in one of those shacks.

It's all some random slot-machine where we're born, to what family and circumstances, and really, however bad our lives may seem at any point in time here in America, what do we have to complain about? Sure, no place seems perfect, but do we dwell on what's good, or what's bad?

Without being too philosophical here, it's how we face the tragedies in our lives that define us. Sure, life should be one endless party! While I wish I could be Spuds Mackenzie the original party animal, we know that it's those times when we ask, "How am I going to get through this?" that really makes us who we are. That leaves us with the realization that our lives are not neat, happy little sitcoms, where everything gets resolved in twenty-six minutes; but at the same time, it doesn't mean life is just one endless parade of suffering and misery either.

Life sometimes seems so unfair. Let's go back to the Bible and see what the ancients said. I'm talking about the Old Testament and the Book of Job, the G-d who didn't allow any shenanigans.

Job is a pious man, living the good life, and prays faithfully to G-d. In all ways, he's a righteous man. So, the Devil goes to G-d and says to him, "You know, G-d, I'll bet if Job's life was made a living hell, he'd curse you. Will you let me do it?"

And without missing a beat, G-d replies, "Okay." Job has done nothing wrong; in fact, everything he's done to that point has been completely on the straight and narrow. But out of the blue, the Devil makes a bet with G-d, and G-d just says, "Sure, why not. It's not my ass here."

Immediately all of Job's family members are killed and all his possessions are gone. It gets worse and worse. He suffers horrific diseases, Biblical diseases like boils, and his skin turns black. The goal here is to really make this guy suffer. (Just the very mention of the name Job is synonymous with suffering. While parents give their children various names from the Bible, like David, or Sarah, one name parents never give to their kids is Job.)

Throughout this ordeal, Job doesn't waver and curse G-d. Eventually everything turns out okay in the end, so I think the real moral of this story is that bad stuff seems to happen, and it can happen through no fault of your own.

We have the choice in this life to either bemoan every calamity and tragedy, or we can choose to accept the situations for what they are. It doesn't mean we have to necessarily rejoice in this suffering; I mean, nobody is a masochist here, but that's our choice. In some way or another, that's the human condition.

Every day we're there at the spring fair, and somebody is holding a plate of chocolate bunnies in front of us. We have that choice, and the choice is completely and absolutely ours, whether we renounce our faith, which essentially is to give up our inner integrity, or just give up and die. Is a plate of chocolate bunnies really worth it?

♥ ♥ ♥

Robert Lansburg is the founder of www.retirementbulletinboard.com, an online resource for baby boomers to network and mutually create solutions for their lives as they now enter their sixties and beyond. This generation will face new challenges and must come up with creative ideas for their future on their own.

He is the president of Auditek (www.auditek.net), a company that uncovers mistakes by utility companies and negotiates more favorable pricing for businesses.

Mr. Lansburg has also written Without Limits, which will be published soon. It is a series of interviews with women who test the very edges of what people are capable of, and the way they define their lives. Among the women he interviewed are a polar explorer, a combat photographer, the first female bullfighter in Mexico, and a noted anthropologist.

Thank God I Was Depressed

ROSEMARY CROUTHERS

Thank God I was depressed. Without struggling through the depression, I would not be the person I am today.

When I retired from my secretarial job that I hated, a huge funk was waiting for me. People today love to call it depression...and doctors are delighted to help by passing out prescriptions. When "it" hit me, I had no job, hardly any contact with adults, no extra income, except for a small Social Security pension, on top of low self-esteem. Why? Because the anchor of who and what I had been all my life was gone. Poof! Evaporated! Just like a snap of your fingers! Who was I if not a secretary? I was nobody! I had no disposable income and no buddies.

What is life without buddies? No one called. I had to initiate lunch dates! I was very angry and hurt, and my husband did not understand. How could a man understand how a woman needs connections? I needed someone to cry with or talk to or laugh out loud with or go to an exercise class with, someone to share stuff with.

So I volunteered as a teacher's aide. I wanted to have meetings to attend, a purpose in life, a reason to get up in the morning. I loved being with the kids, especially preschoolers! After a year and a half as an unpaid volunteer, I was hired as a teacher's aide! I was very excited. It was only minimum wage, but I didn't care. I had purpose in my life again; however, the job lasted only six months.

I then got a job at a deli; that also turned out to be minimum wage with a boss I hated! That lasted six months. I tried another grocery store as a cashier. Hated that too! That also lasted six months. I finally decided if my husband and I could not survive on four pension checks, we deserved to starve! Unfortunately, the one who starved was me! I was starved for people to talk to and dollars to spend.

After almost five years of struggle...lethargy, depression, funks...I am getting the answers I've been seeking. I know God created us to use our minds to find solutions. I also know the answers to relief from the pain I was in were not to be found in drugs. Although prescription medicines are good in many ways for many people, that route is not the one I wanted for myself. I have tried four different prescriptions. One was too expensive, one gave me the energy of a whirling dervish, and the others did nothing. My goal has always been a return to my own personality, my own ambition level, my own energy level.

I want to live to be a hundred twenty and healthy! Healthy means having enough money to be worry-free (debt free), do charity work, and thoroughly enjoy life with enough spare income to go out to lunch with the Red Hat Ladies or an occasional movie.

Along the way, a wise friend, Richard, told me, "You Americans have it all wrong. It is body, mind, spirit. You start with diet. You need to start with your body." On a daily basis, he has always asked himself where is the balance today? What is the priority today? His life has never been consumed with money and wealth. All of that is fine, but he has always strived to be balanced...God, family, friends, work.

So my journey into body, mind and spirit has been a long one. Finally, I understand it is not a onetime event but an ongoing opportunity to meet each new challenge. I'm a slow study, but that's just who I am.

My crisis started when I collapsed at work one evening in November 2004. Rushed to a local emergency ward, I was given the initial diagnosis of heart attack. After two more hospitals, the final diagnosis was stress. Stress caused all my medical symptoms.

I began praying my way through the challenge, praying the Serenity Prayer many times:

God, grant me the serenity to accept the things I cannot change,
courage to change the things I can and
the wisdom to know the difference.
Grant me patience with the things that take time
An appreciation for all that I have
Tolerance for those with different struggles
And the strength to get up
and try again –
"One day at a time"*

Even though my husband and I have a loving marriage that has lasted over fifty years, we do not see eye-to-eye. I have him plus a wonderful son and daughter-in-law who love me unconditionally, super grandchildren, and a few good friends, but it wasn't enough. Unfortunately, part of my challenge has always been that there was never enough.

Involvement in Debtors Anonymous helps me even now although it has been years since I attended a weekly meeting or talked with friends. I attended long enough that the philosophy of the Twelve Steps is permanently imbedded in my brain! Plus my sponsor is only a phone call away.

Then an "a-ha" moment came, when I understood how I bury pain. I realized that the resentment comes from within me and radiates out. The solutions have started to come.

Mostly, my anger is related to money—or, more specifically, the lack thereof. But really it's not about the money. It's about balance. And having plans and goals for the future.

Another "a-ha" moment came after working to get my body in shape even though at times I experience pain—I'm seventy years old! Thank God!

When I am willing to work through the pain, God will appear. Softly. Calmly.

Someone said, "Working outside in the garden is relaxing." So one of the ways I can cope is to go outside and work in the yard. And when it is too much for me to handle, thank God for Antonio, our landscaper down the street!

All this wisdom is mine for the taking; even in the hard times—dreaming and planning are critical. Goal setting is huge! And having a dream!

Years ago a friend told me she managed on $25 a week when her husband was laid off. They had one child and she was a stay-at-home mom. If she could do it, I certainly can figure out where to get more money and how to economize in tough times!

Last year we got lucky. My husband and I are both gear-heads. We joined an association that pays us to show up and run. Now, we can run and afford repairs...even had enough cash to buy a used golf cart, repaint it, and add it to our toys!

Our drag race car is a 1953 Nash Rambler with a hemi motor. There are other forms of expression that are not as expensive as racing. The '50 chopped Merc that my husband built forty years ago is still a crowd pleaser and fun to drive around in.

I still don't have all the money I would love. I know from my head, heart, all the way down to my toes, that it will come. If only I hold onto Psalm 13, the 23rd Psalm, Bible study, the Serenity Prayer and the rosary. I'm learning to cultivate an attitude of gratitude and know that "When the student is ready, the teacher will appear." I am grateful for every drop of rain, the sunshine, a loving husband and family, a few good friends, and the chance to get up and try again one more time.

♥ ♥ ♥

Rosemary Crouthers is a 72 year old "modern woman." As a retired secretary, she now writes stories about drag racing, and Frick and Frac (her two male cats). Inspired by Jesus Christ, her faith and her mother (who lived a full life right up to the age of 91), she is planning to climb the mountain of Machu Picchu in Peru. Rosemary and her husband had two sons; the younger one died in a car accident when he was 19 years old and now resides at his new home in heaven. She is proud to have an amazing family and friends to share her life with.

Thank God
I Had a Dysfunctional Family

SHELDON RICE

"Would you look at your father's gray hair!! Without your aggravation he wouldn't be gray at all." How many times did Ma say that when I was growing up? "Shut the lights, we're not millionaires," Ma would shout at the top of her lungs. The endless guilt and incessant tension in our house were a way of life.

Every soul selects its family when it incarnates. My folks were loving, devoted, generous, and neurotic, making it hard to remain focused on their virtues. It took me decades to replace my resentment with understanding and my pain with gratitude. My frustration, guilt, sadness and self-pity became the catalysts to my present sweet appreciation.

Pa was a sincere, widely loved and well-respected family man. He focused all his energy in earning a living with little patience for my sister, Sally, and me. We would exchange ideas, but I felt depleted by his judgmental attitude. There was a right way and a wrong way, and Pa's opinion was always right. I was frustrated in my efforts to expand his narrow horizons to make him accept my unconventional points of view. The dependent attitude that this fostered led me to crave his attention and long for his acceptance. Despite the difficulties in our relationship, I did not doubt his abiding love. I doubt that I would have survived Ma's distorted domination without his even temperament and sincere desire that I have what he considered the best of everything. My appreciation of Pa's presence in my life fills my thoughts even decades after he passed away. It was his early death from lung cancer that spurred me to throw away my last cigarette and stop smoking after thirty-five years of addiction.

Ma was the youngest of ten children, a first cousin to Pa, and native of the same village in Byelorussia. Left fatherless at age two, she was spoiled by a domineering mother, who modeled for her a bossy and high-strung nature.

For all of Ma's paranoia—and there was plenty—the worst was her attitudes toward food and sex. Her greatest pleasure was to see me eat, with an emphasis on quantity. When I was about two or three, she allowed me to break dishes just so I would finish what she had prepared for me. How angry I must have been to find pleasure in broken crockery! Ma hand-fed me through the second grade and boasted of it in front of me to my teacher. I was so ashamed that I wanted to bury myself. I had to carefully weigh everything I said to her afterwards to avoid further betrayals. As I strove to subconsciously please her, I developed a lifelong habit of overeating.

Sexuality was the other topic of neurosis, the great taboo. Sexual organs were assigned oblique Yiddish euphemisms: penis was pee pee, vagina was nishee, and breasts were tsitsi. Sexuality was associated with dirt and shame. To add to the sexual distortions in my life, Ma never ceased touting her pride to family, friends, and strangers at satisfying my infant suckling needs. Imagine my embarrassment! I must admit that I had a lifelong fascination with breasts until relatively late in life, when I was able to develop a more balanced sexual view. Inevitably, sexual uncertainty was added to my food aberrations, creating a significant measure of discomfort in my romantic relationships.

The most important thing for Ma was to avoid making me cry. Sentiment and emotion were banned as I grew up suppressing my feelings. Ma couldn't let anything be—she was too fearful of losing control. Her way of asserting her inflated ego was by consistently raising her voice, something that drove me crazy. But in order to avoid conflict, I stifled my anger, and after a while I didn't know I had any.

Sadly, my parents spent their last years almost completely alone; she with her incessant television programs and he with a crossword puzzle or Hebrew magazine in another room. It hurt me to see how friends and relatives distanced themselves from Ma's alienating, domineering personality. After Pa died, she rarely made contact with old acquaintances. She spent her remaining years focused entirely on her children and grandchildren, mellowing somewhat with age.

I was a terror in grade school, longing for attention to relieve the strain I carried inside. No one could understand my outrageous behavior at the strict religious school I was sent to in order to instill Jewish values in me. All those years of religious training conflicted with our home life, which was totally non-religious. Of course this tactic backfired years later when I fell in love with a non-Jewish woman. The mere suggestion of wanting to marry her was the closest I ever came to losing Pa's love.

I wanted to distance myself from home for my college studies, but Pa wouldn't hear of spending the extra money. When I finally left home after finishing my bachelor's degree at a local college, I was free at last to find my own way in the world. Little did I appreciate the work I would need to overcome what I then perceived as the negative influences of my dysfunctional family.

My first growth opportunity developed with my best friend right after college. Joel revealed some stunning personal information to me, and then asked me some pointed questions about myself. I would typically change the subject in the face of personal confrontation, but the shock of his unexpected story unlocked something deep inside of me. He showed me how shutdown I was and unable to express my feelings, embarrassed and ashamed to reveal my unhappiness. I well remember the feeling of euphoria as my heart opened to him. For the first time in my life I unburdened myself, and I was elated. A ray of light penetrated deep into my soul as I recognized and released decades of emotion. Best of all, I was open to more change, but I would have to wait a long time to learn how to go about it.

I moved to Israel when I was twenty-eight, discovering a deep affinity for its people and history. During one of my parents' frequent visits they arranged a match between me and Dalia, a native Israeli. They were mesmerized by her extraordinary beauty and sharp wit. I was in a particularly vulnerable state as I had just been rejected in a love affair. I got swept up with my parents' enthusiasm for Dalia and their incessant nagging that I marry. Pushing my doubts aside, I convinced myself of the positive aspects of the match.

Dalia and I married on April Fool's Day of 1965 and remained together for twenty-five unhappy years with but few brief periods of light. I blamed my environment rather than looking inward to make the best of things, the same dysfunctional patterns I had played out with my parents. Despite our personal incompatibility, our marriage produced three wonderful daughters whom I adore. They are a special gift, and I have endless gratitude to Dalia for being a loving mother and grandmother.

In 1987, I faced the biggest crisis and opportunity of my lifetime. I was diagnosed with a tumor between my bladder and spine. I had been practicing a macrobiotic lifestyle for almost two years and had heard of "miraculous" cancer cures. Without hesitation I made the bold decision that I would heal myself with this method exclusively, eschewing all conventional medical treatment. I refused to be concerned about how many people had failed; I was interested only in how many had succeeded. Signing myself out of the hospital, I turned to Dalia and said, "Cancer is the best thing that has ever happened to me." I could almost taste the changes I knew it would force me to make. I had no doubt that I would recover; I couldn't fathom to what extent my illness would heal my life.

I visualized myself healthy and did not discuss my illness with anyone, including my mother, sister, children, coworkers, and associates, in order to avoid unbearable pressure and unwanted pity. I had an intuitive knowing that I was going to be OK because I was so damned stubborn that I couldn't imagine any other outcome. By the end of three years of fastidious practice, a CAT scan revealed that the growth had disappeared.

My illness brought me to admit for the first time in my life that I was vulnerable. My body exposed me as defenseless and needy, emotions I had denied for so long. I lost my arrogance and regained my self. After years of self-reflection, I understood my illness to be the result of the powerlessness and despair I had endured for so long during my unhappy childhood and marriage. With my recovery, my self-confidence soared, and I found the wherewithal to end my marriage. Shortly after Dalia and I separated, I met a wonderful woman named Aviv, the second catalyst in my life for deep personal transformation. She provided me the opportunity to let go of the pain of my marriage through probing, frank, and open conversation. Once again I was learning to let go. Adding to my joy was my youngest daughter's decision to live with me in my bachelor apartment. I was elated, feeling better and better about myself.

With deep self-reflection, I began to recognize that the happiness so long denied to me was a direct result of my previous difficulties. Remembering the anguish of my childhood, I was elated to discover that freedom was mine for the taking. It felt wonderful to feel my feelings rather than hide away behind my masks. I could finally share my life with others and let them develop their own expression. My failed marriage and difficult illness magnified my present happiness and health and showed me my own power. Losing my fear set me free.

It occurred to me then that my spiritual well-being had to be orchestrated by a higher being and was not the arbitrary result of good luck. I had been given so much by the very God I once rejected. Now I knew that God—Source energy—was the basis of my pain and the cause of my cure. The spiritual guidance that allowed me to derive such pleasure from the pain I experienced was the greatest gift of all.

In June of 1995 I met my present wife, Ginat, at a macrobiotic dinner in my home. Within ten days we were engaged, and our marriage has flourished into a loving, co-creative experience. Together we provide macrobiotic services to a worldwide community, welcome guests to our home, and enjoy both family and friends. I look back to my parents with great love and gratitude. I see how my unhappy childhood served as a basis for the joy that I worked so hard to acquire. Only through the resistance I developed towards them could I grow into the spiritual person I am. The extent of their dysfunction forced me to heal my life. It's because of them I have found the depth of joy that I savor today.

♥ ♥ ♥

Born and raised in Brooklyn, NY in an assimilated middle-class Jewish family, Sheldon recognized a strong attraction to Israel in his late twenties and immigrated to that country. He specialized in highway traffic planning during a professional career spanning over forty years in both the United States and Israel. After his retirement in 2000, he and his wife, Ginat, traveled for three years throughout North America in a motorhome.

An intense interest in spiritual writings on subjects of past lives, reincarnation, and near death experiences developed from a dedicated study of numerology. With his experience in discerning personality characteristics and his own practice of the universal Law of Attraction, Sheldon is now a personal life coach, guiding people to health and happiness.

Sheldon and Ginat live in Jerusalem, where they have a center for macrobiotic studies, numerology, shiatsu, nine star ki, palmistry, and life coaching services. Please visit their website www.TheRiceHouse.com for a detailed description of their personal and professional lives.

Thank God...
for Birth and Rebirth

STACEY GLAESMANN, LPC

There's a certain kind of twisted freedom that comes with wanting to die. I got to the point where I didn't care about anything or anyone anymore. Not my job, not my husband or home...not even my newborn baby daughter. From the moment I had given birth to her, I didn't feel "right." They didn't understand why I couldn't "snap out of it" or just "think positively." They didn't realize that I was in a pit so deep that I couldn't see the sun. Every molecule in my body that was capable of producing a positive anything was dead.

It must not have made sense to those outside my brain. I had everything I had ever wanted: a wonderful husband, a beautiful home, a good job, and a sweet baby girl. But the world was gray, and it was as if I had not felt pleasure in my twenty-seven years on Earth. I was constantly on high alert, as if every moment were a breath away from tragedy.

A sea of anxiety threatened to engulf me on a regular basis. It was as though I desperately needed to be somewhere else, yet was powerless to move. Every fiber in my body was vibrating, unable to be still, yet I was paralyzed. I couldn't eat. I couldn't sleep. I couldn't love. My husband and parents knew something was wrong. My eyes pleaded for them to take care of the baby. I just didn't have it in me. I wished I felt something for her – anything. But I didn't. I couldn't. That was when dying seemed tempting...perhaps I could succeed at that.

"How could this be?" I would ask myself all the time. This should be the happiest time in my life! So it became a character flaw—something I had brought on myself and was obviously too ineffective to change. I felt sorry for my family that they had to live with such an impotent wife and mother.

The first time I thought about abandoning my baby was in a grocery store. It was my latest attempt to look "normal" to the outside world. But as I stood looking past the produce, I was lost in a fantasy of turning around and walking out by myself. I would leave her in the car seat in the shopping basket. Surely someone worthy of such a beautiful child would find her and take her in. Maybe this serene goddess would take my place as the lady of the house and my family.

The mornings were the worst. I'd been riding waves of anxiety all night, ever vigilant of fictional bogeymen. The dawn would be proof of yet another one of my shortcomings: the failure to sleep. While the rest of the world was rising from slumber and getting ready for another day of normalcy, I was staring at the ceiling, listening to my rapid heartbeat and wiping the sweat from my forehead, praying that the baby would stay asleep so that I wouldn't have something else to feel inadequate about.

Sometimes, when my husband would leave for the day, I would curl up in the foyer and cry at the closed door. I was desperately sending telepathic messages, telling him how horrible I felt and how much I needed him to come home. Yet I couldn't bring myself to speak those words to him or to anyone else. That would be the absolute proof of my failure as a human being.

Then my daughter would wake up, and so began another day in "paradise."

Somehow, I met her basic needs—food, dry clothing, a soft place to sleep. She spent most of her first two months in various seats, swings, and other contraptions that must have felt warmer than my cold flesh. Though I didn't move off the sofa much, holding her was too burdensome, and I was afraid that she'd "catch" my anxiety.

I tried to find respite in prayer, though I slowly began to doubt there was a God as day after day turned into week after week of the worst time in my life. I got angry with Him, challenging Him to strike me down, and feeling disappointed when again my prayers went unanswered. Eventually I stopped asking for anything. I started to believe that I was paying now for every sin I had ever committed. Again, my failure as a human being was confirmed—this time by the Highest Authority.

I'd watch the clock as if it had the power to give me the relief I wanted so badly. The one thing I did look forward to was the moment my husband would come home. I then could leave the baby-tending duties to him and have an unrestrained cry in the shower. Even as I stood in wished-for solitude with the warm water washing over me, I would still hear the baby's cries as if they were coming from inside my head.

The setting sun would signal the next phase of my endless vigilance. Sometimes, we'd get the baby to sleep by 8pm and we'd fall into bed, hoping to catch some sleep before her next feeding. After a few minutes, my husband's breathing would deepen, and I'd just want to scream.

We'd agreed to take turns with the feeding and diapering at night. But even if it wasn't my "shift," I'd be wide awake, listening and mentally picturing what he was doing: warming up the bottle, changing the diaper, burping her, rocking her, laying her back down. At times, my body would relax enough for me to drift into twilight. But every sniffle, yawn, or squeak from my baby would have me on high alert again in an instant.

I resented the fact that my husband could sleep so easily. I was also jealous that he got to go to work every day. He still had his "normal" life while mine was falling to pieces around me. How I longed to go to work, where I actually knew what I was doing, where everything fit in a nice, neat box. There were no squalling infants there. I knew who I was at the office.

Every once in a while, someone would come by to see me. I resented the intrusion because of the effort it took for me to "put on the face" of blissful motherhood. When tears would start to fall, I would chalk it up to joy instead of misery. My visitor would leave, satisfied that I was indeed a fit mother who could handle it all.

One Tuesday, "the face" just wouldn't fit. I had spent the previous night contemplating how I could escape the miserable life I was leading. The easiest solution seemed to be overdosing on sleeping pills. The only thing I was worried about was that the baby might be alone for a few hours before anyone discovered me. I pictured her, all alone and helpless, crying for her bottle. That image grew stronger and clearer in my mind as my husband went about getting ready for his day that morning.

As he was about to leave, I found my voice.

Please don't go.

That is all it took! Three words had been standing in between my misery and my salvation. The shame melted away from me as I admitted how I was feeling to him, to my parents, to anyone who would listen. The world that I had been holding up over my head was suddenly spinning on its own again. I didn't have to do this alone anymore. In fact, I realized that I had not had to do it alone in the first place.

My recovery progressed quickly as I visited my psychiatrist and therapist. Talking it out, I realized I had been at great risk for postpartum mood problems due to my own personal and family history. It wasn't my fault, and that was the most shocking realization of all. So, who was I supposed to blame? My doctors, for not telling me that this could happen? My baby, for being born in the first place? Or perhaps God, for letting this happen at all? I still wasn't talking to Him, and this seemed a good reason to keep my stoic silence.

Three months later, I was back to work part-time. On the days I worked, I wanted to be home. On the days I was at home, I wanted to be at work. I felt like my life was a continuous stream of dissatisfaction. The depression and anxiety had lifted, allowing me some clarity for the first time in months. What I saw was that I was lacking a real purpose. I worked for the betterment of my boss, but I felt like I was meant for something more.

On one of my days off, I decided to take my daughter to the park to enjoy the early autumn weather. As she sat loading and unloading her diaper bag, I stared up at the clear blue sky and asked God, "What am I supposed to do?" I wasn't really expecting an answer, but I figured that asking for guidance was a good way to break the ice with the Big Guy.

In what seemed like a split second, my mind was filled with images of me sitting across from various women whom I didn't know in an office I had never seen. I was helping them—counseling them—the way my therapist had counseled me. I instantly had the information about where I should go to get the education I needed and somehow knew from the very basement of my soul that this was what I was supposed to do.

Despite severe time limitations, quick deadlines, and botched program interviews, I was one of twenty people selected from all over the country to attend the Clinical Psychology program at the university that I had applied to. I was able to complete the program in two years and had a job waiting for me the week after graduation. I earned the necessary supervised hours for my license in another two years and was soon looking at going out on my own, making my vision in the park a reality.

As I sat across from my first client, who was going through postpartum depression, I saw myself in her eyes. I finished her sentences and completed her thoughts. I assured her that she was not alone and it wasn't her fault. She gave me a grateful look, and in that moment I realized why God had "cursed" me the way He had. I finally understood that the depression had been a gift, not a curse, for without it, I would not have been able to fulfill what I know now is my life purpose: to give hope and encouragement to those with none. Nothing can compare to the experience.

As I hugged her at the end of our time together, I closed my eyes and thought, "Thank you, God, for the darkest nights of my life. For without them, I could not relate so well to this woman. Thank you for the perspective my depression gave me so that I can pass hope to her now."

That one client turned into many, and those experiences gave me material for a book. Thank God I was depressed. I discovered the counselor, author, and speaker who was inside me the whole time. I now touch lives...and for that, I will be forever grateful.

♥ ♥ ♥

Stacey Glaesmann is a licensed professional counselor in the state of Texas. She has just published her first book, titled What About Me? A Simple Guide to Self-Care in the 21st Century. She is also an adjunct professor of psychology at San Jacinto College. Her greatest joy is her family—her husband of sixteen years, Shane, and her daughter, Alexa.

Thank God for Twenty-Nine Months

STEVEN ROBERTS

When the doctor says you have only another twenty-nine months to live, it jars your day.

There are over 1 million Americans diagnosed with cancer each year, and three times in the past twenty years I have been one of them. So far I've beaten the odds and my message is, if I can do it so can you. I thank the Lord every morning I've been able to wake up and share my message of hope and faith.

In the summer of 1990, I noticed a pain in my upper right abdomen, just under the rib cage. I was also experiencing significant night sweating and having trouble sleeping. After several weeks of testing, Dr. Kaye walked into the treatment room where my wife, Jane, and I were waiting for the latest results.

"Good morning," he said. "How are you feeling? How much sleep are you getting?"

"Well, I still have the symptoms we've been talking about," I said, "possibly worse than when we started the tests. Sleeping is still in one- and two-hour installments."

"Mr. Roberts," he said in a suddenly more serious tone, "the Tumor Board has reviewed the biopsy and the test results. I'm sorry to say, you have cancer." He paused. "Your cancer is called Non-Hodgkins Lymphoma, and there are several options to fight it. We'll need to discuss possible treatment options and other consequences. Why don't you two take a minute while I check on another patient?"

Over the years I have noticed that doctors always deliver the news about cancer, or a recurrence, and then leave the room for a few minutes to let us absorb the shock. This process must be taught in a doctors' seminar somewhere.

First Fight – In 1990, Camelot was interrupted by the doctor's announcement that I was "It." I had cancer. It was slow moving but present in the form of a significant tumor in my abdomen and smaller tumors in my lymph nodes. Jane and I looked up and read all the information we could find on this uninvited guest in our lives. After several discussions and additional tests, my oncologist recommended a protocol of chemo treatments every twenty-one days for eight months. We were convinced we had the right medical advice and the right medical team, so we agreed to proceed. Jane added her husband's name to the list of people she prayed for each week at church.

"Am I going to lose my hair?" I asked, knowing the answer. The doctor assured me that I would. "Is there any treatment protocol that will save my life but leave my hair on my head?"

"I'm afraid not," the doctor said. "Several studies are working on less ablative treatments that will not affect the patients so severely, but they are not ready yet. You may want to buy a hat this winter."

My seemingly vain concern was actually an attempt to delay telling anyone other than my wife that I had cancer. After the treatments began, I was faced with announcing my illness to our four kids, my parents and extended family, as well as my employer. Each of these meetings had to be thought out ahead of time and handled with great care. Would I appear to be flawed, weak, less of a leader in my family and at work, less dependable, no longer promotable? These are, of course, silly concerns under the circumstances, but these thoughts went through my mind as I planned to announce my illness. How could I remain relevant to those I loved and those I worked with, if it appeared that I wouldn't be around in the near future?

I survived the eight-month chemo regimen with the average amount of sickness and other effects of the chemo. My body tolerated the treatments well, and I was able to work most days and eventually returned to work full time. I considered myself very fortunate as I rejoined the average pool-of-mankind. One of my supposed friends at work, however, said I looked like an eighty-year-old version of myself. I tried to get him transferred.

Second Fight – Eighteen months later the cancer devil was back. We repeated the chemo treatments, but this time my blood cells did not respond appropriately, and the process didn't work. With my health heading downhill and my cancer unabated, I went to the university medical center in a nearby town. My new doctor entered the treatment room and repeated the initial diagnosis, but with some important added bits of news.

"Mr. Roberts," Dr. Paul said, "I've met with the Tumor Board, and they have recommended that you consider a bone marrow transplant (BMT). If we can get the protocol approved by your insurance company, the transplant could be performed using your own bone marrow. You should know, however, that the procedure is somewhat experimental and therefore dangerous. On a national basis, an average of 10% of patients die during the process, and another 5% die during the 100-day recovery cycle."

Dr. Paul was a straight talker. He added, "I'm not sure if you've been told, but the average life expectancy for your type of cancer, considering when you were first diagnosed, is twenty-nine months." Then he left the room. Jane and I were too stunned to speak. We just looked at each other, blinked back the tears, and sat holding hands. This was the first time we were facing the real possibility that I might not make it. As we drove home that day, I thought that I probably had enough pairs of shoes to last me until I didn't need shoes anymore.

Since I was out of options and my strength and health were in decline, we agreed to go for the BMT. After harvesting my stem cells from my blood, and marrow from my hip, the transplant was set for the first week in May 1994.

The protocol called for heavy doses of chemo for the first two days, followed by the infusion of the transplanted stem cells and bone marrow. The chemo had destroyed my blood cells, white, red, and otherwise.

I had no protection against viruses, especially those from my own body. After the transplant, I lay in the positively charged hospital room, waiting for a sign that the transplant was working. Days and then weeks crept by while we hoped a virus wouldn't find me. The signal would be that new blood cells would start being produced by the transplant (or donation). Each morning the blood test showed zero cells until the eleventh day, when the transplant team reported that I had "nil" white cells. I was assured that "nil" was better than "zero."

For twenty-six days I waited in that room for new blood cells to appear and grow in number. I eventually built up blood cells and strength enough to walk with my two IV poles to a small courtyard. One day I met a nine-year old girl who was also fighting cancer. A volunteer in the children's ward had painted flowers on her head. She smiled about the flowers, but she was despondent over her prospects for recovery and a chance at a normal life. Later I wrote a song about her called "Mr. Will We Make Spring?" I'm not sure she did make it to spring, but I thought about how terrible it was for a nine-year old to go through the chemo fire and wonder about surviving cancer. It made me grateful for the life I'd had. I promised God I would do better, be a better person if I should happen to survive.

Over the course of the next hundred days, I survived an attack of the "graft vs. host" disease, a strange form of blood disorder, and later a blood transfusion from a paid donor (who was subsequently proven to be HIV positive). In any event my CAT scans and other tests showed I was cancer-free.

Third Fight - Then two months after my five-year checkup the devil was back. The previous transplant could not be repeated as my marrow was infected this time around. My best and possibly only chance was a BMT using a donor's marrow, if one with a perfect match to my blood could be found. This protocol was also experimental and dangerous, so the insurance battle had to be fought and won before we could proceed.

We fought along with our doctors and prayed. Finally the insurance company approved the experimental procedure.

The National Blood Bank gave us a 15% chance

of getting a complete match, but there was a one-in-four chance of a match with a sibling. After the longest two weeks we had ever spent, the hospital called to say that my brother Terry's blood antigens were a perfect match. This was incredible. It was clear, God was watching over me.

The BMT was scheduled in May of 1999. The chemo was milder, but for the third time I was going to be bald. The biggest change this time around was that, with the milder chemo dose, there was less vomiting and loss of strength. With a donor's marrow, however, there was a heightened danger from "graft vs. host" disease. I needed to catch it to verify the transplant but immediately put it down before it killed me. An even greater concern was getting the new cells manufactured by the donor's marrow to show up to prove that the transplant was a success.

New blood cells from the donor's cells are supposed to show up in the patient's blood tests around the sixtieth day. We waited through the seventieth then eightieth day and finally cells manufactured by Terry's marrow started showing up. We had planned to inject additional transplant cells the next day. This would have most likely been fatal.

I am now in the tenth year since the second BMT, and I am grateful to my village of supporters—my doctors, nurses and other dedicated caregivers, and especially to Jane for her total focus on my survival. Thank God for guiding all of us on this journey. During the darkest days in the bubble-like hospital room, I did what a lot of people do when facing death: I promised to do better if I survived. One sleepless night in 1994 I wrote this poem:

Five Do-Overs

When we're in big trouble most of us say
If I get out of this alive here's the dues I'll pay
And we make a list of promises we'd do
We'll turn a new leaf, in all things be true

Some would play more and work less
Some played too much they confess
Others promise to love to the end
Or somehow be a better friend

Some want to be in the movies and on TV
Or travel foreign lands and seas
Write a book, fly a plane, sing songs
Just a chance to right all our wrongs

But when I make my do-over list
Five things I'd do, I swear my eyes turn to mist
Remembering who's been always true
And the five do-overs are all about you

I feel the same sense of gratefulness about this poem sixteen years after it was written as I did that night of medically induced reflection. It's about giving myself to others I guess in part to justify why I have so far survived when so many have not. I have attempted to capture this thought in a book I wrote in 2005 called Twenty-Nine Months. (See www.steverroberts.com)

My survival beyond twenty-nine months has meant I have been able to see our four children get educated, married, and employed, and present us with eleven grandchildren. I hold dear every minute. I tell cancer patients to be grateful for what they have and pray for God's guiding hand. The disease is no longer a death sentence. If I can make it, you can too.

♥ ♥ ♥

Steve is a twenty-year survivor of cancer, and this experience has been part of the inspiration for the five books and many poems he has written. Steve's speaking engagements include the subjects of cancer survivorship, writing, and business start-ups. He chairs the board of the Dearborn Library Foundation, works for Habitat for Humanity and SCORE (small business consultants). Steve worked in the auto industry in Europe and Detroit for thirty years, and he and his wife, Jane, live in Dearborn, Michigan, where they chase after eleven grandchildren.

Thank God My Stepfather Died and My Husband Left in the Same Month

WENDI SHANER

I remember getting that dreaded phone call from my mother in February of 2007. "The doctors have diagnosed your stepdad with Stage 4 Lung Cancer, and they are giving him only three to six months to live." That phone call was the most devastating news I've ever received in my entire life. I was shocked and completely mortified. I thought, "Here is a man who was so full of life and vitality, suddenly sentenced to death. How on earth could this be? This is impossible."

Six months before I got that phone call, my marriage was starting to go downhill. I had quit my job to work with my husband, and my mentally challenged brother moved in with us because he was not able to take care of himself. Our financial situation started taking a turn for the worse, and with three grown adults living in a two-bedroom house, it became increasingly stressful. What once had been a happy marriage was quickly becoming destructive. We started fighting about everything: money, my brother, the dogs, our families, the business, our sex life, our backgrounds, or the way the house should be run. There was constant resentment, blaming, arguing, yelling, slamming of doors, throwing things, screaming, and crying. We couldn't get along with each other no matter how hard we tried. I was totally frustrated and couldn't understand why my life was taking a turn for the worse, whereas before, everything had been fine. I really thought God was punishing me during this time.

I started to feel like my personal life was just too much to bear. My self-esteem had dipped to an all-time low. I was forty pounds overweight, extremely depressed, and had stopped caring about my appearance. There were days I didn't want to take a shower, much less get out of bed. I had become a recluse. I didn't want to work. I didn't want to see any of my friends, talk on the phone much, or leave the house at all, except to run my necessary errands. At times, I even contemplated suicide, or leaving everything behind and living in a cave by myself, but I held on to the fact that a very small part of me knew in my spirit that I was going to inspire the world somehow. I delved into reading personal development books, grasping onto any sign of hope that I could. Those books were the only thing that kept me going.

I tried to remain as positive about my marriage and about my stepdad as best as I could, but I was really struggling. I longed to be with my family. I was living in Georgia while my parents were living in Las Vegas. The distance absolutely broke my heart, and I wanted so badly to be close to them. I knew I had a life on the other side of the country; a life that was in complete and utter shambles. My heart hurt every single day that we were apart, and every day of my marriage.

In August of 2008, Mom called to tell me that my stepdad's cancer was getting worse, that the doctors weren't giving him much longer to live. She needed me to come and stay with him because he was no longer able to be by himself. So in September, I jumped at the opportunity to go to Vegas to take care of him for a month. What I had longed for, for over a year, suddenly became available to me. I was stoked about getting to be with my family, even though I knew that my stepdad's time here on earth was becoming increasingly shorter.

In that month's time, I really got to know my stepdad. I listened to his life stories. He shared with me his dreams, his hopes, his desires, and his fears. I got to see how determined he was to live life fully even though he wasn't able to walk or take care of himself anymore. His favorite thing in the world to do, before he got sick, had been to drive. He knew that he was going to get better so he could drive. I believe this was one of the reasons why he lived longer than the doctors had expected.

I also got to see how much he and my mother really loved each other, and what an unconditional loving marriage was all about. This was something that I wasn't experiencing personally, and that I longed for so badly. My mom and stepdad had the kind of loving, deeply committed, affectionate marriage that they only show in Hollywood. Their marriage was what I had hoped to have with my husband, and it seemed that no matter how much I wanted that for us, it just wasn't working at all.

Every time my husband and I would talk on the phone while I was in Vegas, we would fight, sometimes for hours on end. Sometimes we wouldn't speak to one another for days. Not only was I stressed out about my marriage, but I was also stressed out about my stepdaddy and what he was going through. He was so sick, and I was such a wreck. I knew that I had to put my emotions aside and take care of my daddy because I really didn't know how much longer he was going to be with us.

Two months after returning home from Vegas, on December 7th, exactly one month after my stepdad turned sixty-six, I got the phone call that he had died. I knew that his suffering was over, but my heart died right along with him. I was distraught because Red (my stepdad) had impacted my life in such a huge way. He loved me unlike any other father figure ever had before. That month I was in Vegas, I could see why my mom fell in love with him. He was such an awesome guy. His spirit lit up an entire room. He was so funny. He was such a great storyteller. He loved everyone, had a ton of friends, and thought of everyone as his family. The moment you met Red, you couldn't help but like him. His smile was so infectious, and he wanted to immediately hug you. You couldn't help but feel loved. He had that effect on everyone he encountered.

After getting back from the funeral and onto life again, my husband and I went to seek counseling, and were finally starting to work together as a team. It started to feel like we were going to make it, but instead, on December 30th, he told me that he was no longer attracted to me and wanted to be separated because he was attracted to someone else. I felt betrayed, hurt, and completely rejected. I was also extremely angry and told him to pack his stuff and move out.

The first week he was gone, I talked with a friend about what was happening in my life. In the midst of my feeling sorry for myself, he finally had the guts to ask me, "Wendi, do you like being a victim?" I thought, "Man, who does this guy think he is? Doesn't he realize what I just went through and how hard my life is right now?" Then he bluntly told me that the only way I was going to heal was to find gratitude for this situation.

I shrugged off his advice for about a week, until one day I got tired of journaling about being angry and hating my husband, and asked myself, "How can I be grateful for this situation?" Within about five minutes, the word that came to the front of my mind was freedom! I had the biggest epiphany of my life in that moment, and realized that I was set free from a hellish prison. I was free! Free to smile. Free to laugh. Free to sing in the house at the top of my lungs. Free to live life on my terms. And above all else, free to be myself.

I was relishing my newfound freedom! I stopped and asked myself how I could be grateful for my stepdad dying. That wasn't a very easy concept for me to grab onto because I was still grieving his loss. But a few minutes later the word living came to my mind! Yes, living! In the midst of my stepdad fighting for his life, I knew then that I had been given the biggest gift of all, and that was life. That's when I decided that I was going to start living my life again, and live while I was still alive. Suddenly, the cloud of depression and despair was lifted from me, and I was able to laugh and smile again.

To be quite honest with you, I'm very, very grateful that my stepdad died and my husband left in the same month. I feel like I've been given a second chance at life, and I've learned so many wonderful new things. I've learned to cherish my loved ones more. I've learned to grab every opportunity that comes my way. I've learned to not take anyone or anything for granted. I've learned to accept people right where they are and look at their hearts rather than look at their outside circumstances. I've learned how to enjoy life and see the beauty in everything. I've learned to be a kid again, and that it's okay for me to be who I am. If I'm not able to be myself, then I am really doing the world a disservice. I've learned that I have an amazing sense of humor.

I've learned that I'm not a victim in life anymore, but rather a victorious person who's gone through some major things and who now can have compassion for everyone, because I've been there.

My husband and I have decided to get a divorce, and we remain on cordial terms. I really feel like he did me a huge favor. I Thank my friend for being so honest with me about having gratitude for what I went through, I realized just how powerful gratitude really is. Gratitude has absolutely changed my life forever.

❤ ❤ ❤

Wendi Shaner and her husband have divorced since writing her story. They are now friends and chat quite often. Wendi is now attending The University of Metaphysics to obtain a doctorate degree in Spiritual Healing. Wendi has also discovered that she now has a gift in doing energy work with people, doing emotional healing energy work as well as doing energy work in people's homes. She has also started a divinely inspired blog titled, "Moments With the Divine" at www.wendishaner.blogspot.com. If you would like to see Wendi's website, you can do so by going to www.wendishaner.com.

THANK GOD I'M GAY

JASON MANNINO

"And the winner is....Harvey Fierstein!" Harvey doesn't know it, but those words uttered at the Tony Awards on a June evening in 1983 had a dramatic influence on my life as a gay man. My grandmother, Anita Wapnish, is very close friends with his mother Jackie Fierstein, and has been for a very long time. When Harvey was winning his first Tony Awards for Torch Song Trilogy I vividly remember my grandmother calling my mom and telling her to hurry and turn on one of the morning news programs, because Harvey was on. My mom, elated, ran to the television and watched . Though she'd only babysat Harvey when he was young, I believe she was having a very surreal moment seeing someone she knew achieve great fame and success. It sure left a lasting impact on me, an impressionable 11-year-old. Harvey in his boldness and courage has blazed numerous trails in the theater and in the gay community. Harvey's confidence and conviction paved the way for others to "come out," including me. Thanks, Harvey!

Fast-forward four years. That impressionable 11-year-old has become a teenager realizing his own enthusiasm acting in plays and musicals and achieving adolescent success as a chorus boy (I placed competitively in All State Choir throughout high school). Acting and singing was my lifeline. By this time my interest in dating girls had waned to almost nothing. My mom had noticed too. I was one of those quirky adolescents not fully aware of my sexuality. I espoused constantly that I wouldn't be getting married because I wanted solely to commit myself to my acting career. (As if that wouldn't have clued her in!)

My mother was raised in Brooklyn, New York and had gay friends growing up. I also remember her saying that when she babysat Harvey that she knew immediately he was gay. What stuck with me was that she never said anything negative about gay people and never came off as judgmental. Still, it took me a while to come out to her. One night I remember standing in the kitchen of our one level, L-shaped rancher in South Jersey. I was in front of the dishwasher; my mother was rinsing dishes. I don't know what elicited the conversation, but from out of nowhere she asked, "Jason, are you gay?" I froze and the room started spinning. "No!" I snapped, hoping to end the conversation. Mom didn't press, but she let me know that it would be ok either way. I was grateful, and scared.

The idea of owning my sexuality at that time was overwhelming. What came easy, however, was embracing my uniqueness. I was a bit of a character in my adolescence—some would say that I still am—and being in theater supported me in owning that. I was the kid who wore a shoe from one pair on my left foot and a shoe from another pair on my right foot, just for the hell of it. I was the one who wrote an article in the school paper on why people should be allowed to burn the American flag (mind you, I would make a different choice today, simply out of basic respect). The thugs in my high school sent "I'm going to beat you up!" threats for that. I was the guy who told the truth when I wrote reviews for school plays and who got frustrated when it seemed like the other kids weren't as dedicated as I was. The lead character Alban in the Harvey Fierstein penned musical (which I listened to over and over again when I was in high school) La Cage Aux Folles announces to the world in the gay anthem:

"I am what I am:"
I am what I am
I am my own special creation...
It's my world that I want to take a little pride in,
My world, and it's not a place I have to hide in.
Life's not worth a damn,
'Til you can say, "Hey world, I am what I am."

I too knew I was different, and whether I owned my sexuality inwardly or outwardly, my ability to say, "I am who I am. Love it or move on!" was an outward expression of that experience. I believe it was a direct result of my sexuality, albeit, an unconscious one at the time.

It was in high school that I finally admitted my sexuality, both to the outside world and to myself. I still have the journal I kept, in which I wrote, "Now that I am a senior in high school, I will come out to everyone I feel it is important to come out to before I go off to college." Interestingly enough, this was before I had ever had a sexual encounter with a man. This illustrates to me that my gay identity is not just a sexual identity. It is sourced from a deeper level of consciousness. I made this journal entry in 1989, when not many 17-year-olds were coming out of the closet. It took a lot of courage and guts to get beyond my fear and follow through on my declaration. It turned out to be much easier than I anticipated.

Within a month following this declaration I was spending time with my mother watching a talk show that had some gay guests on the panel. Once again, my mother asked me, "Jason, are you gay?" This time I was ready. I said, "Yes, mom, I am." Then she said, "That's okay. I love you." Later that day I went to the super market to pick up some groceries. I bought some flowers and brought them home to my mother in celebration of the freedom and love that comes from authentic expression. Within two months after my coming out my twin brother shocked the family when he came out of the closet as well. We had no idea. As a matter of fact I thought he would take me being gay harder than my straight brother. Nonetheless, unconditional love was always present, and it is a great gift to have a gay twin. I have often wondered, What would my life be like if I had to be someone other than who I really am in order to be loved and accepted? I am grateful that I have never had to answer that question. I am also proud that I had the courage to come out at such a young age. I realize my graceful coming out experience is not common for everyone, and I am blessed in that for me coming out to my mother was a celebration. I am grateful for the blessing of unconditional love I received from her. My profoundly, loving mother died when she was 61. I was only 31 at the time. The gratitude I have for her and her gift of unconditional love is sourced in the depths of my being. Also, I am relieved in that she died always knowing me in my authentic expression.

Serendipitously, in June of that same year I was with my grandmother who was visiting from Florida for my high school graduation. We were watching a talk show with gay guests (I swear!). My grandmother suddenly blurted out, "I wouldn't necessarily like it if one of my grandsons was gay, but I certainly wouldn't love them any less!" In shock, I immediately ran into my mother's bedroom in the opposite corner of the house and called her. I shouted, "Mom, you're not going to believe what grandma just said!" However, my mother was not ready for me to come out to her, and I honored that. I came out to her four years later after returning from a trip to San Francisco where my then boyfriend was living. I explained to her that I had gone there to visit Steve (whom she had previously met) and that he was not just a friend. Her response was simply, "I know." I couldn't help but think, Damn! That was easy! I also learned that until people stop assuming that everyone is straight, "coming out" is something that I will be doing for the rest of my life.

In college I was empowered to start giving back to my gay brothers and sisters through community and campus service projects. As president of the Rutgers University Gay and Lesbian Peer Counseling Line, I supported others who had a harder time accepting their sexuality. I was also trained to teach sexual health and work towards the eradication of homophobia, giving seminars and workshop across campus as a Rutgers University Sexual Health Advocate. Through this work I began to understand true empathy and compassion for others, and discovered my enthusiasm for facilitating others in their process of self-discovery.

Though there are plenty of heterosexual people who are self-actualized, I believe my call towards self love and acceptance might have gone unheeded if I were straight. As a gay man I could have easily given society the power to beat me down and relegate me to a life of self-loathing. However, it is that very possibility that empowers me to choose to love honestly and serve others. I believe a direct result of marginalization is the choice I have made to look inward and heal patterns of my own judgment and fear of those who choose to hate. My experience as a gay man in this society has generated in me a depth of compassion and empathy. This facilitates my understanding that people who choose to hate in the name of "their" God are simply immersed in a human experience that is built on irrationality, fear, hatred and ego, but for them, truthful, nonetheless. As a divine being having a gay experience I choose to remember that those who choose to attack are attacking an illusion they have crafted in their own minds. Even those who have died in the name of self love and expression have not truly died, because love that has known itself as long has man has existed cannot be destroyed. I cannot say when, but I have faith that one day those who attack in the name of "their" god will discover that they only attack themselves.

I am a proud gay man. I celebrate my call from spirit to live and love openly, and honestly. I celebrate the blessings of unconditional love I have received and still receive as a gay man. I celebrate the vulnerability present in loving another man. I celebrate the lives I have touched and the differences I have made for those who have told me, "I have never met a gay man before." I celebrate those whose bodies have been taken by the hands of hatred and disease. I celebrate my gay consciousness and my call to spiritual leadership that will help heal the illusions of hate and fear. I celebrate those who have blazed gay trails before me: Harvey Fierstein, Walt Whitman, Harry Hay, Harvey Milk, Oscar Wilde, Alexander the Great, Tennessee Williams, and so many more. I celebrate the contributions gay men have made to culture, art, theater, music, community service, healing, literature, love, and pushing the boundaries of the mind. I celebrate that my continued journey into self-awareness has kept me honest. I celebrate, and I thank God I am gay!

♥ ♥ ♥

Jason Mannino is a nationally recognized Conscious Career Coach, Life Coach, Speaker and Writer. He combines a decade of corporate and executive recruiting experience with an extensive background in personal transformation to empower you to uncover and embrace your life's true purpose and gifts and integrate them with the work you do in the world, leading to greater fulfillment, contribution, and prosperity. Jason helps you combine your career with contribution, money with meaning, success with satisfaction, love with leadership. Jason is a regular contributor to Huffington Post (www.huffingtonpost.com) and his writing has been seen on line at Wall Street Journal, New York Times, USA Today and more. He holds his MA in Spiritual Psychology from University of Santa Monica, BA in Psychology from Rutgers University. Learn more at www.jmannino.com

Thank God for my Chronic Pain

DR. MICHAEL ANGELOTTO

People have feared and loathed pain since the dawn of time. I on the other hand thank god for my pain.

Before you write me off as a lunatic, take a moment to read my story, it might help you thank God for your pain one day.

As a youngster going through school I was very active and athletic. I was diagnosed with Scoliosis when I was in eight grade. Scoliosis is an abnormal curve of the spinal column. If left untreated it can cause difficulty breathing, organ compromise and eventually sever arthritis of the spine.

My mother was told to bring me to a surgeon and that they could put steel rods into my spinal column. The rods would stop the development of the Scoliosis. They would be there for life and of course be a source of pain themselves.

They would limit my activity and prevent me from doing most of the activities that I like to do. There was also the possibility that I would die during the surgery.

As time progressed I began to experience pain but of course I chose to ignore it.

This did not at all help my condition. My mother decided to take me to a Chiropractor who would treat me, someone who would use a natural approach.

Little did I know that my pain would introduce me to my future career. If you would have told me that I would become a Chiropractor, I would have thought that you were smoking something. I had no interest in the healthcare profession, but this would soon change.

I began a series of treatments from the Chiopractor which included adjustments.

The adjustments were controlled gentle force applied to my spine to correct the Scoliosis. It is a natural healing art which involves no drugs, is safe, and alleviates the pain. A doctor of Chiropractic has been trained very much like a medical doctor in that they learn anatomy, physiology, neurology histology, etc..

However, Chiropractors also receive training in spinal bio mechanics. The Chiropractor corrected my Scoliosis and my pain disappeared. I was so glad to avoid future health problems and it helped me realize at a young age how important my treatments were in order to avoid surgery. Many people live their entire life without taking care of their health. After all, why not buy a big screen TV instead of spending money on your health. This was one of the most important lessons of my life.

When I enrolled at college, I began to study accounting but quickly realized that this was not for me. The only problem was I did not know what else to do.

In my second year of college I was in a bad automobile accident and got to say "hello" to my old friend pain again. At this time, I was into weight lifting and running. I was not interested in renewing old acquaintances with my old buddy pain. I wanted to kick pain to the curb so I could regain my life. I knew pain killers were not the answer. They would mask the pain and had side effects like bleeding ulcers, liver damage, hearing loss and that's just the over the counter stuff!

Think of all the people who are hooked on pain killers.

I went back to my Chiropractor and after an examination and some x-rays he told me that the problem was fixable and I would need another series of treatments. The adjustments relieved the pinched nerves which allowed my nervous system to function properly and magically my pain disappeared again. I felt so lucky. I had now gotten rid of my pain twice! The Chiropractor also shared with me how he could help with allergies, strengthen my immune system, improve digestion and prevent arthritis. He also treated knee pain, shoulder pain and chronic headaches.

As the years progressed I greatly appreciated what this doctor had done for me.

Whenever my friend pain would stop by, Chiropractic would provide relief.

I learned that my health was something to be protected. Health is not something that occurs by chance, it must be worked on. Thank God I learned this at a young age. I also discovered the Chiropractic could be a rewarding career. Chronic pain and ill health can have a devastating effect on a person's psyche. Therefore a chiropractor can help a person's feelings of hopelessness and helplessness. I eventually finished my accounting degree and then went to Chiropractic school. It amazes me how my chronic childhood pain led me to my future profession.

Chiropractic School was challenging. The stress was barely manageable but I believe I was able to deal with it due to my previous experiences with pain.

The pain had hardened me and inspired me to help others with similar problems.

Many people pray for a life of leisure, luxury and fortune. Without adversity and pain I am confident that we would not strive to achieve more. Throughout history the greatest inventors, artists, writers, and athletes have had to overcome adversity. Many have transformed their adversity into inspiration

When I completed Chiropractic school I thought the worst was over, but the worst had yet to come. Starting a practice and treating patients is way more stressful than school. The textbooks can not possibly describe the situations a doctor will face. Children can be especially challenging since many times they don't wish to be there. By the same token nothing is more satisfying then helping a child overcome pain and see the smile on their face.

I know now that my pain was a blessing, not a punishment. It has made me more compassionate to those in need. I can truly relate to their problems. I now thank God every day for my pain. it has made me a person who is truly blessed and who could overcome any obstacle. It has given me my career path and my mission in life which is to spread the word of natural healing. Pain has given to me a satisfaction in life that many people never find. Thank God for my pain.

♥ ♥ ♥

Dr Michael Angelotto is a doctor of Chiropractic practicing in Brooklyn, New York. He graduated from Parker college with honors. He holds an accounting degree and still enjoys weight lifting and working out.

Thank God I Fell off a Chair Changing a Light Bulb and Almost Died

PETER MILLER

When I reflect back on the recent events in my life, I will always remember the two months that lead up to and include falling off a chair while changing a light bulb in my apartment on the evening of April 2nd, 2009. Thank God I fell off that chair, because I have learned some extraordinary lessons that allow me to savor my inspired life more than I had before.

I was involved in the production of a powerful feature documentary, *The Prosecution of George W. Bush for Murder*, based on the book by Vincent Bugliosi. I had arranged to screen it in Chicago and immediately following the screening, I had planned to travel to Los Angeles and San Francisco. Quick trips like this are routine for me. The highlight of my time in San Francisco was a ride on the Fire Boat to view San Francisco Bay, an adventure set up by my dear friend James Dalessandro. I loved it. I returned to New York with plans for a long overdue trip to Brazil with my best friend of many years, Albert Marchetti. The time I spent with Albert was extraordinary.

Upon my return from Brazil, I had been invited to lecture at Augusta College in Augusta, Georgia. I then returned to New York and then traveled to Honolulu, Hawaii with my daughters, Liseanne and Margo for their spring vacation. This was not a regular trip to Hawaii because my friend, Anthony DeStefano (author of *Ten Prayers God Always Says Yes To*, www.TenPrayers.com) had introduced me to a unique accountant and world renowned tandem surfer, Bear Woznick. Bear did some work for me during the trip and we went to the beach every day. We canoed on Waikiki, and Bear taught my daughters how to tandem surf. We went swimming with dolphins, truly enjoying this tropical paradise. This trip was a whirlwind of activity.

Having traveled extensively for over a month straight, I returned to New York and proceeded with the daily tasks of managing clients, and opportunities that were afforded to me. I presently run PMA Literary and Film Management, Inc. (http://www.pmalitfilm.com), my globally positioned literary management company, Millennium Lion, Inc., my motion picture production and development company, and I co-own a publishing company, The Story Plant (http://www.thestoryplant.com) with my partner, Lou Aronica.

I receive non stop phone calls and 200 daily emails. I have placed over 1,000 books throughout the world, produced several films, with some 20 more film/television projects in development, and managed many clients' careers. With my good fortune who could foresee an impending accident that would put my professional routine on hiatus?

In New York on April 2nd, I met with an old friend, Jon Furay. We shared a pitcher of sangria and had a light dinner at Don Quixote. Jon and I parted company and I walked to my nearby office. After I finished a few tasks there, I got on my bike and rode to my apartment.

I love riding my bike; it's something I've been doing every day for the last nine years. Riding my bike give me moments of peaceful stillness in a life that always seemed to be moving full speed ahead. Soon, life would force me to slow down.

I got into my apartment and turned on the light in my bedroom. One of the lights in a three-light fixture above my bed blew out. I have changed hundreds of light bulbs in my lifetime, and didn't think twice about changing this one. Instead of standing on the bed and changing the light fixture above it, I decided to use a little chair to stand on. I removed the light bulb, replacing it with a new one. As I attempted to get off the chair, it tricked out from under me, and the centrifugal force drove the top of the chair into my left calf. It felt as if someone had struck me with a hammer.

Immediately, my brain said, "ice," so I got a huge bag of ice, lay down on my couch and iced my leg several times before falling asleep. I woke up the next morning only to discover that my left calf was the size of a watermelon. It throbbed excruciatingly.

I called two of my friends, Dr. Albert Marchetti and Dr. Volokitin and they suggested that I call my doctor, Dr. Satish Dhalla. He told me that I needed to go to the emergency room immediately. I take Coumadin, a blood-thinning medication; because I had my aortic valve replaced 9 years ago by an artificial St. Jude's Valve. Coumadin is a necessary preventive medicine that thins the blood to avoid getting a blood clot.

After speaking to Dr. Dhalla, I dressed and hobbled out to hail a taxi. After some trouble lifting my leg into the back of the taxi, I proceeded to St. Vincent's Hospital where I checked myself into the emergency room. Shortly upon my arrival, a surgeon, Dr. Yoh, examined me and said, "Mr. Miller, we're going to need to operate immediately, or you're going to lose your left leg." At this point, my left leg was throbbing in pain, I had no feeling at the bottom of my leg, it was gray and swollen, and I couldn't move my toes. Doctors told me I had what is called "Compartment Syndrome," wherein the body shuts down in a certain compartment because of the bleeding. I had a serious hematoma in my left calf as a result of the constant bleeding.

I was told that I could lose my leg if they didn't perform a fasciotomy, a procedure that involved cutting two ten-inch incisions on each side of my calf, which would drain the blood out of my leg. If they stitched up my left leg prematurely, I could wind up with a dead calf muscle and a "gimp" leg. When I heard this, I was scared to death. How did I go from Rio De Janeiro, to swimming with the dolphins and riding my bike to the possibility of losing my leg? Little did I know at that time that I would be in the hospital for 15 days, the first 7 which would be in the ICU. I also didn't know that this incident would end up being a gift dealt by the universe that would change my life.

When your life changes so dramatically—from the hustle and bustle of meetings, phone calls, emails, dinners, drinks, travel -- to being bedridden with your leg elevated for a week, watching it bleed -- you have an opportunity to look at your life from a different perspective. This perspective, for me, became one of tremendous gratitude for the countless blessings that I have been given, and a new light switched on in my brain that said, "embrace your circumstances." It took an event like falling off a chair, winding up in the hospital and almost losing my leg to grant me one of the most wonderful wake-up calls of my life.

When you wind up in the hospital, you can meet all kinds of people. My circumstances were unique in that I wound up in a room next to a 400 lb. gang banger with a stab wound and a 24-hour police guard. In comparison with the gang banger, I was beginning to realize that my circumstance wasn't so bad. On the second day of my hospital stay, while mulling over my misfortune, a Franciscan monk, Christopher Keenan, came into my room. To me, he seemed like an angel. He cheered me up by offering me Holy Communion the next day, Sunday. God came to me! It had been about thirty-five years since I had been to Communion, so this was quite special, and the next day I received the Blessed Sacrament. Coincidentally, another monk came to see me the following Wednesday. I now had taken Communion twice in three days. How lucky was I? Very lucky.

While in the hospital I was blessed with many visitors. My daughters and their mother, Giselle, my friends Mike DeSimone, Jeff Jenssen, Stefan Radtke, Bob Tulipan, Joshua Simons, Rhodi Hawk, Michaela Hamilton and her beau Gene, Gabrielle Bernstein, my brother Robert's former wife, Betsy, her friend Randy, my longtime friend and consigliore Tony Lover, and my niece Sarah Miller and her husband Jay Gaussoin, who brought me the corn beef I craved. I was showered with gifts, including flowers from Diane Ladd. My dear friend Anthony DeStefano not only arranged a steak dinner for me, but also arranged to have the original Patsy's Restaurant cater an Easter brunch for me, which was extraordinary. My client and friend, M.

William Phelps, sent me a beautiful flower arrangement that brightened up my room. I even had some amazing business meetings from my hospital bed. I want to give a belated thanks to Richard Roffman and Andy Korge for coming to see me and then following up with the fabulous gift of stone crabs and key lime pie. My daughter Margo brought her two best friends, Eleanor and Evie, to visit me, and when they left, I cried because I realized what a special angel she is.

The pressure of running three businesses while in the hospital, and my responsibility to dozens of people was overwhelming. My business operations could not have continued during my hospital stay if I had not taught my assistant, Adrienne Rosado, to write checks. Business became seamless as my assistants, Nick Kaufmann and Amina Henry, with the help of my daughters, delivered bills and mail to me. I realized how lucky I was to have such great people surrounding me. I wanted to continue to build a culture that I could appreciate. It would create a win-win situation for all involved.

While I laid in bed, trying not to worry (I love the saying that "Worry is interest paid for money never owed"), I knew I was not going to be able to travel to the London Book Fair. I had spent the previous 2 ½ months choreographing my greatest international book fair, complete with some 40 meetings with publishers, editors, authors and media from around the world. If my ability to network the global market was successful, it would be half of my clients and projects. Fortunately my brilliant assistant, Adrienne Rosado, and asked her to go in my absence. Thank God I had a great assistant, who now has the new title of Director of Subsidiary Rights. She went to London and did a fabulous job. So, because of my leg injury, I learned how to delegate and put my trust in others. I must acknowledge my brother Robert for coaching me through the hospital routine, which can really wear you down. I needed 4 units of blood, IUs of antibiotics, Heparin, etc. Getting an infection in the hospital can set you back or kill you. Naturally, despite my optimistic attitude, I was still frightened.

On the morning of the seventh day in the hospital, my bandage had to be changed. The doctor ripped the adaptic bandage off my left calf too abruptly, causing not only excruciating pain, but also more bleeding. As a result, the opportunity for me to leave the ICU and be in a private room was delayed. I was incredibly angry that the young surgeon was unaware of the proper procedure that would have prevented this. Fortunately, I was off of Coumadin and on Heparin, another, less severe, blood thinner. My body was healing, and the bleeding finally stopped on Friday afternoon. I also received an amazing email from Beverly Hills based Dr. Julia Hunter who encouraged me to take a lot of vitamins and minerals to promote my healing. It was extremely helpful to me to receive encouraging alternative medical advice and healing from such a well-respected expert.

I woke up the morning of Easter Sunday when my surgeons came in and looked at my wound. Lo and behold, I was healing beautifully and there was no infection. Despite the lack of attention to the bandage of the previous 50 hours, I was fine. I kept thinking how lucky I have been. I was learning so much about myself and I was realizing the deep appreciation that I have for the wonderful relationships I have with my friends and clients, and the deep affection that I have for my children. I was also realizing how to cope in situations where I have little control.

A particular example of this is when Adrienne came to visit me on Easter Sunday, and she told me that we shared a common injury in having damaged left calves. She told me that when she was 9 years old, she was walking on the street and a stray bullet hit her in the leg. She was in the hospital for 2 weeks, and it took her an additional 6 months to heal. I felt such compassion for her—a little princess having to suffer such horrible pain for no reason. I already liked Adrienne, as she has been a valuable associate for several years, but now we have a special bond. It was amazing to learn that even when you feel like you're suffering alone, there are sometimes unexpected people who will know exactly what you're going through.

My time in the hospital allowed me to think about what it would be like to spend the rest of my life without my left leg.If this accident happened to somebody who did not take Coumadin, it would not have been such a painful, complicated problem. It made me think that I have to explore how to discontinue taking Coumadin and to figure out how to protect myself from a similar injury. It led me to the realization that perhaps I am simply doing too much in my life. I realized that if I hurt myself, I hurt my family, I hurt my business, and I hurt my clients. Thankfully, the experience strengthened my relationships and it brought me closer to these people. This lesson was a true gift, one I am grateful for. Thank God I fell off that chair changing that light bulb!

Life is a journey with mountains and valleys to overcome. My accident and recovery made me think of a play that I was in when I was in college, *The Time of Your Life* by William Saroyan. There was a soliloquy performed by the main character that went something like this, "There are 24 hours in every day, and twenty-three and a half of them are spent worrying, waiting, contemplating, and sleeping, and we live every day for half an hour of joy." Well, despite the accuracy of that soliloquy, I want to challenge this philosophy and recognize the joy in my life beyond the half an hour. I am committed to honoring my fulfilling and prosperous life and sharing that wealth with everyone I know.

When I reflect back on my work, I don't regret anything. I only look forward to doing bigger, better and greater things for my clients, my family, and myself. As a result of my life being pulled out from under me, I can truly say that my heart and brain have been enriched with gratitude because of my sincere appreciation of the many blessings I have been afforded with.

The most valuable gift I received in this experience was recognizing the value of clarity in everything I do and with whom I do it. So Thank God I fell off a chair changing a light bulb, as I have some new skills for appreciating all the wonderful gifts that have been bestowed upon me.

♥ ♥ ♥

I dedicate this story to my good friend Demian Lichtenstein for connecting the dots here. Luv ya like a brotha. Roars LION - Peter Miller - New York, NY – Summer 2010 website: www.pmalitfilm.com

THANK GOD I LISTEN TO MY INNER WISDOM GUIDE

DIANNE PORCHIA

When we married, we were young, we were in love, we owned a lovely home in Beverly Hills, we drove nice cars, wore fashionable clothes, ate at all the "in" spots in town, we were a healthy, active, attractive couple with money to travel the world both for business and pleasure.

Early in our marriage I worked alongside my husband helping out with office duties for his various entrepreneurial enterprises. We had oil and gas syndications in Kansas, home business opportunity, and eventually commercial real estate development and management, where my background in interior design was an asset.

By the late 1980's life was fairly fat for us. My husband became partners with his old college buddy who was making "big league" real estate deals. They rode around in his private limousine with a chauffeur / bodyguard and took routine trips to New York on the luxurious VIP charter airlines. I was told I didn't need to work in the office anymore and so I quit and rented studio space to become an artist. I even enrolled in a bachelor's degree program at Otis Parson's School of Art & Design.

The sense of power and privilege that money and good fortune brought us also seduced us both. Like a great many Los Angeles men in that position, he began having extra-marital affairs. I always suspected this might be happening, but never had hard proof, so I continued trusting that, "I was his third and last wife," as he would reassure me.

In this "big league" business world, marriage and family were an asset, while affairs and mistresses were the expected norm for men of money and power. The smart wives got "paid off" with expensive jewelry, lavish shopping sprees, and trips to les cliniques in Switzerland for the latest longevity injections and treatments.

Girlfriends got gifts too. The smarter men would have their jewelers stock plenty of women's Cartier watches and diamond earrings for that necessary and spontaneous little, "Love Interest Endearment." I settled for going to art school, getting involved in charity work and acting as our activity and travel director.

It is no wonder that my husband felt overwhelmed as a provider, guilty as a father, fearful of intimacy with me and depressed with his life. Our seemingly lavish lifestyle was in fact riddled with law suits by disgruntled investors, adversarial relations with two ex-wives, disconnection and guilt with three children, exorbitant attorneys' bills and work and personal relation stress that filled our beautiful home. This necessitated frequent getaways. Being our travel director was my way to balance out the stress and try to bring relaxation, romance and sex back into our lives.

I thought if I could get my husband away from the bad influences and stresses of his daily life, that our underlying love would re-ignite and we would live happily ever after. To the contrary, during our five year self-exile, my husband only became further depressed, our sex life dwindled , and he continued having affairs. I became an angry, cynical wife and directed my pent up sexuality into suggestive art projects.

After sixteen years of marriage, it came as quite a shock when he asked me to move out of our home, rather than work it through as a family. When I refused to move out, he moved in with a girlfriend. This was how our marriage ended.

Shortly after our separation, my husband filed for Chapter 7 bankruptcy, which forced me into the same action under an "innocent spouse clause." I was willing to remain married on paper to defend him through an investigation by the U.S. Treasury Department. I was still hoping we could reconcile and get through this very challenging time in our marriage.

We had been good companions, we had a family history together and our greeting cards still spoke of enduring love. Inside, however, I had become numb to emotion. My heart was like the walking dead. My inner light was barely a flicker.

I found myself approaching mid-life divorced and without the financial wealth and security that I believed everyone strived for. I had to start all over again. With no nest egg to fall back on, no retirement in place, a big bankruptcy mark on my credit, heavy competition in the workplace and no knowledge of computers, I was really scared. I felt abandoned, lost and overwhelmed, and lacked self confidence to succeed.

Nonetheless, something inside me, which I have come to know as my Inner Wisdom Guide, told me I intuitively knew how to heal my Self from my percieved loss and depression.

I sought understanding, purpose and meaning to my challenges by examining the "bigger picture" through spiritual books. At Esalen Institute, I experienced emotional release through massage and met my first spiritual teacher, a Native American healer named Charles Martin, aka Wain Chungka, who taught me to recognize my intuition as Spirit Guides, and receive opportunities that came to me through coincidence or synchronicity.

I had a choice to either hold onto a "victim" perception of the "wronged wife", (which I knew would only keep me "stuck"), or to focus on the energies of healing myself and moving forward in my life.

I made a daily meditation of mountain biking to the top of the fire trail where I lived in Mandeville Canyon. Each ride, I asked for the beauty of nature to heal the hole in the pit of my stomach and replace it with love, light and gratitude.

When the day came for me to stop grieving over the loss of my marriage, start dating and have adventures, I asked for exactly this in my meditation. When I stood up from my prayer to stretch my arms, I looked down the fire trail and saw a very attractive, tan and muscular man completing a run. I had literally just finished asking the Universe for adventure and men to date, and here was one! I peddled down to introduce myself not knowing that this was the beginning of the lifelong loving friendship I now have with the man I call my brother, Bert.

As we talked on the mountain top, I learned that Bert was one of these extreme adventurists who jumped out of air planes, dangled from ropes on El Cap, explored hidden caves and ran around naked with Indians in the Amazon. Having just come out of a sixteen year marriage where adventure meant laying on the beach on some remote tropical island with four-star accommodation, I had never before met anyone quite like Bert and I was immediately fascinated.

I learned that Bert was not the kind of man for securing a stable committed relationship with, however... he had a twin brother named Ben who was. When Bert invited me on one of his more tame adventures to a remote desert oasis with hot mineral springs near Death Valley, Ben and I connected. This was the beginning of the most deeply loving and sexually passionate relationship of my life up to that time.

Through that first introduction to Bert, I have formed an amazing family of friends who in our collective hearts we each know we are there for one another through deaths, births, illness, divorce, marriage, alternative relationships and through times of personal challenge.

The privileged lifestyle I gave up in divorce once represented my ultimate goal in life. However, through reinventing my self, my beliefs and my priorities in life, I successfully redefined the "brass ring" with quality friendships, a purposeful career path and meaningful and loving relationships. Amazingly, I enjoy a very abundant life on very little money. I am blessed to live in a beautiful big house in Topanga Canyon with mountain beauty that fills my soul daily. My shared home is filled with music, creativity, joy and laughter. I have the freedom to enjoy each day as I choose and experience heartfelt fun and adventures with a large and intimate group of quality friends.

Lessons:

♥ Be careful what you ask for, you just might get it.

♥ Be open to all possibilities of answers to your prayers, they may come through people or opportunities you do not immediately recognize.

♥ Trust your Inner Wisdom Guides to show you the way, they are aligned to your heart and soul.

♥ ♥ ♥

Dianne Porchia, M.A. spiritual psychology from University of Santa Monica; B.A. Fine Arts from Byam Shaw School of Art, London; certified in massage, Jin Shin acupressure, cranio-sacral therapy, energy work and dance. Passing Performance™ stress reduction for maximizing mind-body performance; W.I.S.H.™ Whole Integrated Self Health and Commitment To Love™, unique mind-body-heart-soul approach to lifestyle changes and heart-centered communication skills for deepening relationships and balanced wellness based on personal values, integrity and passion.

Thank God I lost everything

SUSANNE GAIL

At thirty-six years of age I thought I had everything – a comfortable peaceful life with a husband and one child, a prestigious home in Florida, loyal friendships, and freedom from having to seek employment. Something was empty, inauthentic and fruitless inside of me. I ached for more. I was hungry, and I could no longer hide from, nor fill the holes in my life with the distractions of work, volunteering activities, people, things, or success.

Finally, I was willing to confront the nakedness of my spirit. I was provoked to seek God and to satisfy my soul no matter what the price. My marriage, my home, my identity and my deep-rooted perceptions from my past were of little consequence and the rewards I gained were profound.

Little did I know that God was looking for me. He wanted me to come home and to know Him; and in knowing Him, I would see who I am in Him. He wanted to shake me into another dimension. God wanted to birth a vision in me, so He got me to a place where I was so dissatisfied in my life.

I will take you to the first place in my life where I died and had to learn to live again.

I lived two lives at the same time. I was free about expressing love, understanding, appreciation, and empowering humanity. I generously gave of my time, talent and treasure to my family, to my friends, and to my community service work.

However, behind my benevolent smile, I was bound by a silent suffering...

I died as I was raped, tortured, left numb and dissociated from my innocence at eight years young.

The incident occurred after school, around 3:30 in the afternoon, when my friend and I rode our bicycles to a nearby playground on our way home. We entered a large concrete tunnel that is usually buried underground. While we were playfully talking, two young men jumped down from on top of each side of the tunnel and blocked the two of us inside. My heart raced in fear and my mind started to think of what actions to express in order to liberate us from these two guys. One of the men held me down, covered my mouth, and told me not to scream; the other was occupied with my friend. I could not distinguish what was going on with my friend as she retreated into her own world of torment. I made a struggled effort to speak to them in hopes of getting them to stop physically attacking me, yet they proceeded to batter the two of us for what seemed like hours. I screamed silently within, "Make them stop; I'm scared; I better go along with them; I'll show them, they won't get to me; pretend it doesn't matter and maybe they will go away; why is no one here to protect me?" I remained frozen.

In this moment, I emotionally detached from my physical body. It was as though I became an observer rather than a participant of the experience. My strength, power, inner wisdom and life were taken from me as I plummeted into the abyss, feeling dirty, shameful, scared, and unable to speak a word to anyone. After it was over, my friend and I never spoke about what happened and our friendship dissolved.

I was determined to prove to the world that I was still my parent's special girl, and that the rape experience did not take away my power or abilities. Therefore, in my early teenage years, I worked as a babysitter to earn money to pay for my own clothing and other personal items. I excelled in visual arts as means of self-expression. I actively participated in extracurricular activities, fundraising for charitable events, and volunteering for community service work .

I focused on work. In my teenage years and twenty's, I was bound by what I played with, finding temporary relief in burying my pain through my involvement in being excessively busy with work and extracurricular school interests. I searched for ways to wash away, to cover-up to deaden my shame, grief and anger and to claim back what was taken from me.

By 21 years old, I saved over $20,000 and bought my first new car. In my early twenty's, I had a lucrative breakthrough when my mentor showed me how to build an entrepreneurial health products business. Because of my personal health issues and my healing remission, I became passionate about marketing natural health products. Within two years, I was earning a six-figure income, was promoted to being a corporate trainer, traveling throughout Canada and the USA, while educating people on how to start their own business.

In addition, I purchased a commercial building and I started a natural health clinic. Within two years, I experienced the manifestation of all my dreams come true. My need for applying my talents and for serving others filled the void, and helped to rebuild my self-esteem... temporarily. Something was nagging inside of me and I felt empty, thus, I found myself on a spiritual quest for answers.

It was at this time that I met my boyfriend. Within five years I had assumed a quarter of a million dollar debt, and had to sell my business, my commercial property and home at a loss to pay off the debts.

After liquidating all assets, leaving my family and friends in Canada to move in with this boyfriend in Florida, I got married and started a new life being a homemaker and step–parent to my husband's daughter.

As I reflect on the past fifteen years, I endured many traumatic life hardships. The death of my boyfriend and my girlfriend in car accidents; witnessing my friend's father's gun-point suicide, major health issues throughout my teenage years, a quarter-of-a-million dollar financial loss of my once-prosperous business, lost my commercial property and home, and the grief of a marital divorce, home foreclosure, and family alienation that eventually precipitated the final defining moment that changed the direction of my life forever.

After twelve years of marriage, I started to have flashbacks, waking up in the middle of the night anxious. I found myself feeling empty, dead, alone, and screaming inside that no one understood what I was feeling. I had everything; a husband and children, a beautiful home in a prestigious area, and plenty of money. Something inside of me was still missing.

I had discovered that my husband had planned the divorce years before, took all the marital money and equity from our fully-paid off home, and I was now facing foreclosure. Where was my five-year-old daughter and I going to live? I had no income or work experience to fall back on. This was my final straw and this is where I decided the drama stops.

I was polluted by compromises to my character. The darkness of my past sins, fear, pride, weakness, grief, depression, hopelessness, and strife tried to pull me back to where I was before. There was no peace, no victory, and no freedom. I began to face the compromises, justifications, and rationalizations that I had made. I felt broken, depressed, angry, and alone. I cried out, questioning who was I and where was God? I heard no answers. I felt that God had abandoned me. I hated life, and I was unable to see any way out of my bad situation.

Overwhelmed with my weaknesses and shortcomings, I felt an intense sense of worthlessness, like I was a failure that had let everyone down. I struggled to face another day, waking up in the middle of the night with anxiety attacks, crying out to God. Nothing comforted me. I was overtaxing myself.

I wanted to be around people who were warm, affectionate, patient and consoling. I needed to know that someone cared about me as a person. I needed a good listener that could reassure me that I would be alright; not people who would lecture or make judgmental statements, such as "You shouldn't feel like that" or, "That's the wrong attitude".

Late night religious motivational speakers on television became my saving grace. They always seemed to have relevant messages for me at the precise moment I turned on the television. I eagerly watched these speakers day and night. I sought to understand and apply some order to my chaotic situation.

In the depth of my hopelessness, feeling broken, and like a failure – I cried out to God to take me Home to Him, to deliver me from my sorrow. It was in this moment that God answered my prayer for help, and I found my true self. I decided that my 30-year drama stopped here and now.

Now, I will take you to the place in my life where I learned to live.

As a child, regardless of the life events that occurred, I managed to look at the world with pure and rational eyes, with a deep love and understanding for the human condition and a belief in the "goodness" of humanity. Because I learned to detach from my feelings at an early age, I realized that we are all children at heart. A child is good at their core; even when their behavior may reflect something less than "Godly." Therefore, I was committed to having God reveal how to live a healthy, prosperous, and fulfilling life.

As I write this story, I have completed my marital divorce. In looking at all of my past experiences, I realize that they served a bigger purpose of healing and clearing the old and outdated consciousness, and of restoring a new vision for my life.

I believe that everyone has been created in the image of God. Since I am made in the image and likeness of God, I am further called to be an example of God's brilliance, and to let my Godly Self shine brighter than the pain and rage of any of my life circumstances.

I say to myself that "the light of God surrounds us, the love of God enfolds us, the power of God protects us, the presence of God watches over us. Wherever we are, God IS, and so it is". Amen.

♥ ♥ ♥

Susanne is a Holistic Organizational Life Coach, a Visionary Entrepreneur and Midwife to Dreams, a Philanthropist, a Mother, and a student of Life. For over 10 years, Susanne has been a self-employed entrepreneur, generating a 6-figure income through marketing natural health products. She has owned and managed her own natural health clinic center, housing diverse styles of holistic practitioners. In addition, she has been a "midwife to dreams" and special events workshop coordinator across Canada and USA.

Susanne's journey progresses from a troubled past – that included rape, financial poverty, betrayal, death and divorce -- to experiencing the abundant life of a true overcomer. Her vision includes creating order in the world around us, sharing "wholistic" education and fostering creative expression through books, video, (cancel the word - computerized) games, and television media programming for children and adults, and more. For more information on projects contact her at: iamexpressions@yahoo.com or (954) 213-5242

My "Dear" Death Experience

CHARLENE ACKERMAN

At the age of 39 I was told I had breast cancer. My immediate thought was, "Please God, let me raise my sons, then we can talk cancer." Kurt just turned 11 and Mark was 14. At the time breast cancer survival rate was only 1 out of 3. I survived! I got to enjoy watching my young sons become men. I even enjoyed what some parents would call rebellion; I saw it as a step toward manhood. Then... 13 years later... I was diagnosed with kidney cancer. My sons were grown. I was completely ready and willing to accept what God had in store for me. I was grateful that I had been given the gift of seeing them grown, married and starting a family. I so looked forward to being a grandmother, yet I knew God had answered my prayer. I couldn't believe how calm I was with the removal of my kidney and recovery. Once again I was spared. My mother had kidney cancer several years previously and hers had spread. She later died of lung cancer.

When my youngest son married I immediately began the shift from Realtor to Hypnotist. I knew at the age of six I wanted to be a hypnotist. My brother was a terrible tease and when I heard a hypnotist can make you do things, I loved the idea of telling him what to do. Of course, the first thing I learned when I entered the field, is a hypnotist cannot make you do anything the subconscious mind will not accept.

It immediately became a passion. I simply could not learn enough. I was constantly reading books and listening to "how to" tapes so that I could teach myself hypnosis.

Following my mother's death from lung cancer, I began annual Great American Smoke Out Clinics with the proceeds going to American Cancer Society. I received the honorary, "Member of the Year" award for promoting this nationally at conventions. I was living my dream.

As my business expanded, I sponsored some of the biggest names in the field to give seminars for my growing student base. I knew I had reached the top in November of 1997 when I had the opportunity to bring Ormond McGill to Janesville. I had always admired him. He had entertained our troops in WWII. He was dearly loved by everyone that knew him, or even knew of him. Life was GOOD! I wondered ... "where do I go from here?"

May 19, 1997: I felt an extremely painful tearing on both sides of my body followed by a night of severe vomiting. I knew it couldn't be my appendix because the pain was on both sides. Besides, following a previous abdominal surgery (to remove tumors), my doctor told me, "I was going remove your appendix, but it was so shriveled it could never give you a problem."

May 20: Confined to bed, extreme pain... thinking... this too shall pass. That evening my fever shot up, I was trembling and my teeth were scattering. I admitted myself to the Emergency Room and was sent home. Diagnosis: Urinary track infection, call doctor in three days if pain persisted.

May 21: Feel huge mass on right side, I am nearly immobile. Go to Urgent Care. Ambulance ordered to take me to the hospital. Dr. called hospital to tell them of my condition. The ambulance took forever. Several hours later when I arrived at hospital I ended up parked in the hallway, as they could not find any record of my scheduled arrival. Following x-rays... they said they needed a CAT scan... doctors were waiting to perform exploratory surgery. It was hours later that they were able to give me the CAT scan and the surgeons had left for the day. Surgery delayed till after 5:00PM, the next day as all surgery rooms were filled.

May 22: I lay in the fetal position all day due to the pain. Following surgery, as I was lying in my bed in near oblivion, it occurred to me "I could be dying? I am dying!!! I can't die; Ormond McGill's coming to town." It immediately flashed through my mind, "How could you possibly be thinking of Ormond McGill on your deathbed? You're a wife, mother and grandmother."

I saw two spirits off to my left that appeared to have come to assist me on my journey. Instantly, I felt myself transported into Universal space. I could see in the vast distance what appeared to be Earth. It looked to be about the size of a child's large rubber ball. Lights sparkled in vast numbers around the globe. I received a message; I knew her as the Virgin Mary. She has been with me before during dire situations. She said, "It's okay to go. The seeds have been planted; your work will go on." I knew the lights represented my students. I had planted the seeds. The work I loved would go on. Why were they so scattered? Lights were everywhere.

I experienced an overwhelming sense of peace and joy. I saw my students going out and assisting others. Fascinating!

I had a sense of how small we are as individuals in this vast universe. People those close to me would mourn my death, but in reality my passing would be as insignificant as one less grain of sand from Earth, or one less drop of water from the ocean. Death is nothing to fear. It brought me an incredible feeling of unconditional love and peace. I realized the insignificance of material things

I was ready to go. I reached my arms out to the two spirits who were watching, waiting - then they began to fade, leaving me behind.

I pleaded, "Here I am, take me with you," as they faded away.

I spent eight days in the hospital being pumped with mega doses of antibiotics. At one point a fever threatened the possibility of further infection, requiring additional surgery. I was spared. The fever broke. The doctor tried on several occasions to tell me just how serious my condition was. I did not care, and turned away. It wasn't until my post discharge checkup that I learned that I had peritonitis and gangrene.

My journey back into the real world began. My recovery proved slow and tedious. My body was healing, but I regretted that I had not died. The magnificent peace that I had experienced was something I could not shake. I went through weeks of depression. Everything became such an effort: dressing myself, chewing food, swallowing, driving a car, turning steering wheel, door knobs, keys, lifting my feet, walking, everything! Even talking became a conscious effort! Carrying around the physical body just seemed like too much effort. I remember thinking I might have to wait another twenty years before I would have another opportunity like that. I knew of course that death must come naturally in order for me to enjoy such peace.

I did not know how to climb out of this hole. It just seemed to be getting deeper and deeper. I looked everywhere I could in a desperate attempt to find answers. On a tape by Caroline Myss, she said to ask yourself, "Why am I alive?" So I did. I bought myself a notebook to keep a journal. My first entry, written July 5, 1997 was written to God in anger. I asked, "Why am I alive?" I added, "Help me to live better." I remembered a quote I had heard and I wrote, "Better to walk an unknown path—don't contaminate." Then I wrote, "Okay, God, you win!"

The next day I was driving home when I saw my three grandchildren in the front yard. They lived a block away from me. As I walked in the door, my telephone was ringing. It was my grandson; they had been waiting for me, they wanted to come over. When they arrived, Nick, my oldest grandson said, "I hope we don't ever live too far from you, Grandma." Music to my ears!

Next entry, exactly seven weeks (note date of entry) from the day my appendix ruptured:
A New Beginning: "7/7/7 3:00 AM Why am I alive? Grandchildren!!!!!"

My depression was gone! Over! Done! Finished! I know now why I am alive!

Life took on an exciting new meaning.. Communication with Virgin Mary through dreams and her touch continues to guide me on a journey of "planting seeds". On May 22, 1999 I was in Taiwan teaching hypnosis to a class of primarily psychiatrist and counselors, planting seeds. I have learned over the years to expect something very special, even magic to happen on May 22. I call it my "ReBirthday."

I began focusing on a program I have presented to 100's of college students in Taiwan; I call my program, "Esteem4Teens."

I have spoken and taught in over a dozen different countries since my "Dear" death experience, with nearly 20 trips to Taiwan.

My current inspiration is working with PTSD (Post Traumatic Stress Disorder) for our returning Veterans. I have been guided to a marvelous technique which has worked near miracles in helping victims of PTSD. I have spoken at numerous hypnosis conventions on my "Esteem4Teens" and PTSD program.

I am writing a manual to teach other therapists how to use the gift I have been shown, and have already scheduled my first class in Sedona, AZ.

I can now say in all honesty: Thank God I am Alive!

♥ ♥ ♥

Charlene Ackerman has written a book, "Why am I Alive?" following her NDE (near death experience). She refers to her experience as "DEAR" death experience.

She has been practicing hypnosis since 1988 and teaching hypnosis certification since 1992. She knew at the age of six, she wanted to become a hypnotist. She has several awards. NGH "Member of the Year" and "Instructor of the Year". She has also been named "International Hypnosis Trainer" as well as "Hypnotist of the Year" at Mid-America Conference 2006. Her practice is ever expanding on an international level, and in August 2006 began teaching in China. She is a well-known speaker throughout USA, and has been given the honorable name of "Mother of Hypnosis" in Taiwan.

Thank God
We Surrendered
He Said, She Said...

CHRISTIAN AND CINDY GRANCOURT

Christian:
I first heard about "The Secret" cruise in May 2007 while doing some telephone sales work in Sydney for one of "The Secret" teachers, Dr. John DeMartini, of whom I was a student. I had also been a student of Tony Robbins and had been attending his seminars for over 10 years at that time. I had been studying with Dr. John DeMartini developing my own personal growth with a view towards a career in human transformation. I thought that having wisdom from these two great teachers and would allow me to offer the world valuable service.

While working for Dr. DeMartini's sales team, I received a phone call late one evening from a man on the other side of Australia who was hoping to buy some tickets. I informed him that no more tickets were available for his city but instead of expressing disappointment and ending the phone call with a friendly goodbye, he continued to converse with me.

He suggested that I should attend "The Secret" Cruise . I spent a day or so looking into it but decided against it because I couldn't justify the $5000-$6000 total cost for the trip and seminars. So I let it go.

Cindy:
I had a crazy summer. My schedule was completely insane, having traveled extensively due to my nightclub DJ career. I'd hit all the hotspots; two tours in Vegas, tours in Los Angeles including the Playboy Mansion, one tour in Boston, one in Denver, one in New York City, one in Portugal and one in Ibiza, Spain.

My personal life was in major transition as well. I'd left my marriage of 18 years and filed for divorce. I was on a search for freedom and personal growth. I'd found a lot of answers in "The Secret," which I had watched in February of that year. Quite honestly this movie spurred me to take action towards my divorce. I signed up for a success-coaching program with Jack Canfield in July and began my journey to reconnect with myself. Life seemed uncertain, but my focus was on faith and surrender.

My fall schedule showed no signs of letting up. I had a Dallas and Houston tour, and a Halloween booking was sure to follow. This left only a few weeks in between the tours for the dream vacation which I had already booked to Tahiti.

I was in no position to book myself another personal type of vacation; truly, it was the farthest thing from my mind. I received a myspace message from Susan Bagyura, an author booked on the "Bob Proctor Secret Cruise". Susan asked if I was attending the cruise and would I like two tickets to the author's private reception? Wow! What cruise? An author's private reception with Bob Proctor and Michael Bernard Beckwith? Whoa! That would definitely suit my purposes.

I went immediately to the website and listened to Bob Proctor on video as he explained how amazing this cruise ship to Mexico would be. We would be surrounded with 2000 other like-minded folks, an entire ship full of success-oriented people, all there to receive information on how to create multiple sources income. We'd be hitting Cabo San Lucas, Mazatlan and Puerto Vallerta. This sounded too good to be true!

I decided to surrender. "This cruise is going to change my life. I'm going! I don't know how yet, but I'm going!" Did I mention that the cruise was only one week away?

Christian:
Two months after deciding against going on the cruise, I was driving to the post office to mail in an application for "The Oneness" program (a three week spiritual retreat in India) that happened to coincide with the dates for "The Secret" cruise. On the way to the post office, my friend Richard called me. "Hey Christian, are you going on "The Secret" cruise in October?" Now wait a minute. This is the second time I've been told about this cruise in as many months. That instant, my intuition was telling me to be on this cruise. I decided to surrender it and forget about what I wanted to do in India. I went home and booked my trip to San Diego...

Cindy:
Lying on my bed that evening, completing my module for my Jack Canfield coaching session, I wondered where I would get the money for this trip. I needed $2300 dollars. I surrendered. It didn't matter, I thought, because I was definitely going and it would have to manifest itself. I had already made the decision and somehow it was all going to have to work out. I was tired, but I felt I needed to stay up and complete my module. I also had this underlying feeling that good news was coming my way. Soon, the feeling became so powerful that I knew I must check my email. I put the things I was working on aside and made my way to my office to open up my email. Sure enough, great news was waiting. I received an email from my good friends, Yves and Cynthia, who booked my Tahiti trip saying that they had misquoted me on the price. They originally quoted me $7500 which I had already budgeted and put aside. Now, he was saying that the rate was $5200, putting EXACTLY $2300 back in my pocket, the precise amount that I had asked for just a couple of hours before!! I now had the money to go on the cruise!

Christian:
Although I knew I was being drawn to the cruise, I didn't know why. I just knew something was going on that I had to surrender to. I had such diverse and advanced knowledge in the field of personal growth, that I didn't

feel that the content of the seminar was what was drawing me there. It was too simple, too basic compared to what I had done in the past. So then, what was it? I decided that it could possibly be for networking for business contacts or people that I had to meet for some other reason. Not far from the back of my mind was also the possibility of a love interest. I had made a list of everything I wanted in an intimate relationship several years back during one of the Tony Robbins events but I decided to not to recap the list while in my Santa Monica hotel room. I spoke out aloud to the universe, "You know what I want and what I need so I surrender to whatever you want to bring to me".

Cindy:
Once I booked the trip, the following day I began looking more deeply upon my intentions for this trip and what I would like to accomplish. The first thing I thought of was the most obvious goal, getting a copy of my original music track, "The Secret", directly into the hands of Bob Proctor and Michael Bernard Beckwith. This was an opportunity to go directly to the source, speak with them and place a copy into their hands. Perfect.

Secondly, I thought about what else this trip may open up for me. Surely, it would be a nice vacation to Mexico. Surely, I was bound to learn something valuable from the seminar speakers. Surely, I would be inspired by the success stories of others. All of these things were possible positive outcomes from the voyage. I relaxed and felt satisfied with myself that I wasn't being frivolous. Ahhhhhh. Big Sigh.

Now, how about a little something for me? Hmmmm. Wouldn't it be nice to meet a wonderful man on the trip? A romantic shipboard romance? As visions of Leo and Kate swirled around in my head, it seemed to make sense. I wanted to be in love. Mad, glorious love. Who knows? Maybe, I could even find someone with substance on this ship, unlike the nightclubs. Surely, a spiritual man would be drawn to something like this.

A list. Yep, that's what I needed. In my coaching sessions with Jack Canfield, I had written a list for my perfect man and relationship. When I wrote the list in mid-July of 2007, I cautioned myself to be careful with what I asked for because I have the ability to manifest. When I get clear in my head and even THINK about things, they manifest. Then, when I write it out and/or visualize and use affirmations, just WATCH OUT! Thus, I knew that I should be specific on my list and so I wrote it and literally forgot about it, surrendering and letting go of any attachments to it. Now, reflecting on it, I remembered I had a list. I got my list out and reviewed it, adding a couple more items to it.

Voila! I had set my intentions for "The Secret" Cruise. I decided. I declared it. I affirmed it. I visualized it. Then I surrendered.

Christian:
I left LA and flew down to San Diego to board the ship and cast away a few hours later. On that first evening I was scheduled for the 8:15 dinner sitting, but was feeling a bit seasick for the first time in my life. This was odd, since I was born on a tropical island, was used the ocean and never got seasick. Despite feeling ill, I headed down to the restaurant and forced myself to go and be. Once I got there I ran into a waiter and mentioned my queasiness. He suggested that I retire to my room on a light meal of green apples and crackers, which apparently works wonders for seasickness. I welcomed the remedy and despite my disappointment, surrendered to his suggestion of retiring for the night.

Cindy:
The next week, I made my way on board Holland America's Oosterdam. When I received my information packet, I noticed they made a mistake on my dinner time. I had requested the 6:15 sitting and they scheduled me at 8:15. I made a mental note to myself to change that, but I found myself so lost in the exploration of the ship that I had missed the 6:15 sitting, so I readied myself for the 8:15.

In the dining room, I was assigned to a table of six. There were two couples and an extra seat at the table. I wanted to change my dinner time to 6:15 for the following evening, but I found myself enjoying the NYC and Aussie couple so much that I decided to surrender and stick with the time that I was "mistakenly" given. What great energy there was at our table!

Christian:
After my evening of seasickness, the following evening was the "formal night." When I arrived at my assigned table, my seat had been taken. After I failed to show up the previous night, my instinct told me that the other couples had offered it to a friend, believing that they had a spare seat at their table. I mentioned it to a waiter hoping he would help me find another seat. Instead he told me to just kick the person off my seat. I didn't want to be a 'buzz-kill' as they looked like they were all having fun, so I surrendered to finding myself another seat.

Looking around the dining room, I saw a table for four, with two ladies and two empty seats. I asked if he could join them and they acquiesced, so I sat down and we opened up a friendly conversation. Moments later, two men approached the table saying that they had made some arrangements earlier in the day to join the two ladies for dinner. They then left for a moment with one of the girls and came back to announce, quite rudely, that they had found me a seat at another table so I should leave. I was a little offended by their lack of good graces, so I stood up and told them "Thank you, no, I am quite capable of finding my own seat." Although disappointed, I again surrendered and when the other girl apologized I responded with "Thanks but don't worry, everything happens for a reason."

I left the table I in search of another seat. I spotted one across the dining room, and approached the table in the hopes that I could put an end to the whole musical chairs fiasco.

Cindy:
After deciding to keep my 8:15 time slot for the night of the formal dinner, I made my entrance decked out in a floor-length aqua blue shimmering gown. I was in good spirits and looking forward to the interesting conversation at my table. Ten minutes into the dinner, I noticed someone moving towards our table out of the corner of my eye. "Hello, is this seat taken? May I join you for dinner?" a sexy voice with an Australian accent inquired.

We all looked up and immediately there were a chorus of "yeses". Yes, please join us. Wow. His name was Christian and he took my breath away. What a beautiful man! He was tall, dark, handsome, elegant, regal and upscale...all of which were in my list. As we spoke through dinner, I mentally checked off items on my list, one by one. I even had a specific age that I was interested in. Thirty-five. Christian had just turned thirty-five the previous week. Christian had a belief that he would meet or be married to his wife when he was thirty-five.

We talked throughout dinner that night like there was no one in the world but us; we connected so deeply. We headed to the lounge after dinner and chatted some more. We had a more magical and romantic moment than Leo and Kate could ever have dreamt about. We spent the night on my deck under the moon and the stars with the wind blowing through our hair while we spoke of our dreams. We spent an enchanting week together in Cabo San Lucas, Mazatlan and Puerto Vallarta Mexico.

Thank God we surrendered. There were so many things we'd each surrendered to that allowed our romance and deep connection to occur.

Christian:

Once we had established our connection that evening, there was still a lot more to surrender to. Cindy had been married before and also had two children; whereas I had never been married. The thought of taking on being a stepfather to two girls was daunting. I was also uncertain of how my life would be with an ex-husband potentially making things difficult for Cindy and I. There were still a number of things for them to work out. They still weren't legally divorced, still needed to sell their house, and still shared custody of their children.

My life was pretty easy at that time. I had just myself to worry about. Was I biting off more than I could chew? What would my parents think? I had many moments where I was afraid, but the love, the connection, and incredible way that we came together was enough for me to refuse to allow those fears to come between the fulfillment I was sharing with my ultimate life partner.

Cindy:

Amongst all of the other things that we both had to surrender to, there was the fact that I had just filed for divorce six months prior! I was really in no hurry to jump back into another serious relationship. I had left my ex in April of 2007 and met Christian in October of that year. I was enjoying being single and I had actually decided that I would never marry again!!

We married seven weeks later in Bora Bora, Tahiti on the beach at the St. Regis Hotel.

Christian:
I didn't even ask her!

Cindy:
So romantic! He simply surprised me with a traditional Polynesian wedding on the beach. I had to find out that I was getting married from Etienne, our butler!

Christian:
We married each other again exactly three months later on the beach in Santa Barbara, California, to make it official. We married again one year later in Melbourne, Australia for my entire family to witness.

Cindy:
We are enjoying our love so much that we have decided to get married every year! Vegas here we come!

Christian:
One of the most important things we found out when we came together was that our union was not only for our love, but that we were to share a life's purpose together.

Cindy:
Yep! We currently share a business together in which we have a variety of companies ranging from Professional Speaking to Event Entertainment.

Christian and Cindy:
Thank God we surrendered. We found our twin souls over International Waters, on a romantic cruise ship and began our amazing journey of love and purpose, all because we said "Yes" to surrender. Thank God we surrendered!

♥ ♥ ♥

Christian and Cindy Grancourt experientially know the simple yet powerful keys to attracting love, nurturing love and growing love in a relationship. Their epic tale of love and adventure is a romantic and inspiring story that teaches principles for achieving a blissful relationship that is possible for every person to attain and maintain.

With extensive and complementary backgrounds, Christian and Cindy Grancourt bring together over 30 years of experience combined in the Personal Development Field.

Together, they offer a wealth of knowledge and wisdom concerning a number of areas including business consulting, success coaching, life skills, professional speaking, hypnosis and all aspects of the relationship field.

Christian and Cindy reside in sunny Santa Barbara, California with their two daughters, Zoe and Hannah.

Thank God
I had 5 panic attacks Per Day from Post Traumatic Stress

ELISE FRANCES

Becoming a mother is one of the most challenging and life changing experiences that a person who loves being in control can go through. The biggest lesson you learn is that while you cannot have control of every outcome, it is wise to take responsibility.

There is absolutely no greater blessing than holding your newborn child that grew inside you in your hands for the first time. Both the love and newfound responsibility hit you like a ton of bricks. This can be empowering and it can be debilitating.

We were a young family and we had found the most perfect house with a little white picket fence, ornate windows and amazing original features. Behind the property line was one of the most beautiful nature reserves I'd ever set eyes on. There was an abundance of bush land filled with eucalyptus trees. With that came the inhabitants of rainbow lorikeets, bandicoots and kookaburras. My husband and I immediately agreed we must do everything in our power to secure our home here for our little family. We had two precious daughters Tallulah and Evangeline.

Evangeline was barely walking at the time. Things couldn't be any more perfect in our nature haven, but there was one thing that I just couldn't' seem to get out of my mind. It was like a niggling tapping on the shoulder. A gentle daily reminder that bothered me on a daily basis. It was a mother's intuitive whisper...that feeling at the pit of my stomach. But every day, I did ignore it. The back of the balcony was amazingly high. Perched high up amongst the trees, the balcony stood about 4 meters from the ground.... Down below it was a concrete paved area.

For months, I had encouraged, mentioned, gently urged and finally nagged my husband to fix the balcony. It had a huge gap between the palings which happened to be the perfect size for a little toddler to fit right under. I visually could see an accident happening over and over in my mind.

I believe you get what you think about. A major life incident was about to happen and it would spiral my into a life full of fear and mental debilitation. As a family, we had just finished eating our evening meal and Todd had sat down to watch the children play as I went to fill the dog's water bowl.

As I stood up, from patting my beautiful dog, I heard Todd call out "Tallulah, what have you done?" When a man's voice sounds weak and desperate, it is not a good feeling. Eva, was lying face down on the ground, at the bottom of the hill. She had fallen from a great height onto the concrete head first. Her father was standing above her, paralyzed in disbelief.

He called to me as I ran toward them screaming desperately. "Oh my god Todd, is she moving? Is she breathing? Is she alive?" My heart pounded like I have never felt before. I couldn't feel my arms or legs. I couldn't even tell where I was! It was like a vice was on my head and I was talking under water. I couldn't even hear myself screaming.

I pushed Todd out of the way just as Eva let out the loudest most delicious healthy belly scream I have ever heard. I was shaking uncontrollably, Tallulah was crying and saying "sorry mummy." They had gotten into a tussle over a toy and little Eva had lost her balance and rolled under the fence.

The neighbor had heard it all and had called the ambulance. They arrived with their emergency gear within minutes. As they looked at the drop from the balcony in disbelief they whisked Eva up on a spinal stretcher and into the ambulance to go back to the ER. They had to get her to the hospital to check for internal bleeding. The looks on the faces of the paramedics clearly communicated fear, although they tried not to show it. I knew this was a dire situation, and the panic ran through my body.

This was to be longest night of my life. I would wake up my daughter and check her vital signs constantly. It left me exhausted and emotionally drained. At the end of the longest 24 hours in my life, we got the news that Eva was going to be fine....a broken arm and nothing else. A miracle. No head injury, no internal injuries. She had survived the fall by reaching out with her arm. I was the person who wasn't "fine."

Soon after the event, I began noticing that I was increasingly agitated and nervous. I developed severe physical manifestations of Post Traumatic Stress Disorder. My body chemistry had changed in response to my daughter's accident. My sense of control had been taken away from me. My ability to protect my children had been questioned. My confidence had been shattered. What kind of mother was I? It was my responsibility to make sure the balcony was safe and I had passed the responsibility to someone else. It was my partner's role as the house handyman to fix these things right?

My confidence had changed. I was a woman that had lived and traveled the world solo. I had been in some of the most challenging situations and I had survived them. There was nothing I previously had thought that I couldn't achieve or accomplish. I was confident and very sure of myself.

I first realized I was no longer myself when I was driving along a three lane freeway with trucks screaming past on either side. My heart began to pound just like it had the day of the accident. My hands became sweaty and behind my neck was hot. I was dizzy and unable to focus. All I could think about was being squashed off the road. I thought I was having a heart attack. I pulled over to the side and thought I was surely going to die.

There was an ambulance that arrived thinking

a woman was having a heart attack only to find me suffering from a severe panic attack. They assured me I would be fine. Living like this was not fine. Things became increasingly worse. I reached the point where I was waking in the middle of the night with tingling all down my legs like spiders were biting me.

I wanted to completely escape my body. If I could have had myself committed to a mental institution I would have. I kept thinking if I tell the doctors I am crazy, they wouldn't believe me anyway. What crazy person have you ever heard that walks themselves into a mental institution?

I may not have been classified as insane, but I couldn't continue on the path I was on. At my worst point I was having up to five panic attacks a day. The list of things I was no longer able to do was growing rapidly. I was unable to eat at restaurants for fear getting food poisoning, unable to drive over bridges, unable to go to a doctor for fear of catching a disease, unable to use a public restroom, unable to eat food other people had cooked, unable to take medication, unable to swallow food due to the fear of choking. I had once clocked up over 300 flights and now was unable to even contemplate getting on a plane. I washed my hands over 100 times per day and woke in the middle of the night thinking I was being bitten by spiders. I was even unable to go to sleep at night, I feared I would stop breathing.

How could such a confident woman be reduced to a fearful little girl? I knew this was not the life I was meant to live. What had all of my experiences taught me about myself? I was powerful and able to create what I wanted. I was not going to succumb to this state of being. This was temporary; I was giving away my power.

The more I feared a panic attack, the more I would focus on having one. I had created a vicious cycle that I couldn't stop. No amount of meditating, deep breathing or drugs could stop it. I realized I had to retrain my mind.

At the core of who I am is a self motivated woman. I had to bring that part of me to the forefront.

One panic attack turned in to five a day as it was all I could focus on. I knew I had the power to stop these patterns in my mind. I just needed to make that decision. I began to retrain my mind. I started focusing on inspirational self talk. Whenever a fear would enter my mind, I immediately replaced it. If I was fearful of driving over a bridge, I would tell myself how many examples of times I had successfully driven over bridges before in my past. If I was fearful of choking, I would slow down and eat my food more slowly.... I would coach myself out of my fears. I learned to apply this to every part of my life. I rewired my brain to look for the balance in every situation. I asked myself empowering questions.

I forgave myself for being irresponsible, and allowed myself to "Let Go" of trying to control every situation. I saved my life. I used my knowledge to empower my daughter by example. I'm grateful for my panic attacks as they have given me the gift of empowerment.

The panic attacks have dissipated. I haven't had one in over 3 years now....... Thank God I developed PTSD because if I hadn't I would never have realized how I can empower my life. Because of my PTSD I am here helping others empower themselves through NLP and inspirational healing. Because of my PTSD I am now aware of the balance that exists. Thank God I had Post Traumatic Stress Disorder.

♥ ♥ ♥

Elise is a writer, speaker and filmmaker, committed to helping people discover their true purpose in life. She uses her intuitive connection to cut through people's barriers and get to the core of what may be holding them back in their lives. Elise lives in Sydney with her two beautiful daughters and is committed to helping pre-teens navigate through the images and messages in the media to experience a positive love of self.

Thank God I Lost My Dream Job and Found My Dream

STEVE BHAERMAN

Next time you utter the phrase, "a funny thing happened," consider this. Maybe that "funny thing" is just an example of the Universe's sense of humor, where you think you're headed down one path and you're really headed down another. Like the time I thought I was a college professor, but a funny thing happened . . . and I ended up becoming a comedian instead.

The story began when I found my dream job. Actually, "found" is not the right word. From the moment I heard there was something called the Weekend College where I could teach autoworkers as part of Detroit's Wayne State University, I "stalked" this job. I knew this job was mine, and every week I called the department head to ask if I'd been hired. I must have been such a nudnik that the guy hired me just so I'd stop pestering him. The day I found I'd been hired, I literally cried with gratitude.

The job was even better than I imagined it would be. I had a knack for making the classes I taught — like Labor History and Ethnic Studies interesting as well as educational. Sometimes the men would bring their wives to class, because apparently it was the best edutainment around.

More than one student told me I was the first professor they'd ever had who actually spoke to them like a person. They leveled with me on the first day. "We're just in it for the money," one of them told me. Apparently, under this program their stipend from the G.I. Bill was higher than their tuition, and they got to keep the difference. "Well then, I'm in it for the money too," I replied. After all, I was being paid more than I'd ever been paid to teach before. "Tell me," I asked, "do you have to pass your courses in order to get your stipend?"

They admitted that they did. "Well then, we have some work to do, eh?" Those men worked very hard that year and were proud of what they learned and accomplished. They also found many more valuable reasons for being there than just the money. How popular was I? Toward the end of that first year I traded in my Ford Pinto for a new Honda — considered a traitorous act in Detroit — and no one torched my new car.

That summer there were no classes, and I took off to research a book I was writing on education, expecting to have my job when I returned in the fall. And that's when the not-so-funny thing happened.

Wayne State needed to replace the part-time employees with tenured professors — most of whom hated the notion of teaching the autoworkers as much as I enjoyed it, I was out of a job. For a semester, I tried to piece together other freelance teaching jobs, but it didn't add up to a living.

Meanwhile, I had moved to Ann Arbor. I decided I needed to get a job, and that's when I saw the ad in the paper. The Ann Arbor Department of Parks and Forestry was looking for an equipment operator.

Since I had operated farm equipment before, I was hired. My job was helping to take down trees that had Dutch Elm Disease, and this had my Jewish mother from Brooklyn a little concerned. She was afraid I might catch Dutch Elm Disease. Seriously.

I assured her that people didn't get Dutch Elm Disease, although dogs get it. "Dogs get it?" she asked, concerned about Buster. "What happens to dogs?"

"They lose their bark," I told her.

For the first several months, the job was great. I enjoyed being outdoors, using my body, and giving my brain a rest. At night, I worked on what would be my second book on education. My first, an account of my experiences starting an alternative high school in Washington, D.C., had been published by Simon & Schuster and had been widely reviewed. Even without a teaching job, I figured, I could get back in the game with another book. As summer gave way to fall and then winter, I started getting depressed. It's one thing working outdoors in the summertime.

But in September, the college kids who'd been working part time returned to school. Then there was me — college professor and published author — and here I was getting up each cold, dark morning, putting on a jump suit, and spending the day chipping brush. At least I had a job, but not one my mother was likely to brag about.

I did have one ace in the hole, and that was the book I was writing. It would be a way to get my untracked career back on track. But the book didn't seem to be working either. Simon & Schuster passed on it, and my agent was having trouble selling it elsewhere. Nonetheless, I persisted, writing every night. I was sitting at the dining room table one cold night working away at the book, when I distinctly heard a voice.

I'm not accustomed to hearing voices, particularly when they are not attached to people, but I heard this one. "Let go of this book," the voice said. "The book is your past, and you need to focus on the future."

"What's the future?" I asked. The voice was silent.

I was at work a couple of weeks later — a bone-chillingly cold February day — and they put me with a new guy, Larry, who turned out to be a brilliant psychologist disguised as a truck driver. As we rode and worked together, Larry came up with an idea. "You're a writer," he said. "Let's start a little newspaper." And so, for the sheer fun of it — and to alleviate the boredom — I said, "Sure." It was a decision that would change my life. Larry and I ended up producing an anonymous humorous biweekly publication for the twenty-five or so people we worked with. We called it States Wire Service, and our masthead slogan was "All the News Before It Happens, Guaranteed to Be Fallacious If Not True."

The premier issue — typed and reprinted at the campus copying shop — was surreptitiously dropped off by a girlfriend and left on the lunch table before everyone cruised in for lunch. I walked in, ignored the papers sitting there, and walked to the men's room. All of a sudden I heard a whoop. And then another. The guys had discovered the paper — and it was all about them. For the next two years, we continued to tell the truth through humor. We created what could best be described as an ongoing, interactive situation comedy.

We would write something in the paper, and our fellow workers would respond to it. We started a rumor in the paper that one young and ambitious groundsman was "campaigning" for foreman. We even wrote a speech for him in the paper. One morning, I came to work and there he was, standing on one of the lunch tables, dramatically delivering the speech we had written for him.

Other times, guys (I say this because it was an all-male workplace) would try to do things that would get them in the paper or at least mentioned briefly in our gossip column, which we called — because of the general sci-fi, outer-spacey tone of the paper — "News From Uranus." During this time, our nemesis was Foreman Don. A former marine, Don was tough, tough, tough. He was a man of few words, and as soon as the paper appeared, he became a man of even fewer words. One day, he was out on the work site and remarked, "Every time I say anything, it gets in that damn paper." Naturally, in the next issue we reprinted that very quote.

A few years ago, I had a reunion with my friend Larry, who had stayed on to become union local president. "You know," he told me, "over the years, Foreman Don and I became friends, and you know what he said? He said, 'I loved that paper. Boy, do I miss that paper!'"

As per the ritual we developed, foremen were not allowed to be seen buying the paper and had to give their quarter to a worker to buy it for them. Each time an issue came out, a different worker sold it — so the entire shop felt they had ownership of it. At a place steeped in habitual unconscious behavior, all of a sudden there was a spark of creativity. Two of the workers — both highly intelligent but illiterate — returned to school to learn how to read. Those who worked in other city departments would get hold of the paper, and wished they, too, could have a crazy newspaper about them. Within months, I'd forgotten about that serious book I'd been writing, and it forgot about me. I discovered two important things: The first thing was, for the first time I recognized the power humor has to generate I Lost My Dream Job . . . and Found My Dream sanity, balance, and creativity. The second thing I realized was, I was really good at it. One day, while generating material for the paper, a funny name flew into my head . . . Swami Beyondananda.

A year later, after I'd "pre-tired" (that's when you leave a job before you get really tired of it) from the Forestry Department, a friend and I decided to start a publication to reach Ann Arbor's newly forming holistic community. We knew that people took their health, growth, and spirituality way too seriously, so we decided the paper needed humor. We gave Swami Beyondananda the inside back page feature, and the Swami's been running the show ever since.

Very quickly, the Swami became the most popular feature in our magazine. Swami's early columns like "Teach Your Dog to Heal," "Tantrum Yoga," and "Everything You Always Wanted to Know About Sects" made their way into syndication around the country. In late 1986, my wife, Trudy, and I took to the road with the comic Swami act, and the Swami and I have been inseparable ever since. We've met wonderful people, been to great places, and watched thousands and thousands of people laugh. It turns out the joke was on me, and a fortunate joke it was.

My good fortune reminds me of the young immigrant who came to America from a little Jewish village in Poland. He needed work and, being a very religious young man, he went to the local synagogue and applied for a job as a shamus — a janitor. He almost got hired. But when he revealed he couldn't read or write, he was turned away. Desperate yet resourceful, he bought a little pushcart and sold cheap items on the street. He sold a little more, he bought a horse and wagon . . . and finally, he opened a storefront. Long story short, after twenty-five years he owned a huge department store. Still religious, he made a large donation to the synagogue. There was a big ceremony, and the successful businessman handed the rabbi a check — which was signed with an "x." The rabbi was surprised. "You can't read?" "If I could read," the man said, "I'd be a shamus."

How fortunate I was to have a job I loved, and then lose it only to find a truer calling. Thank God the universe had a bigger plan for me than I had for myself. Thank God I lost my dream job and found a dream I never would have dreamed.

♥ ♥ ♥

Steve Bhaerman is a writer who performs comedy internationally as Swami Beyondananda, the Cosmic Comic. As the Swami, Steve is the author of *Driving Your Own Karma*, *When You See a Sacred Cow, Milk It for All It's Worth, Duck Soup for the Soul*, and *Swami for Precedent: A 7-Step Plan to Heal the Body Politic and Cure Electile Dysfunction*. Steve is currently working on a more serious book with cellular biologist Dr. Bruce Lipton, called *Spontaneous Evolution: Our Positive Future Now*, to be published in fall 2008. He can be found online at www.wakeuplaughing.com.

Thank God
My Favorite Uncle Molested Me

ALISON NAIL

I wish I had some sort of amazing introduction that would make the words between a capital letter and a period be so profound that it would not be necessary to read the rest of the words below. My story is not unlike many other women's (and men's) stories I have had shared with me. My story, however, reveals the dynamics of surviving each day without the mentality that I am a victim.

I accept responsibility for what has happened in my life. Perhaps grasping that our lives can seem so minute at a young age, the abuse, the rape, the mental mind games only went so far into my core. I realized, somewhere in the depths of me, I chose this life. I chose my family. I chose my circumstances in life.

Now, this may seem like a feasible concept to adapt to in our adult lives. Many people have asked me, "How does a child choose to be in a home that abuses them? How does the child choose to be molested, yelled at, beat on, left for homeless, given weeks-old food to eat? How does a child choose this?" My answer—some souls return to teach, to grow, and to nurture others. Sometimes that picture is not what people think of as "ideal," and there is room for the responsibility of the person's own actions. For me, I realized at the age of nine, that no matter what happens to me—it isn't just some random "thing" that happens to me. The series of events in my life created a whole scenario that would allow me the insight to facilitate others on their lifelong journey and healing.

I carefully chose my favorite pastel, multi-colored dress, my bright pink heels, white stockings, with just a touch of eye shadow to match my shoes. I celebrated – no – relished the thought, that out of all the people my favorite uncle knew, he had chosen me to accompany him to a live performance of a Broadway musical about cats. This was a special night; I was nine years old, I felt like Cinderella and was honored to have this opportunity to dress up and spend quality time with one of my most treasured family members.

Hearing a loud, strong knock on our front door, I quickly ran down the stairs to greet my uncle, who glided into the living room. His arms wide open, I jumped in and strangled his neck with my arms, and he laughed with joy, "I am so glad to see you," he said. "My-oh-my, don't you look beautiful!" My round cheeks turned pink.

As we drove from my three-story green farm home, my uncle and I headed into town in his full-sized, classy town car. He asked me all kinds of questions regarding school, extracurricular activities, and my writings of poetry and imaginative stories. I contemplated, "No one asks these types of questions about me! He must really care!" My uncle made comments about how attractive and mature I had become in my own growing stages. He said, "I know that as a young woman, you have taken on a lot of responsibility that maybe your parents shouldn't put on you. I would never do that to you if you were my daughter."

We reached the parking lot of theatre, and he told me to wait inside the car.

He came around to my side of the car to open up my door, and he took my hand. I graciously said, "Thank you," and tried to let go of his hand. His grip on my small hand tightened, and he took me inside the theatre with his other arm around me. He seemed to walk with a sense of pride, but I felt a rising nervousness creeping through my soul.

Upon entering the theater, we sat in the third row. The fluorescent lights dimmed overhead. His lethargic fingers began to trace my right knee. My knee instinctively jerked, with my foot hitting the back of the chair in front of me and bumping the patron sitting there. Profoundly embarrassed, I sank deeper into my seat; his clutch became more solid. He whispered some strange words in my ear; I couldn't hear what he was saying because the blood rushing to my head was pounding so loud. We left the musical before it was finished. The car took us to his apartment. This was the first step down a long and brutal journey to endless, secretive events of being repeatedly tormented by my much-loved uncle.

Countless events took place that my mind refused to remember—seven years of abuse, of rape, of being penetrated, of mind games and threats.

Then I met the man of my dreams, the love of my life, the perfect relationship - well, almost. Every time he came close to showing his love for me intimately, my stomach would hurt, my head would spin, and I would get highly agitated with him. I didn't understand why this was happening and became so frustrated and depressed that I sought the help of a university counselor. He and I spent many afternoons recollecting the vision of the abuse my childhood had endured.

The last session with my counselor ended in reading a book about a little girl who told the same life story. I had to read in front of my classmates. The last illustration and typed lines in the book said I had to appreciate my attacker. I could hear my fellow classmates suck in a deep breath. "Appreciate?" Through my tear-filled eyes, I said, "Yes. I appreciate him. Just as she, this little girl, appreciates. There is no asking. There are no expectations; only Appreciation." I had not realized that this was what I needed to do to begin to heal. It just took one click. The "moment of click" happened for me in that appreciation, and then my story moved into unexplainable, uncontainable gratitude.

I continued to struggle with the long-term effects of the molestation: multiple miscarriages, lack of self-worth, as well as many failed relationships from believing that I am nothing but sexual property. Even so, in my daily meditations and prayers, I start with gratitude.

"Thank you, God, for attending to my soul through the abuse. I know without you, I would not have made it in this life."

And as the law of attraction would have it, I started to come in contact with men, women, and children who were victims of all sorts of abusive atrocities. When I share with them the specific details of my story, typically their first reaction is, "How do you deal with this? When does the pain ever stop? When will I start to feel good? How do you wake up and still smile?"

"First," I reply, "I discovered the full acceptance of appreciation. Appreciation that identified my abuser as having never received love to satisfy his own inner hurt. His hurt only blinded his eyes, which in turn created a mind that needed to hurt someone else – me." I share that there is no one definition of appreciation, but rather it is a decision I make each day, to let go of resentment and untie myself from the thoughts that bind me to the abusive events.

In that appreciation, I saw my uncle as separate from my family tree, separate from the offense itself. I kept asking myself, "Why does one being desire to hurt another?"

A soft voice entered my thoughts: "It is only from his lack of understanding of how to express his own pain that he hurts others. It has nothing to do with you."

"Second, every morning, I wake up and express gratitude for my circumstances. It definitely didn't feel good for a while – because my hurt brain and memories couldn't understand. But gratitude for the events in my life slowly changed my heart. My heart began to expand greater than my brain with love, gratitude, and appreciation – mostly for myself."

"Third, I pulled from every resource I could to assist in my healing. I tried self-help books, audio CDs, support groups, counseling, writing, prayer groups, and seminars. But then, no matter what resource feels right at the time, I identified that my journey is my own. Every other person's experience is different from my experience. Each person's healing path may not fit mine. I could learn from and 'take notes' on their abuse events and healing; however, I learned to say to myself, 'You are your own greatest source of strength. Look how far you have come!'" Although all of these resources were definitely helpful, I acknowledged that moving through my own restoration is a lifelong journey.

Every day, I have to remind myself to do these steps. But with the memories of molestation, violation of trust, and exploitation of my innocence, I have been given the greatest gift – the fulfillment of my life purpose to create awesome godly spaces of healing and encouraging others to move through their own roadblocks to fulfill their life purpose. After being in contact with over two hundred people in my lifetime, I know that I have facilitated many of those two hundred in their healing. I have come in contact with women, and many men, who have shared their stories with me, seeking healing from their past. But most importantly, I have gained a strength... a tenacity that defies the odds. I have found an unconditional love for myself. I embrace each moment, living in the present.

Thank God my favorite uncle molested me.

❤ ❤ ❤

Alison is a Spiritual Catalyst for Change to Empower Women. She is also an inspirational public speaker and writer and enjoys traveling, showering love on her nieces and nephew, hiking, and meditation.

The Power of Perfection™

Is it possible that you are already Perfect exactly as you were, are, and will be in EVERY moment? Has it been 10 years and you're still searching for "success" or "happiness"?

Sometimes the hardest place to find a tree is in the forest. The quality of your life is determined by the quality of the questions you ask yourself. It's a lot simpler to find the Perfect Answers by asking the Perfect Questions.

Are you ready for a clear and specific technique that describes exactly how to balance any emotion and, in doing so, honor the true perfection that exists inside you?

Discover The Power of Perfection™—a complete education series on how to honor and love yourself, and live the life that you would LOVE.

For more information visit
www.thankgodi.com

Special Bonus

Learn more about Thank God I... Published Authors as they read their stories and share more insight in exclusive interviews at http://www.thankgodi.com/mygifts

Manufactured By: RR Donnelley
Breinigsville, PA USA
September, 2010